TOM EMISON

UNTHINK EVERYTHING YOU THOUGHT
YOU KNEW ABOUT
STRATEGIC PLANNING RETREATS

Publishing Services provided by Paper Raven Books
Printed in the United States of America
First Printing, 2021

Paperback ISBN= 978-1-7369346-0-9
Hardback ISBN= 978-1-7369346-1-6

PRAISE FOR CHUNK

"*Chunk* is a fresh look at strategic planning for your company. Tom shows you how to bring 'Magic' to the strategic planning process for your organization while avoiding the magical thinking that plagues a lot of organizations."

—Russ May, President & COO (retired), Midwest Sign and Screen Printing Supply Co

"Tom successfully distills his experiences as a father, husband, friend and business advisor to champion strategic leadership and planning as a *discipline*, not an event."

—Tyler Nottberg, Chairman & Chief Optimist, U.S. Engineering Company Holdings

"*Chunk* is not your typical business strategy book for your bookcase. Nope! *Chunk* reads more like a novel, chock-full of lessons learned and earned by Tom Emison, a music-loving and passionate strategic clarity evangelist eager to help people and businesses succeed. Do yourself a favor; buy *Chunk* and read it now!"

—Jon Buggy, Architect and Director, RSP Architects

"*Chunk* is *the* playbook for delivering an epic strategic planning retreat!"

—Wade Sandy, CPA, CCIFP, Partner-in-Charge of Construction and Real Estate, Eide Bailly LLP

"An epic workbook for companies committed to improvement. Love the timing. As companies transition from the baby-boomer strategy (just bury yourself in your work and good things will happen) onto the next generation, this is a great tool. Godspeed!"

—Kevin Donnay AIA, President/CEO, WiDSETH

"Strategy is about stretching limited resources to fit ambitious aspirations. *Chunk* needs to be one of those resources. Read it and you'll be stretched. You'll be inspired!"

—Jeff Prouty, Chairman & Founder, The Prouty Project, Inc.

ACKNOWLEDGMENTS

The COVID-19 pandemic was the motivation for this book, but my clients were the inspiration. So was my dad, Jim Emison (RIP), a retired U.S. Marine and CEO of Western Petroleum Company. My appreciation for the art of strategy comes from the countless hours as children we saw our mom, Connie Emison (RIP), drawing, sketching, painting, and creating. I thank my brother, Bill, and my two sisters, Betsy and Cathy, for their years of support.

Thank you, Dr. Marty Knight, Professor and Varsity Swimming Coach (retired) from Hamline University, St. Paul, MN. You are a big reason why later in life I won three U.S. Masters Swimming National Championships. To Dr. Richard Fowler, who taught me positive self-visualization, thank you. To Dick Ebert, retired CEO and Co-owner of Ebert & Sebastian, Inc., I am in awe of you still. Russ Agosta (retired) from Grant Thornton, thank you. Because of you, I worked with the exceptional Richard "Jake" Jakowsky at Anderson Electric. Wade Sandy, Partner at Eide Bailly, remain curious, Trail Boss. The leaders at The Prouty Project, you have truly set the bar high, friends. To the many leaders at Young Presidents' Organization (YPO), it was an honor to serve as a resource for you.

I thank the Associated General Contractors of America and your local chapters. Thank you to the Construction Financial Management Association and your local chapters. Thank you to the many publishers of my feature articles and white papers, especially the publishers of *Building Profits*. Thank you to the Building Futures Council think tank and the brilliant Jack Chiaverini of Perini Corporation.

I have dozens of clients to thank. Most are CEOs in U.S. architecture, engineering, construction, and real estate companies ("A/E/C/RE" or "Built Marketplace"). To the many executives who led those companies, thank you. A few clients deserve special thanks. Thank you to the amazing Jim Johnson, CEO of GE Johnson Construction Company. Thank you to the gifted Tyler Nottberg, Chairman and CEO of U.S. Engineering Organization and his exceptional President Tim Moormeier. Thank you to the daring Chupa Nelson, Chairman of RA Nelson and Associates. Thank you to the tasteful Pat Rodgers, CEO at Rodgers Builders in the Carolinas. Thank you, Steve Hauschilt of Graham Construction in Iowa. A joyful thanks goes to the exuberant co-conspirators, Ron Krank and Ron Erickson (both retired), from KKE Architects (now DLR Group). Doug Hutchison, Chairman and CEO at Meisner Electric, what an amazing journey you have lived. Bless you, Randy Knecht, CEO at Journey Group. Thank you to the perhaps-gone-mad Whitney Peyton, President (retired) of CBRE, Minnesota. To the determined duo of Chip Reid (retired) and Mike Taylor at Current Builders of Florida, thank you. Kari Karst at BX Civil, thank you. A very faith-filled thank you to Paul Thrift and John Thompson at Thompson Thrift. Nancy Anderson and Russ May of Midwest Sign and Screen Printing Supply Company, thank you. Mark Swenson, FAIA, and David Graham, AIA, of Elness Swenson Graham Architects, you are simply the best. Kevin Donnay, AIA, CEO at Widseth, what a remarkable leader you are. Dave Dobosenski, CEO at St. Croix Regional Medical Center, you are an innovative and inspiring CEO. Bruce Engelsma, Dennis Diessner, Pete Diessner, Al Gerhardt, and Phil Boelter of the Kraus-Anderson Family of Companies, every minute with you was (and remains) a blessing.

All of you and many others demanded a lot from me, as I did from you. Most of you do not know it, but while I was in the front of your retreat room facilitating your strategic business decisions, *I* was the one getting an education. You placed your trust in my processes. "As iron sharpens iron, so one person sharpens another" (from the Book of Proverbs 27:17 NIV). I will never get the misguided logic that caused all of you to place your faith in me as a business advisor and retreat facilitator. But thanks.

There are a lot of conference center hosts, executive wellness center staff, hotel meeting room organizers, catering personnel, resort staff, and A/V techs to thank. It is mindboggling how many of these specialists helped to make so many epic strategic planning retreats successful.

Thank you to Tom from Christian Counseling for Men in Wayzata, MN. To my AA sponsors, my Celebrate Recovery sponsors, and others who have toiled alongside my mess I call a life of sobriety, bless you. Cindy Lannon, God bless you, sister.

Pastor Dan Johnson of Plymouth Covenant Church, thank you. Annie Young, you are completely blind, an award-winning artist, *and* an accomplished triathlete. Keep the faith, Annie. To the Jesuit priests at the Demontreville Men's Silent Retreat Center in Minnesota, thank you. Ann Bancroft, expedition leader across the South and North Poles, thank you. Thank you to a dear friend, the Honorable Jim Ramstad, U.S. Congressman from 1991 to 2009, who passed away during the writing of this book. Thank you to the countless competitive swimmers in U.S. Masters Swimming. The Y's Guys Masters Swim Club in downtown Minneapolis—Darrell "Bubba" Smith, Mike Burns, Mark Sells, and the gang—awesome work. Thank you to the many roadies who cycled thousands of miles with me to raise money to fight multiple sclerosis. To my fellow Pirates in Tight Pants roadies Gary Bolenbaugh, Geoff Gray, Lucy Gray, and Mike Blanchard, "*Yar!*" The journey really is the destination.

A huge thank you to my team at Paper Raven Books. The cover design, the valuable editing, the interior illustrations, the countless patient conversations you had with me, and your marketing planning for the successful distribution of *Chunk*—it is all deeply appreciated.

Finally, thank you to Pammy and to our three grown children, Emily, Mac, and Ashley. As Willie Nelson sang, you were always on my mind. For 30-plus years, I flew from client to client, city to city, and retreat to retreat. Your support was (and remains) my biggest blessing. Pammy, the many sacrifices you make as a wife so I can help clients with work—I cannot begin to know. Thank you. Emily, your passion for the written word and your search for truth inspire me. You are courageous, Majessa. Mac, your way is now the Rocky Mountain way, and I am so very proud of you, your career, and your golf swing. Always bet on Mac. Ashley, you are one of the most thoughtful people I will ever know.

TABLE OF CONTENTS

RETREAT

The term "retreat" has two contemporary meanings. The first meaning is the idea that a military platoon can better achieve their goal by retreating before proceeding. The second meaning is spiritual, as in going on a church retreat to reconnect with God and your fellow church members. You are regrouping before proceeding to connect once again to the essence of your organization before creating a simple, compelling, and sound business strategy. In a retreat, you are a special band of brothers and sisters on an incredibly important assignment to reimagine your company so you can create new, exciting results. Imagine the possibilities.

AUTHOR'S NOTE

The COVID-19 pandemic raced across the world in 2020 as I was writing this manuscript. I shelved *Chunk* the entire month of May 2020, quite puzzled as to how to proceed. I figured, who wants to read a business book about gathering leaders together in intimate gatherings for offsite business planning retreats now, when about half the civilized world is quarantined? By June 2020, I recognized how essential real time together was becoming to my family, friends, colleagues, and other business leaders. Thousands of companies saw their business models swiftly interrupted. Supply chains got decimated. Entire categories of leadership team meetings and interactions (like strategic planning retreats) were suspended, or sloppily squished into awkward virtual meetings. It dawned on me that, in the 2020s, there will be a lot of corporate reimagining going on, and there will be a rush on strategic planning retreats. The pandemic reinforced the need for leaders to experience independently facilitated retreats in person. For a while there in 2020 and 2021, it meant such meetings were physically distanced and folks wore masks. But, that will change over time. Hey, your company cannot wait for things to return to normal before having an epic strategic planning retreat. There will be no return to the way things were; this pandemic was the Black Swan (i.e., mostly unpredictable and somewhat catastrophic) event that many leaders had been warning us about for decades. Your leadership team needs to think together in the same room.

It's about connection, or re-connection more accurately. Virtual strategic planning meetings may work as a temporary facsimile, but you need time together. Connection. The years of 2020 and 2021 were epic. Your future will be, too, when you reimagine everything in an epic strategic business planning retreat.

INTRODUCTION

THE STRATEGIC BUSINESS PLANNING RETREAT NOT WORTH HAVING

"Eye to eye on the opponent
A strategy for me to explore
A beginning before any score
I am ready with my silver sword…"
EXCERPT FROM "STRATEGY GAME"

BY PRESERVATIONMAN

From Meaningful to Meaningless

It was just before 8:00 am on Day One of our three-day strategic planning retreat when five old white guys half-heartedly pierced the strategic planning retreat room. Their body language? Tired. Defeated. The cultural diversity they presented included (1) bald, (2) gray, and (3) bald *and* gray. By 8:05 am, a senior vice president was reading the *newspaper* in a strategic planning retreat that was supposed to have started five minutes earlier. Three top leaders were not even present.

Ever the optimist (re: naïve fool), I got the strategic planning retreat started. We worked our way through a group discussion of their strategic situations currently. The late arrivals eventually showed up. We did okay separating strategic symptoms from strategic causes. We backtracked through some of the documents I had sent them before the retreat, including important material they had obviously not read. They seemed to absorb some of my information and insight. I had organized their retreat into chunks, or small decisions that allow a strategic plan to emerge from the meeting. We moved through the agenda and completed the various exercises and topics I had prepared for them (the chunks), but we never spoke of the soul of their company. The discussions were okay, and opinions were aired. But their conversations were shallow and opaque. My facilitation methods were working. Sort of. At the end of the first day, there was some progress. As we wrapped up, I did what I always did at the end of the first day and asked the CEO to stay late for a one-to-one debrief. I had come to treasure these one-to-one meetings with my clients to compare notes and hang out at the end of a long retreat day. We excused the rest of his team to the hotel bar while he and I talked over the day and prepared for the next. I braced myself because the day had been blasé.

That is when my crisis became clear. We sat at a table across from each other, me with my notepad and pen in hand. I asked questions about how he felt the day had gone. *Just listen*, I thought. *Take notes. Listen to him. Then adapt tomorrow to what you learn from him right now.* I had performed dozens of such one-to-one end-of-day check-ins with CEOs. Then, casually leaning back in his chair, he dropped it.

"I don't plan to implement most of this strategic plan. We didn't implement our last plan either," he announced apathetically. I physically winced. Glancing up from my notes, I twisted my head like my Labrador retriever back home. He piled on, "This time away in an offsite is okay for team building, but I don't expect much will change in our company. I am only doing this retreat thing because I have to give something to our board chair in a week or two. That'll shut him up. Then we can get back to real work. You know. You got to go through the motions." With great effort, he rose from his chair, nodded his head toward me, and started to leave while I did an excellent impression of a deer in the headlights.

The memory of that conversation still discourages me years later. We wonder why so many American businesses have lost their edge globally. We ask why top leaders lose personal steam and why employees are not fully engaged in their own companies. Why do leaders develop strategic business plans that do not express true strategy? Why do some just go through the motions? I had gone from slightly deflated at 8:00 am to aghast at 5:00 pm. I was failing. This CEO was only holding this offsite strategic planning retreat "thing" to satisfy his boss? I thought I had seen a glimmer of hope that the team was at least trying to engage in strategic thinking that day, however imperfectly. As it turned out, *I* was engaged, *I* was excited, and *I* was intent on excellence.

But *I* was alone.

It was *not* a planning retreat worth having. He was right; nothing would change in his outfit with that attitude. His appalling lack of leadership had a negative and immediate impact on my engagement as a retreat facilitator, something I had guarded against for years. I had learned that, on occasion, a subtle hint of disengagement from the client could pop up during retreats. But, until then, such disengagement had been predictably fleeting. Clients always rallied. We would roll into an epic planning retreat with powerful outcomes and a completely new corporate vision. They got engaged. And sometimes, whew, they were inspiring. My retreats were never about small-minded strategy or filling in the blanks in some oversimplified strategic plan template.

But the nonchalant way this CEO admitted his apathy got me detached. I thought about quitting on the spot. This charade was nothing more than a stunt to satisfy his board chair. Lyrics from "Pigs" by Pink Floyd ran through my mind: "Big man, pig man, ha, charade you are."[1]

Sure, I was being paid, but that was not the point. Paid to do what? To run a now meaningless strategic planning retreat for Chief Executive Pig Man, who envisions a strategic plan that he will not implement? I took more notes, nodded my head a few times, and followed him out of the room. I skipped their sumptuous private dinner and instead went back to my room, guzzled an energy drink, worked out (plyometrics) in the hotel back hall stairway, showered, ordered pizza, and stuffed my face. Emotional eating: guilty. Then, I got marginally ready for Day Two of their three-day offsite retreat with me, Mr. Not-Very-Epic Strategery Guy ("strategery" is a derisive term from the occasionally misspoken U.S. President George W. Bush).

Rethink Your Business, Now

Looking back now over the past 30 years I have spent designing, facilitating, and documenting all types of business retreats, this one experience stands out as a real failure. A flop. I can count a few other retreats like that. I figure I have about a .750 successful retreat batting average, which is exponentially better than the .100 batting average we read about in contemporary business and academic literature describing strategic planning retreats and implementation. That's right; according to many sources, only 1 out of 10 strategic plans succeed (success being defined as producing results that exceed their initial quantitative and qualitative expectations). But my botches just killed me. I took it personally when a planning retreat stunk. I still do.

Business strategy retreats are not exciting to some leaders, and that is a problem. Even if you are not a retreat facilitator, strategic thinking is an essential leadership attribute for you to hone individually and as a leadership team, especially during times of rapid change. Big picture visioning (more on this and other terms later) is the corporate competency that can set extraordinary organizations apart from their average counterparts. Most business leaders periodically think deeply about their business. But only a tiny fraction think deeply about their business *together* on a regular basis. When offsite strategy retreats are not a corporate priority and are not organized into discreet chunks of decision-making, it preempts the leadership team from developing this capacity to see—and later seize—a shared vision; to think deeply together, to connect.

I have heard that some CEOs say it is lonely at the top. Lonely? Sounds to me like they are isolated and probably doing their job wrong. The most effective CEOs I have met are not lonely at all. They are leading something special and seem to know it. They are directing a team that thinks hard together. The model of the Lonely Dictatorial CEO who spouts fountains of strategic wisdom is a relic from a bygone era, like shag carpet and fake-wood-paneled executive offices. Strategic leadership has always been a team sport. Now, this is even more true. When a planning process is rendered down to an isolated leader holding a meaningless offsite session, it handicaps the entire company. Financial performance erosion, loss of employee morale, fading customer experience, loss of market relevance, poor succession planning, and orderly liquidation can all be traced back to shabby strategic planning retreats, idiot-proof planning templates, and a lot of lonely (re: isolated) CEOs.

Friends, you have to *think* together in a strategic planning retreat. This is highest-level teamwork. That thinking has to be about competing differently than your competitors, not just better. I cannot imagine a more important time for you to do that than now. It's why you picked up *Chunk*, right? If you are the top executive in your organization, you cannot facilitate this strategic retreat yourself; you likely already know that. If you are a chief strategy officer, perhaps you can facilitate such a retreat, and I hope *Chunk* will further complete your understanding of the art and science of strategic planning retreat facilitation. Even then, the amount of objectivity you must bring to the entire process is higher than you may think. Odds are that you need to hire an outside, objective, and transformative retreat facilitator. Huge new business opportunities/risks will present themselves. It is exciting. Seizing them requires transformative, connected thinking together, not just another run-of-the-mill offsite session.

Strategic planning retreats are stimulating for high-performing executive teams. So, over the decades, I catered to those types of leaders. I aimed to always make strategic planning retreats transformative. As the years clicked by and my portfolio of retreat experiences grew, I started adding more and more creative exercises, components, or chunks. I incorporated methods into the retreats like improvisational acting, role playing, and short-movie productions using my Apple iPhone iMovie app. More awesome chunks! I found that, the more the leaders were engaged creatively, the more memorable their experiences were. And that vision of theirs? Now instead of just another boring retreat, their vision was seared into their corporate strategic spine. Boom! Success.

To develop that kind of vision in the business retreat, I focused hard on *place* (delivering my work in outstanding executive retreat sites) and *process* (following a proven flow of chunks that I tailored for each client). In wonderment, I would facilitate the meeting while leaders connected to each other and their business like never before. They told me these retreats were *un*like others. I saw hardened U.S. construction company executives choke up with excitement about their new corporate direction and executive purpose. That is how engagement can start right from the top of an organization.

Much of what we read in the business world suggests that, in order for the corporate culture to prosper, a clear tone must come from the top of an organization, aka the C-suite. This tone must align to (or from) the corporate culture. News flash: epic retreats are where leadership tone is established, not from page one, section two of some generic online strategic plan template. After one planning retreat years ago, my client Eric spent the next year personally focused on losing weight and improving his own well-being. At the time, I had no idea just how transformative that strategic planning retreat had been for Eric. A year later, he ran his first marathon at age 50. Both he and his company were rejuvenated. Another client was so excited by his new company strategic business plan after our retreat that he got on a plane the next week to go sit down with his business risk and insurance broker and show him the strategic plan, including his new leadership succession plan. My client and his insurance broker could not have been more delighted.

That is what an epic strategic business planning retreat is about.

Epic strategic leadership retreats galvanize the trajectory of your entire organization and the individuals who lead those organizations. Leaders and supervisors are positively yearning for this type of experience. When I was writing this book, the COVID-19 pandemic deterred thousands of strategic leadership retreats and erased entire categories of leadership team interactions. Out went the nice, breezy strategic retreat conversation over coffee followed by handshakes and in came the tiled-screen virtual meeting awkwardly interrupted by unstable internet connections and "Tom, you're on mute." The disruptions to business models, the paradigm shifts for customers, the required blend of both long-term perspective and short-term agility, the accelerating technology breakthroughs, and the new way executive teams have to collaborate all beg for time thinking together. What you need now are real and stimulating strategic conversations to reinvent your company; and I argue these need to be in person in an epic retreat.

Who Is *Chunk* Written For?

I wrote *Chunk* for business leaders who want to survive and thrive in the 2020s and beyond. The ones who will benefit most are those who want to plan well, develop brilliant business strategy, and foster top leaders in offsite retreats but do not know exactly *how*. Maybe that is you. Maybe you know that you need an outside partner to deliver an epic retreat experience for your leadership team. But what should you be looking for? How do you avoid the cliché corporate retreat with boring and predictable team-building experiences? You might be caught up in the mechanics of business strategy and overlooking the art. You may be a department leader who wants to read this book before your next group offsite. You might be a business owner who senses something major is missing from your leadership team, but you do not know how to organize an epic strategic planning retreat, much less lead one. Maybe you are a private equity group leader coping with market disruption in our volatile, uncertain, complex, and ambiguous (V.U.C.A.) world (V.U.C.A. was coined in 1987 by the brilliant Warren Bennis and Burt Nanus).[2]

You might be a retreat, resort, or executive conference center general manager. You may be a CEO, CFO, CIO, or anyone from the C-suite. Maybe you were voluntold to facilitate the next offsite company retreat (gulp). You may be a business school professor. Your next retreat might be for a not-for-profit board or a new venture you are launching with a partner. You could be the senior pastor of a church or the superintendent of a public school district. No matter your role and background, my message is plain: transformational strategy happens in transformational strategic thinking retreats.

If you know that *companies* do not develop business strategy, *people* do, then read this book. If root-cause strategic situation analysis gets your blood flowing, this book is for you.

If you are the type of leader who observes an industry dynamic you see in another sector, or another aspect of life altogether, and you think to yourself, *You know, that is similar to what is happening in our company,* you are going to like *Chunk.* If you think hard about whom to invite to a corporate planning retreat, the objectives, the agenda, the crucial conversation(s) needed, and the flow of the meeting, this book is for you. If you want to *witness* business leaders change paradigms in 48 hours, then keep reading. Maybe you are a board member intent on strategic innovation. This is for you. If you know that a vertical market acquisition is a creative business endeavor (not just a financial deal), then read on.

Hey, if you want to disrupt your fragile competitors (hint: they are *all* fragile) instead of being disrupted, guess what? Your disruption will stem from the uncommon dialogue you lead in your planning retreat. If you see signs of groupthink in your top team (i.e., if you hold meetings that discourage creativity and individual responsibility) and you worry it is marginalizing your competitive position in the market, this book is for you. If you understand that all types of personalities come into the strategic retreat environment (i.e., all learning styles, all social styles, all backgrounds, etc.), this book will suit you. If you want to shove corporate politics, unproductive egos, and tribalism to the side and really get down to the best strategic ideas during a retreat, keep reading.

Chunk will prove that an astonishing amount of successful business strategy boils down to the deep experience a group of leaders have together in an offsite retreat. They will assess their strategic situation, create a new vision, cement their hearts and minds together, select their new success measures, and so much more. Each of those components is a chunk in the strategic decision-making process. The *place* that is home to these experiences and the *process* used to deliver them really matter. I hope to inspire you with a pretty chunky business case for epic strategic planning retreats.

Brilliant strategic planning retreats are not made of byzantine business school content, market share calculations, asset turnover computations, or product-line evaluation matrixes. These are valuable tools in a retreat, along with dozens of other utensils. I use them all of the time. But they are the trappings of business strategy paraphernalia. Some business leaders get overly caught up *in* them and enamored *by* them. I am not inspired by most of that stuff. Neither are most CEOs or retreat participants. Helping your company emerge from where it is today does not rest on tools. It will be your capacity for original strategy (determining your strategic *essence*) that will produce your outcome, not tired metrics from status quo strategic planning toolkits.

A myopic focus on metrics will get your company sideways. I am about to become very unpopular with some of you. But, I have never fully understood the misguided fixation some business leaders have on corporate metrics. Most such neuroses are based on misquoting the brilliant Peter Drucker who said, "What gets measured gets managed."[3] Many stop there and blindly go about rash metric setting processes they saw in some two-minute video clip. What many people do not know is that Mr. Drucker went on to say, "...even when it is pointless to measure and manage, and even if it harms the purpose of the organization to do so." So, please go back and read that entire quote now. All of it. The thing is, strategic slackers do not bother with Drucker's whole statement. And here's a surprise: some say Mr. Drucker never even said nor wrote those words in the first place. Still, corporate managers across the U.S. just recklessly put corporate metrics in place. Lots and lots of measures. It feels good to measure sh!t. Unfortunately, the partial Drucker sound bite is now so embedded in the U.S. businessperson's vocabulary that corporate America is predisposed to counterproductive levels of metric measurement instead of actually driving strategic innovation. It's like stepping on the scale every hour to constantly measure your weight loss instead of entering into a fitness and nutrition program. More measurement does not always drive better results and often produces damage.

These corporate metrics lemmings should all be pulled aside and given a short dressing-down for two reasons. First, plenty of good and bad things happen in businesses every day that are beyond measure. In most companies, much of what does get measured does not matter, while many things that desperately do matter do not get measured at all. It makes me crazy. In organizations whacked on metrics, the dysfunction will disfigure the strategy and confuse leaders. They will accurately measure their way to corporate oblivion. Second, our U.S. business metric obsession has led to countless misguided efforts by hundreds of corporate leadership teams who now equate metrics with strategy. Metrics are *not* strategy and can be distracting. They have a place in supporting strategy, I know. But it ain't first violin.

Much of what I bring to *Chunk* does not come from the business domain at all. For example, I have taken part over the years in a men's silent retreat at the Jesuit retreat house in tiny Lake Elmo, MN.[4] That is where I learned how critical guest speakers can be to a riveting planning retreat and how essential it is to follow and trust an agenda. I have swum for hours with the surfing line up at Pine Trees Break in Hanalei Bay, Kauai, Hawaii. That is where it was so easy to see that every group in life has a fascinating social order; I learned how relevant sociological and psychological principles are to strategic planning retreats. The Brave New Workshop Comedy Theatre,[5] led by the sidesplitting John Sweeney, showed me the importance of teaching participants about improvisational thinking in their planning retreats. Competitive group bicycle rides, conversations with professional musicians, yoga class with my daughter, Emily, weekly lessons from our senior pastor at Eagle Brook Church, walks through museums, silent auctions at charity events—you can find staggering strategic imagination in unlikely experiences. We can probably all agree that the range of scholarly work on strategic business planning is vast. But, the range of seemingly unrelated yet highly applicable strategic business planning insight is exponentially greater. It is not an exaggeration to say one can find pertinent strategic business planning wisdom walking across a field, looking at the tree line in the distance, and asking, "What strategy is at work by Mother Nature over there by those trees?" This is the level of analogical thinking needed in your company now.

I read business books by much more accomplished business writers. I'm a newbie. To say I have been impressed by these authors and leaders is an understatement. I have been deeply influenced by their works. Rather than give you my recommended reading list of over 75 strategic leadership books and resources, allow me to cut the list down to these really tasty ones. Start with *Crucial Conversations* by the keen Kerry Patterson, Joseph Grenny, Ron McMillan, and Al Switzler. Blend that with *Good to Great* by none other than Jim Collins. Dice in some of everything ever written by Michael Porter (that is quite a lot). Then toss in a dash of *The Fifth Discipline* by the able Peter Senge. For an appetizer, devour some savory *Range* by David Epstein. Serve it on *The Strategy-Focused Organization* by the sharp Robert Kaplan and David Norton. Pile on a heap of *SEAM* (well known in Europe, not as much in the U.S.). Chase it all down with *The Art of War* by Sun Tzu. If you have room for dessert, indulge in a scoop of *Blue Ocean Strategy* by the gifted W. Chan Kim and Renee Mauborgne. If you want to smoke a little something before you sleep, light up anything written by the sage Daniel Pink or the sunny Richard Florida. These are just some of my flavorsome influencers (writing this paragraph made me hungry!).

Strategic Thinking Is Not Hard; Strategic Thinking *Together* Is

Your strategic faculty for change as an organization will be in direct proportion to the *quality, length, and consistency* of the epic planning retreats you provide yourself and your leadership team. You need high-quality places where you can think deeply together, great resorts or retreat conference centers, not dreary basement conference rooms. You need processes that are lengthy, not rushed; consistent, not spotty; expansive, not expedient. Some organizations still understand why these factors matter. But many, maybe even yours, have lost their way strategically. They have lost appreciation for excellent strategic thinking retreats. This will badly penalize them going forward. I have discovered three reasons why some companies have lost their way:

1. Some organizations fairly well suck at strategic *thinking.* Nothing amazing is sought in a retreat, so nothing much is achieved. They set low retreat expectations and achieve them. Participants walk away unchanged and equipped with a strategic plan that is really just a list of operational improvements to the business. So much for repositioning the company.

2. Many organizations cut back on epic retreats because some leadership teams avoid essential and hard conversations. Strategy retreats can be difficult exchanges filled with mental gymnastics. Not every executive team wants to have those hard conversations like:

- Selling a business unit
- Downsizing a location
- Rebranding a division or product line
- Facing the same, big, ugly internal leadership team dysfunction that has been hounding them for years
- Moving the current president confidently into retirement
- Innovating dangerously in the supply chain (e.g., an architectural firm that decides to enter into construction management)
- Redirecting a team who should now report to a new boss
- Selling to a competitor
- Adding major overhead
- Appreciating as a group that the recent seven-figure investment in new technology is failing
- Overhauling corporate governance

3. There is a third reason that is a bit baffling: upbeat conversations in epic retreats that leaders also want to avoid (in addition to #2 above). I know, odd, right? I can understand a leadership team avoiding a *difficult* conversation, but what about *fun* conversations such as:

- Opening a new geographic location
- Implementing Lean, or any operational excellence initiative
- Adding a new market sector

- Moving toward a very enticing new company vision
- Doubling the size of a service line
- Tapping a new distribution channel
- Decentralizing to give leaders more autonomy
- Acquiring a competitor
- Acquiring a supplier
- Leadership transition
- Becoming technology-driven, not just technology-oriented

Some leaders steer away from these excellent strategy conversations because it feels like too much risk and change. In ordinary retreats, these conversations never make the light of day. But epic retreats positively burst with them because capable leaders know that taking measured risks is fun and is the recipe for corporate growth.

I call it "the right sort of crazy" when I witness zeal for brilliant business strategy. I got my start consulting in the late 1980s when offsite retreats were all the rage. They were highly anticipated opportunities for the best and brightest leaders in a company to come together, grow, and innovate, to get a little strategically crazy. Biannual two-day offsite strategic planning retreats were typical in many businesses. Some were intimate gatherings of just five to seven top leaders. Others were large, participative collaborations. Some retreats included leaders from multiple companies (e.g., my client company and their key customers or suppliers), collaborating for the first time on a partnered business strategy. I led most such offsite experiences near the end of the client's fiscal year for many years. Enormous efforts were made communicating the vision, mobilizing the vision, connecting the broad financial plan to the vision, and so on. These leadership teams were finally working *on* their company, not just *in* their company, which is a universal goal of executive teams in midsized companies (I define these as businesses earning between $25,000,000 and $500,000,000 per year in sales). This investment paid off hugely once when my client used his strategic planning process and retreat as a lever to move confidently into retirement.

"Tom, this team-oriented planning process has allowed me to put my signature on the company one last time. I think I can now accelerate my transition. What do you think?" he asked me. "Yep, I guess I agree with that. But, more importantly, it looks like your team supports that, too," I answered.

Get this: there were internal and external communication plans *for* the strategic plans. It was a best practice and still is. Monthly and quarterly meetings during execution of the strategic plan were mandatory and exciting. I had clients who modified their executive compensation programs to reward leaders who led or participated in their strategic action plans. There was desirable leader attrition because of bold new corporate strategic plans. In other words, leaders who did not share the new company vision and did not want to drive organizational change were fired, resigned, or preferably shifted into other roles. Executive turnover was—and remains—an important barometer of actual strategic thinking. A strategic planning retreat that is designed to retain all of the leaders will usually produce a white-bread plan. The goal isn't executive leader retention; it's strategic advantage in the marketplace forged by a team devoted to that strategy. A strategic plan that is not a change mandate is usually just a laundry list of tactical improvements that makes a leader feel good about the retreat but leaves the company unchanged strategically.

Something shifted slowly. We seem to have no time anymore. Is the Earth spinning faster or something? Instant gratification and shallow thinking have diluted folks' strategic thinking. Thoughtless strategy sound bites and idiotic 10-point strategy quizzes now prevail. Or maybe I am becoming a management consulting artifact at age 63. Perhaps some leaders have forgotten the Eisenhower Decision Matrix (often also attributed to the iconic Stephen Covey [see below]) that reminds us not all things urgent are important and many important things are not urgent. Epic planning retreats are rarely urgent and are always important. Your company probably *right now* needs a major commitment by top leaders to seriously and independently facilitate strategic thinking in a safe and healthy (and inspired!) setting. It needs to be organized into well-coordinated decision-making chunks.

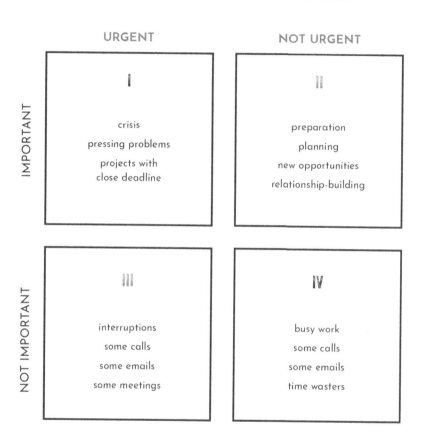

THE URGENT VS IMPORTANT MATRIX

	URGENT	NOT URGENT
IMPORTANT	**I** crisis pressing problems projects with close deadline	**II** preparation planning new opportunities relationship-building
NOT IMPORTANT	**III** interruptions some calls some emails some meetings	**IV** busy work some calls some emails time wasters

Perceived lack of time for a superior retreat process at an expensive (i.e., inspired) location is a common excuse from weak top brass. They evidently have time for their businesses to fail due to sloppy marketing strategy but not enough time for 10 top leaders to get away for three days and do some profound rethinking for the future. They have time to see their customer experience slowly fade but not enough time to think about how to make (and keep) it exceptional. They have time for profits to slip gradually but not enough time to be best in class. They have time for undesirable employee attrition but not enough time for engagement. They have time for due diligence late in an acquisition process but not enough time to justify that acquisition in the first place. They have time to react in dysfunctional corporate departmental tribes but not enough time to proactively reason across such silos. They have time to fill out the latest strategic plan template du jour but not enough time as a leadership group to really think together. They allow time for top leaders to grow tired, ordinary, spiritually bereft, unwell, or divorced but allow no time to grow excited and brilliantly united.

Lousy Offsite Strategic Retreats Are Now a Cliché

"Our offsite sucked, but we had some good food!" When I overheard a guy make this comment about some other business retreat he had attended, I felt pained. Gradually, planning retreats have become ordinary. Moreover, technology has changed how we work together at the executive level. Three-day transformative offsite strategic experiences are now the exception, unfortunately. Even two-day retreats are hard for some to justify to the bean counters. So, one-day retreats (with half a day of golf and half a day of filling out a strategic planning template) or a poorly orchestrated virtual planning meeting of some sort have become the norm. Over time, we have forgotten what sociologists and psychologists have known all along: we need to think together, to debate together, and to envision our future together as a top leadership team. This requires time together, face-to-face, in an inspired *place* and using an effective planning *process*. Quality time right now, in your organization with your team, thinking strategically, is the way to secure your future. Not a half-day sit-down or some puerile strategic planning app on your mobile device that unconvincingly promises to bring you and your leadership team together as never before.

Writing this book during the pandemic, I realized how important it was to have methods for leaders to think strategically using virtual platforms such as Webex, Zoom, Microsoft Teams, GoToMeeting, and others. These were not totally new to me. In 2019, I participated in 25 hours of virtual business meetings. In 2020, I spent 330 hours of my work life in virtual meetings. So, the virtual executive team meeting hit me like a snowball to the forehead. While these cybernetic gatherings proved invaluable during our time of global crisis, and while they can be a temporary facsimile for face-to-face gatherings, nothing provides a profound business strategy experience like meeting, dreaming, transforming, and action planning in person. Connection matters. Relationships matter. Still, we must find ways for epic retreats to unfold virtually, too. I suppose it is all just part of the Next Normal we are all conjuring across all of humanity. Of course, meeting live provides the best experience, even if it has to be performed in a physically distanced manner with health and safety protocols new to most of us. I am talking about an epic offsite strategic planning retreat of real depth that will help you reimagine your company for the Next Normal.

Leaders across all industries agree that strategic thinking is a core competency in high performers. So, why are some organizations reductive in the strategic planning process and place? Some top brass have lost their bearing, right? High-performing organizations rely on strategic planning all the time. They aren't lost. Don't let naysaying critics convince you that great strategic thinking for an entire company can be done in a lame two-hour workshop.

Chapter Challenge Questions

At the end of each chapter, I offer challenge questions for you and your leadership team to consider. These will help you get the most out of this book. Please read them fully and answer them in the margins. Doing so might engage you more actively in reading *Chunk*. Then, please move on to the next chapter.

1. When was the last time you were in a lousy strategic planning retreat? Looking back at that experience, how did the process and the place contribute to the failure?

2. By contrast, when was the last time you were in an exceptional strategic planning retreat? How did that retreat make you feel as a leader? What got galvanized inside you? How did it create new capacity for growth in that organization?

3. I maintain that your leaders are yearning for outstanding strategic thinking opportunities, together—like those

in a retreat. When you think about your company leadership team, are there two or three very critical strategic conversations that need to happen, not in isolation, but in a group retreat? How could having those conversations as a group be important for your organization? Why?

CHAPTER ONE

STRATEGIC PLANS THAT ACTUALLY GET IMPLEMENTED

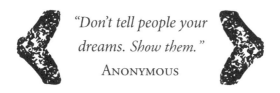

"Don't tell people your dreams. Show them."
ANONYMOUS

Strategic Jamming

Steve Winwood, Jim Capaldi, Chris Wood, and Dave Mason formed the band Traffic in 1967. The band was inducted into the Rock & Roll Hall of Fame in 2004.[6] Most people do not know that Traffic's singer, keyboardist, and guitarist Steve Winwood actually was a singer for the Spencer Davis Group at age 14. Can you imagine that? At 14, I was pointlessly riding my Sting-Ray bicycle around the neighborhood, skidding black rubber patches onto my best friends' driveways. At the age of 19, Steve officially joined Jim, Chris, and Dave to start their new band, Traffic, after meeting them through jam sessions at a club called The Elbow Room in Birmingham, England. Jamming is a process, one that is necessary both in music and in your business. Jamming is a good way to describe a strong leadership group in an epic strategic retreat experience.

Prosperous organizations (and stellar musical groups) know creative work (including business strategy) is not an event; it is a process. Strategy is a creative mindset and the offsite retreat is the pivotal moment in which that mindset is unshackled. It's not a cost; it's an investment. Mindlessly completing some strategic plan form in a rushed one-day session—c'mon, you are better than that. If you want a strategic business plan that gets implemented and is continually improved upon, then recognize that the planning retreat investment plays a central role in corporate success. In strong organizations, the epic planning retreat can be an essential executive team experience. It must be maximized. It must be significant. It has to be both heavy and light; wide open but directed; creative but results-oriented; substantial yet whimsical. Every item on the agenda needs to be weighed, facilitated, openly explored, and eventually captured in writing. Every participant must feel exceptional, even the naysayers. Especially the naysayers.

My background is in the creative process, not finance. I do not come to business strategy or the facilitation of planning retreats with a business school degree. I do not have an MBA or any other letters after my last name. I did not take a single business or finance class in college. If you have not deduced it yet, I am a liberal arts type. I am from a Midwestern town, Minnetonka, MN, home of Tonka Trucks, Minnetonka Moccasins, and a little private company called Cargill. My first real job after college was as a copywriter in a small advertising agency. The job that transformed me as a young man before that

28

was on an offshore oil rig supply ship in the Gulf of Mexico, where I spent weeks at sea. The most important leadership lessons I have learned have been in AA meetings, endurance bike rides, Bible study, U.S. Masters Swimming, industry conferences, and one-to-one real strategic moments with CEOs in executive retreats, not in business school classrooms. Strategy is manifestly a creative process. Creative strategy *is* strategy. Your company is going to have to compete differently than your competitors, not just better. Your planning retreats need to be about reimagining your direction, not repeating the same old strategy and tired meeting agendas. I take strategic inspiration from many sources, including the creativity and musicianship of the various artists I admire, which is why you will find in *Chunk* an excellent collection of music references that I think have business strategy connections.

So, company leaders need to creatively "jam" on their company direction. Guess how Traffic came up with the name of their band? Jim Capaldi came up with it while the four of them were waiting to cross the street in Dorchester, England. What if you made your business strategy that clear? Not massive Excel spreadsheets, monstrous (make that monotonous) PowerPoint presentations, three-ring binders with hundreds of pages of business gobbledygook, or—even worse—a dumbed-down and generic strategy framework found online. What about just pure and clean expressions of enlightened strategy that glue your stakeholders to your company, help you focus your limited resources, and frustrate the hell out of your competitors?

Buzz, Browse, and Bite

Back in the late 1970s when I was working on the oil rig ship, I met a young man who was a roustabout like me. It was around three in the morning when a crane dropped him down inside a personnel basket onto our supply ship. He came down to help me with placing equipment and supplies on our sprawling deck. We started chitchatting while we waited for loading and unloading instructions from my (probably stoned) ship captain. The pungent smell of diesel exhaust and sea air washed all over. He shared with me his dream of one day opening his own business, and his face lit up as he passionately described his vision. "No more of this sh!t work on the rigs," he told me. "At my shop, you'll be able to get your hair cut, buy music, and eat dinner, all in one experience. Because, you know, that's what guys want." My first thought was that mixing bits of cut hair with vinyl and food was a terrible idea, but being Minnesota nice (i.e., pleasantly agreeable to everything and everybody), I kept that to myself. Still, I admired that he had a plan in mind, a strategy. Most important, he was excited about it.

Decades later, I thought back to that experience and understood he had been onto a customer-centric vertical marketing strategy. He had a strategy without a written plan. It may have been a bit hapless, as I have never heard of such a business model (the Cut Hair—Buy Music—Eat Dinner Vertical), but he had a strategy and passion. I really hope he was able to make that vision a reality. I would call it "Buzz, Browse, and Bite."

Other than my brief stint on the Gulf of Mexico and vacation trips around the world, I have lived in the Minneapolis-St. Paul metro area all my life. I have worked at client locations all across the U.S. and Canada in every conceivable planning retreat location you can imagine. But, when I mention Minnesota, "The Land of 10,000 Lakes," and my Midwestern background, it clicks with people. It's a community with a bustling creative scene and is home to legendary artists such as Bob Dylan, Prince, Garrison Keillor, and F. Scott Fitzgerald. Minnesota has a vibe and is home to a disproportionately vast advertising and marketing communication market. Compared to cities of a similar size, the Twin Cities have an exceptional number of high-quality advertising, public relations, and marketing communication firms. Not all of them are the biggest agencies in the global creative community; some of the firms I most admire here are small shops. But the sheer number of awards won by advertising agencies the last 40 years is staggering. The Twin Cities used to be flyover country, but for many years now it has been competitive creatively with New York, Seattle, London, Tokyo, and Amsterdam. And, as far as the music scene goes, everyone rightly places Dylan and Prince on the musical pedestal, but those two giants are part of a much broader creative populace. Growing up and working here instilled an appreciation for creativity.

After college, I found a job as a writer and account executive in a small ad agency in the Twin Cities. I was early in my recovery from drug and alcohol addiction and was still learning about the business world. One of my office duties included bringing coffee to meetings and planning sessions. I had no idea what was going on in those meetings. Big words were being tossed around, especially the words "strategic" and "planning." It seemed these leaders were high on collaboration and building creative alliances in settings away from the daily grind. I learned that many of the best advertising and PR campaigns germinated in retreat settings where originality could flow. While I was stuck in mind-numbing staff meetings, hallway gatherings, or scavenging leftovers in the lunchroom, the higher-ups were holding offsite retreats with clients. I was intrigued.

Five years later, I joined a boutique strategic consulting firm that specialized in strategic business planning, including offsite executive retreats. My mentor was the president and co-owner of the firm. He sold and delivered strategic planning consulting services. He was like a deity to me back then (well, not our Lord, but definitely brilliant). He was a Wharton School graduate and a theatre minor with an uncanny ability to call on an unknown CEO on Monday, get an appointment for Wednesday, talk strategy with the CEO for an hour, have a signed letter of engagement by Friday for $85k (in 1988 dollars) worth of strategic consulting, and start comprehensive and detailed strategic business planning the following Monday. No bullsh!t. No wasted time.

His name was Dick Ebert. He took me under his wing and showed me just about everything I needed to know to deliver epic strategic planning experiences for clients. Meeting him was my lucky break. It was only later in my consulting career I realized the primacy of *place*, not just *process*. I studied and absorbed Dick's thinking and methods. Later, I added my own processes to his. He was a simply remarkable facilitator. I wanted to build on his success. So, over the years, I have kept enhancing and synthesizing like that. For reasons I do not fully grasp, I feel that I owe it to Dick to relentlessly keep helping teams unlock their strategic thinking potential.

When I worked for Dick, I could do in one month what he could accomplish in, oh, about a week. I was developing my own clients and preparing for my own retreats with clients. I was inefficient and feebly educated when it came to business and finance. But Dick graciously looked past my deficiencies and was willing to invest in me. I had an aptitude for building client relationships in an industry that was notoriously cheap about things like offsite strategy retreats, research, and development. This industry is architecture, engineering, construction, and real estate (often called the Built Marketplace) and it is big. Some estimate it at 13% of the global economy, and most of the businesses are closely held. They wrestle with the profound need for strategic planning but have trouble justifying the expenditure of time and money to do that planning. I did not win a lot of new client consulting engagements at first. But I was meeting CEOs. I was learning. It was a start.

Dick had a gift for offsite strategic planning retreat design, especially the agenda structure and the process. So did his whimsical and keen partner, David Sebastian. In four years under their tutelage, I won eight new strategic business planning consulting clients. If my clients were satisfied with my work, they would refer me to other leaders they knew. These other leaders were also in the Built Marketplace. They all either knew each other or knew of each other. Very early in my career, I realized that I was really serving one industry, not many different industries as had been suggested by others. Viewing the industry as one ecosystem enabled me to help clients navigate that ecosystem. Seeing the range of possibilities for one company in the industry required a wide-angle camera view of the entire industry. As the years progressed, I branched out to other sectors, like healthcare, wholesale distribution, and not-for-profit. Ironically, this broader strategic planning consulting work in other industries made me a better specialist in my target market, the Built Marketplace.

Crusty Dad Wisdom

When I first started meeting with business leaders, I was so nervous that I would panic in my car before walking into their offices. Actually, the nerves kicked in days before. I would sleep poorly and get light-headed. I had two young kids at home who inspired me every minute to work hard and to remember *why* I was working hard. Then, the day of an important first meeting with a CEO, my self-esteem would plummet, my inner self-talk would take a turn for the worse, and my fear would soar. I felt professionally inadequate. But I would keep the meeting and proceed anyway. To compensate, I worked like a warrior before winning a consulting engagement and during my delivery of that engagement. One July weekend when I was hanging with my dad, I got some much-needed advice to get over myself.

I was helping the old man in his garage in picturesque Deephaven, MN. Dad and I were engaged in small talk while doing chores. Talk turned to the subject of work. I admitted to him how hard it was for me, a know-nothing newbie to business strategy with no formal business education sitting face-to-face with seasoned CEOs and *advising them* on matters of business strategy in their own company. He just listened and slowly swept the garage floor. I explained what I was doing day-to-day in my job and described how, even though I was gradually learning, I still felt so nervous. He kept sweeping. I bottom-lined it for him: I was inadequate and did not deserve to be at the strategic business leadership table with any CEO. "I'm just a recovering addict in the wrong job," I said, absentmindedly rehanging his rakes and brooms on hooks on the wall.

He stopped sweeping. "Stick (his nickname for me since I was age 10, not because of my golf game but because I was skinny as a stick), you are as deserving as anyone else he is gonna see that day. And I can tell you, as a CEO myself, he's a bit nervous, too. If he is any good at all, if he has even an ounce of humility, he knows he does not have all the answers. He is older than you, smarter than you, and he knows his construction business better than you ever will. You are right about all that. But, you have two things he doesn't."

"Like what?" I asked, disinterestedly.

Dad started sweeping again. "The first is obvious: you are independent. You are outside. That's important. Second, you are young and can bring some magic. That is what he is after from a strategic business advisor: magic. It's not about your credentials. To him, it's not about S.W.O.T.s, or forecasts, whatever. You know and I know that what he is really after is some magic in an offsite retreat with his team. He is not a magician. He knows that. He is willing to pay your company a small fortune if you can deliver some magic. You are not in the wrong job. Don't be intimidated by him. Just get to know him. Listen to him. His sh!t smells same as yours. Get over it."

As we walked into the backyard to coil up some garden hoses, I felt lighter. Turns out some of the best executive advice you can get is from your crusty dad in his dusty garage. He and I did not see eye to eye on all things. But, in that moment, he led well. He was supportive, and I gratefully turned an important corner professionally.

Thirty years later, I have now had the blessing to design, lead, and document over 230 strategic business-planning processes. I have worked with over 75 CEO clients across the U.S. and have delivered dozens of workshops, seminars, and even a few keynote speeches. I have written nearly 30 articles and whitepapers on business strategy. I led a podcast series on strategic innovation (*Build Me Up!* by Kraus-Anderson).[7] During this span, I won three U.S. Masters Swimming National

Championships and over 100 Minnesota Masters Swimming victories. I raised over $100,000 on my charity bikes rides to fight multiple sclerosis (MS). None of this would be possible or meaningful without my wonderful family. I have had the privilege of raising two wonderful children, Emily and Mac. Later in life, I had an unexpected and divine appointment with the love of my life, Pam, and her splendid daughter, Ashley. Pam and I were married October 10, 2009.

Among these accomplishments and family blessings, there were these strategic planning retreat moments, extraordinary moments in offsite retreats at fantastic *places* in which I used proven *processes*. I simply cannot tell you how powerful these planning retreats were to me. They were career altering. It was humbling to see the sagacious CEO of an architecture and engineering firm give his retirement speech through his own tears to his executive team, who were also emotional. It was inspiring to see up-and-comers in a large real estate development company take the lead on crucial conversations and bring solutions, not just problems. It moved me to see a choice made in a mechanical engineering company to close a losing operation to free up resources to expand nationally. I witnessed a large construction management and general contracting company pick a growth strategy that moved them up the customer value chain. It was just cool to see a rural health system reimagine their strategy for healthcare innovation. I saw a distribution company rethink its place in the supply chain and prepare the company to be acquired. The retreats were made of exceptional stuff, and those awe-inspiring moments over the years have fulfilled me.

Wait, What?

I was the strategic planning retreat *leader*? But I am a recovering drug addict and alcoholic with no formal business school education. The juxtaposition always surprises me. Clients say I do crucial and valuable work for them in these retreats. Maybe my lack of academic credentials is irrelevant because no one has ever mentioned it to me. They rarely even ask about my education. So, I just kept outworking my consulting competitors. I compensated for my lack of financial acumen with all-nighters. I read voraciously from a very wide range of fields. Maybe my clients sensed all this.

The thing is, these strategic planning retreat successes happened a lot. The strategic plans we developed in these retreats got implemented. The stereotypical strategic business plan that sits on the shelf gathering dust? That was not my experience at all. What I understood then, and still do, is that only an epic retreat can produce a plan that leaders commit to and implement. I developed my Epic Strategic Planning Retreat Formula, which is my thrive mandate for you:

EPIC STRATEGIC BUSINESS PLANNING RETREAT FORMULA

FORMULA FOR STRATEGY FAILURE

One Reductive Retreat at a Lousy Location

+

One Ordinary CEO

+

A Lame Process

=

Zero Implementation of Organizational Change
aka a plan that sits on the shelf collecting dust; aka a
flat tire

FORMULA FOR STRATEGY SUCCESS

One Inspired Retreat at a World-class Location

+

One Committed CEO

+

A Rigorous Process

=

Infinite Implentation of Organizational Change
aka a plan that smashes the competition; aka An
extra gear

This meant every planning retreat I led (and still lead today) *had* to be epic. It had to be UNlike anything they had tried before. It's why the title of my book, in bold letters on the cover, has that big UN in there; UNordinary, UNboring, UNcomplicated, and UNbelievably better than retreat participants are expecting when they enter the retreat process. I could not stomach the idea of a client strategic plan not being implemented. What would Dick Ebert say if I delivered something less than actionable strategic transformation? Competition has always been in my soul. I looked at every single strategic planning retreat as a challenge to improve upon the last one. Executive planning retreats became a focus and then a passion. I would come back to my firm and try to relate a recent client retreat to the leaders in the firm. I would explain the process we had delivered for the client, the retreat dynamics, the location, the testimonials, and the next five-year strategic plan for the client organization. I would paint how good it feels professionally to be there with the client C-suite leading this work for and with that C-suite. The leaders in my firms did not always get it, to be frank. They appeared a lot more interested in counting beans than anything else. So, after 30 years, I shifted gears.

Boom

I decided after all of those years delivering client retreat experiences to join a large client as a member of their senior leadership team. No more flights crisscrossing the U.S. with the energy-sapping schedule of running a three-day-retreat, catching the red-eye flight to the next retreat, flying home to coach my kids' sports teams, and then waking up to the next week to do it all over again for another offsite planning retreat for another client in Somewhere, USA. In 2015, I joined the Kraus-Anderson Family of Companies. That is my story. Not a rags-to-riches tale. More like supply ship to business retreat room. My personal account is not special. But it is helpful for you to know the context in which I offer *Chunk*. I am a veteran of the strategic business planning retreat *place* and *process.* I love the work and the distinctive moments, and I cherish the relationships with clients. I can promise you this: if you capitulate to some oversimplified strategy retreat and just go through the motions, you'll get nothing. If you are considering trying to run your own corporate retreat for your own organization, consider this: even retreat facilitation consultancies hire outside facilitators to lead their planning retreats. I love the creative process and I know with certainty that strategy *is* a deeply creative endeavor, not just financial. I do not have a doctorate in organizational development nor a master of business administration; my MBA stands for Must Build Another. There is always another epic strategic leadership retreat to build.

Other strategic planning consultants and retreat facilitators will disagree with some of what I advise in *Chunk*. Some will find fault with my planning paradigms, processes, and more. That's cool. I have done that to myself actually in my quest to keep improving my own expertise and tools that actually work in retreat settings. Others will question my curiously strong obsession with retreat place. There are other ways to reimagine your organization and perform strategic business planning. I get that. I wrote this book because I had an unusual experience in my 30-plus years as a strategic planning retreat facilitator: my clients' strategic plans were well implemented. This fact alone makes this tome worth sharing. But there is much more I will share to help you discover your new strategic direction.

I know that in only two-and-a-half days you and your team can develop, discuss, summarize in writing, and prepare to implement a comprehensive and detailed three-to-five-year strategic business plan for your multimillion dollar organization. I know from experience that it will secure your long-term competitive advantage in the markets you serve in a disrupted (and disruptive) world. On top of that, you will be able to sharpen yourselves personally and restore yourselves physically. When put that way, the investment you make in a two-and-a-half-day strategic planning retreat is just smart corporate risk management.

Chapter Summary

Say what? No MBA? No business and finance pedigree? Nope. But, with a few hundred retreat planning experiences under my belt, the methods and techniques of sound business strategy—especially in the retreat setting—have been an amazing sandbox. It is a creative process, friends, and not just a business process. Coming from a geographic location steeped in creative leadership has helped me. Did I count my billable hours? Yes, at first. But then others did that for me, which allowed me to focus on counting organizational transformations. I wanted to give clients some magic while helping them avoid the magical thinking (i.e., the "If we can dream it, we can do it" fallacy) that can creep into offsite strategic planning retreats.

Chapter Challenge Questions

1. I compare strategic plan jamming to rock and roll musicians. How is it analogous? How could you transform your company if you gave leaders enough time and space to get jammin'?

2. I am a recovering drunk and lack the typical business school background you would associate with a business advisor and strategic planning retreat leader, yet I have led hundreds of retreats. How could your life experiences (no matter how bright, or dark) provide important context for developing your own strategic retreat smarts?

3. Why do some executives count corporate beans and others count corporate transformations? How do you cope with disinterested naysayers who may not be too excited with strategic planning, or who loathe the idea of an offsite retreat?

CHAPTER TWO

Getting Started with the Strategic Clarity Roadmap

*"The advice I like to give young artists,
or really anybody who'll listen to me,
is not to wait around for inspiration.
Inspiration is for amateurs; the rest of us
just show up and get to work. If you wait
around for the clouds to part and a bolt
of lightning to strike you in the brain,
you are not going to make an awful
lot of work. All the best ideas come
out of the process; they come out of the
work itself."*

Chuck Close

Skimp on the Process and You Get Lame Strategy

If you were a kid in the 1970s, Creedence Clearwater Revival was legendary. Even though they were from way down south in hot Louisiana bayou country and I was raised in frozen Minnesota, the music was universal for my generation. They had nine Top 10 singles in three years, and in '93 their success and influence was officially recognized when they were inducted into the Rock & Roll Hall of Fame.[8] Despite the obstacles that came with collaboration among four independent creative minds (which sometimes led to some very public conflicts among the band members), they found a way to combine their talents and make something magical. There was a flow to their work, their musicianship, and their spectacular contributions to rock and roll. They had a creative process. Like all great rock bands, all great strategic thinking retreats also start with the process. So, let's start talking about the broad process of initiating and preparing for an epic planning retreat. This will serve as the foundation to explore more insights about the retreat experience itself in upcoming chapters.

Many people do not understand the importance of process. They may point to a broken business situation (e.g., loss of a key customer) and point the finger at a person to blame. They do that because it is easier to just blame a person than it is to examine a more systemic problem. In reality, it is almost always a process to blame, not a person. Fewer still understand how to sell a strategic planning consulting process from the outside, or even from inside an organization when you're pitching it to top management. Strategic planning is intangible. Perhaps you see a strategic planning retreat as an isolated event. You look to a date on the upcoming corporate leadership calendar and say, "We have a planning retreat coming up in four months" and focus on the event. Maybe you do a little pre-reading and some pre-retreat homework. Then, the event happens. After that, little changes. It was mostly just an operating planning retreat, not strategic at all. It was a moment in time, and now it's back to work.

In contrast, epic strategic planning retreats happen because of a process that is complex and quite arduous work before, during, and after the retreat. This work is all worth it later when the company establishes its sustained competitive advantage in its markets. Having designed dozens of these processes, facilitated so many planning retreats I have lost count, and helped to capture them all in writing, I know this: when you skimp on the process, you get lame results.

A process is something that happens across time with inputs, actions, and outputs. That is simple enough even for me. It is important to realize the epic retreat itself happens in the middle of the process, not at the beginning nor the end. In successful organizations, the process is repeatable. That epic retreat? It is right in the middle of the strategic planning process. Before we get to the overall process and its intricacies, consider how you sell this process to the boss if you are a senior leader. Or how do you sell it to yourself if you *are* the boss? Why must the process be similar but vary slightly from one year to the next? Why are the very best strategic planning retreat facilitators so insistent on a strong process? Why do great retreats require so much pre-work? Why are oversimplified strategic plan templates, frameworks, and other contrivances so easy to find on the internet but produce nothing? Why is the end of the strategic planning retreat the starting line, not the finish line? Let's answer all of those questions in *Chunk*.

The Process Is Cyclical, Not Linear

The strategic planning process is a cycle. It is not linear; rather, it is iterative. I am not innovating here. Most everyone knows this. Taking my inspiration from two of my hobbies, cycling and competitive swimming, I see strategy (and strategic planning) as cyclical. In thoroughly evaluating the processes I have led and the many tasks associated with each phase of the process, I have organized everything into my Strategic Clarity Roadmap (below). In each phase of the process, I tailored the action steps slightly differently for each client. But there was a pattern. This cyclical pattern is repeatable annually (and slightly better each time) within a company at the department, location, or business-unit level. The more often I stuck to that process, the more often the client was successful with their strategic plan implementation. Think of the strategic business planning process like an annual family summer vacation. It can be a bit adventurous and not everyone has to be on board with the vacation plan every time; just being together and building memories are what matter most. The next summer, you do it again and maybe change up a few things to try to make it better than last year, continuing to grow more connected as a family throughout the process. And you keep repeating (and improving upon) this vacation each summer (although, once the kids are teenagers, I make no promises about the harmony of your family vacations!). The process keeps getting better, or should.

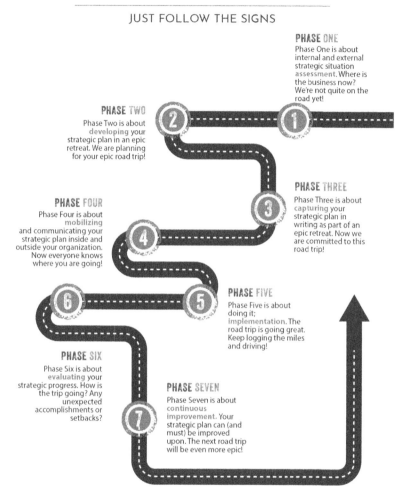

THE STRATEGIC CLARITY ROADMAP

JUST FOLLOW THE SIGNS

PHASE ONE
Phase One is about internal and external strategic situation assessment. Where is the business now? We're not quite on the road yet!

PHASE TWO
Phase Two is about developing your strategic plan in an epic retreat. We are planning for your epic road trip!

PHASE THREE
Phase Three is about capturing your strategic plan in writing as part of an epic retreat. Now we are committed to this road trip!

PHASE FOUR
Phase Four is about mobilizing and communicating your strategic plan inside and outside your organization. Now everyone knows where you are going!

PHASE FIVE
Phase Five is about doing it; implementation. The road trip is going great. Keep logging the miles and driving!

PHASE SIX
Phase Six is about evaluating your strategic progress. How is the trip going? Any unexpected accomplishments or setbacks?

PHASE SEVEN
Phase Seven is about continuous improvement. Your strategic plan can (and must) be improved upon. The next road trip will be even more epic!

The epic strategic business planning retreat itself only takes place in the "Develop" and "Capture" phases of the Strategic Clarity Roadmap. But the retreat is part of a much larger process we know as strategic business planning and implementation. Each phase of the process is critical. If you are to build a corporate culture in which epic planning retreats are the standard, then you must become brilliant at all of the phases. Within each phase, I never completed the same activities the same way twice. For Client A and Client B, I tailored the activities in the phases differently. For Client A in Year One of my work for them and Client A in Year Three, I modified the activities within the phases. Tailoring the process within the phases is both judicious and fun.

The Strategic Clarity Roadmap includes a diagnostic part (Research), a prescriptive part (Develop and Capture), and an action/improvement part (Mobilize, Implement, Evaluate, and Improve). The next chapters will go into detail on these individual parts. But let's just talk generally about how to get started. How did I do it? How did I get started with the CEO? Why was the CEO always my direct client (i.e., the decision maker)?

Just Listen Like a Chief Strategy Officer

To start, I *always* consulted with clients under the umbrella of an engagement letter, or written recommendation, as if I were a chief strategy officer. This was true whether I was delivering a strategic planning process recommendation to the CEO within my own company or to a potential client. I never referred to it as a proposal—or worse—a bid. Consultative selling from the point of view of a chief strategy officer is about relationships. It is about thorough recommendations based on exceptional listening. I do not think strategic planning services can be packaged and sold as a commodity, which is why I have so little respect for uncomplicated strategic plan templates that are not only uncomplicated but are also devoid of value.

Perhaps you are a leader in an organization, so all you are trying to do is get your top executives to understand the importance of process and place. For you, it will not so much be about the sales process as the process of building a solid business case internally. These two things are nearly the same: the practice of (1) building internal consensus to invest significantly in strategic planning process and place and (2) the consultative selling practice of winning an engagement to help a client invest significantly in strategic planning and process. These two are nearly identical. I learned this after three decades of management consulting, followed by several years as an in-house vice president of strategy for my own employer. It turns out that persuading new and current clients to consider my approach to strategic business planning is virtually indistinguishable from persuading my CEO in my own company to consider the same thing.

So, my process (before I ever wrote the engagement letter) began with really getting to know the CEO and their business. I was interested in learning as much as I could. To this day, I am still taken aback by the fascinating nature of strategic leadership teams. I was inquisitive about each client's market and their organization, meeting the CEO face-to-face, building rapport, asking questions they expected to be asked and some questions they did not, taking good notes, genuinely caring, building more rapport, finding emotional fit, determining if he or she wanted anything to do with me and vice versa. It was about curiosity. I learned to get this done with more speed and ease as I gained experience.

The CEO Does Not Always Have Vision

Okay, on to the process of developing a broad approach to a written strategic planning recommendation. When meeting with a CEO, keep a few things in mind:

- Forget their title; get to know the person.
- It is a job, not a divine position.
- They are busy, but not too busy for you.
- Most of them are brilliant and generous. That right there tells you how to succeed in business.
- They have been in some exceptional strategic planning retreats, but more lousy ones.
- CEOs have a fraud sifter. You had better be yourself and be valuable right now, or buh-bye.
- Some of them lack *strategic* vision. They may know finance, marketing, or operations. But, candidly, not all of them really have great strategic vision. It can be their executive Achilles' heel, if left undeveloped.
- They all are driven. Some are obsessed. They *love* their organization.

In such meetings, I suggest presenting the Strategic Clarity Roadmap to them. Use their words (not yours) to describe the outcomes you might generate together. Ask questions totally focused on their competitive market position and the threats to company long-term strategic security. You want to end the meeting with them thinking, *Maybe this strategic planning process and place is more important than I thought.*

The strategic planning process that actually works is *not* the process the CEO thinks they need. Many prospective CEO clients thought I was only a meeting facilitator when in reality I was a business transformer, or a strategic-purpose-agent. Therefore, all I did at that point was tailor my Strategic Clarity Roadmap on the spot, focusing on the results it would generate and the activities I would perform. You can do the same. If they start asking questions about cutting some steps from the process, ask questions like, "Sure, we can cut that (e.g., financial performance assessment in Phase One). We can cut other activities, too, in order to save money. So, what parts of this valuable process that you've told me you want and that has been proven effective do you want to cut?" Or, "Yeah, we can do this down the street at your club, that's convenient. But, you have told me you are looking to reimagine your company for a new strategic direction. I think you should consider an actual executive retreat location, not your club. Can you let me try to get you a smart deal at an inspired location?" In my experience, they usually have no objections to me keeping the project scope about where I deem it appropriate. They are just trying to save a buck, and I do not blame them for that. Almost every time, the client went with the full, bigger process and the more appropriate place I had recommended.

I learned that the entire retreat process (and the client's appetite for spending) varied greatly depending on certain characteristics: if it was a for-profit business, a not-for-profit, or an educational organization; a new business, or an older business; a Midwest company, or an East Coast company; if the CEO is new to their role, or if she has been in that role for a while. Hence, I placed even more importance on tailoring the activities within each phase. Such customization is critical. No two companies are alike, nor are any two leaders.

In the Strategic Clarity Roadmap, there are three main parts: diagnosis, prescription, and implementation. Within these parts are seven phases. Your main concern when starting an engagement with any client should be to get across this idea of a cyclical process every year. After three to five years, you will together activate the same reliable phases, but the activities you perform within each phase will change.

Chapter Summary

There are three main parts to epic strategic planning: diagnosis, prescription, and implementation. Within those are seven phases of work to be completed in the Strategic Clarity Roadmap. Within each phase, there are numerous activities to perform. If you skimp on that process, you will skimp on the results, I promise. But, getting the CEO to talk openly and deeply about their strategic challenges can be hard. Akin to a journalist, you just need to get them talking. All you need to do is just listen.

CEOs have very few Achilles' heels, but one of them can be vision, or the lack of it. This is often why they hire an outside resource to lead strategy development and epic retreats. It is more important for CEOs to participate in a retreat than it is for them to facilitate that retreat.

Chapter Challenge Questions

1. How does your organization create and manage business processes to work *on* the company, not just *in* the company?

2. If you are the CEO of your organization, how would you like an internal leader to approach you on the topic of strategic clarity and offsite retreats? How well do your leaders listen to you? How well do you listen to them on matters of business strategy? How does this help or impede strategic collaboration?

3. The Strategic Clarity Roadmap is not magic, but it is a proven process. I have suggested it is iterative, or cyclical. How does iterating help an organization with strategy? How might a linear "one and done" planning process every five years not work? Why do you think you would (or would not) make a strong chief strategy officer?

CHAPTER THREE

Prescription Before Diagnosis

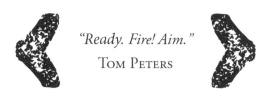

"Ready. Fire! Aim."
Tom Peters

Music as Medicine

Doctors are now prescribing music therapy for heart ailments, brain dysfunction, depression, learning disabilities, post-traumatic stress disorder (PTSD), Alzheimer's, and early childhood development.[9] I find this freaking amazing. Maybe this explains why my blood pressure drops when I listen to Jean-Michel Jarre's "Oxygene" or why I can get amped up for a big U.S. Masters Swimming race by listening to "Eruption" by Van Halen. The thing is, no doctor in their right mind would prescribe any kind of therapy without diagnosis first. A doctor who prescribes treatment without understanding the patient's needs would be sued for malpractice. So, the first part of an epic planning retreat is an exceptional diagnosis of the situation facing the retreat team *before* any planning begins. At this point, we are in the research phase of the Strategic Clarity Roadmap in this chapter. We are not in the retreat room and are not ready to facilitate decisions quite yet. As many of my friends down South say, "We're fixin' to get started." This chapter is all about preparing to hit the target.

There Are Not Too Few Tools; There Are Too Many

There are countless strategic business diagnostic methods. Strategy pros know about these, and you may, too: Strengths, Weaknesses, Opportunities, Threat (S.W.O.T.), Strengths, Problems, Opportunities, Threats (S.P.O.T.), Strategic Assessment Model (S.A.M.), Political, Economic, Social, and Technological [P.E.S.T.], Porter's Five Forces, Value Chain Analyses, Early Warning Scans, and War-Gaming. One could use these methods for all of the major functions of an organization and even at a broader level if there are multiple locations. For example, if a business has 20 U.S. locations, a P.E.S.T. analysis could be performed for each U.S. location and, more than likely, for the organization overall. There are countless books, guides, templates, buzzwords, apps, and individual and group exercises. There are diagrams, flowcharts, tutorials, and entire MBA programs devoted to strategic business planning assessment. So, the problem is not having too few tools to work with; rather, the challenge is having too many to choose from. Though the exact tools are different from one another, the goal is usually the same: gathering data, information, and insight to guide informed decisions that can be confidently made by a cross-functional leadership team to (later in a retreat) establish a long-term competitive advantage for their organization. This is the definition of strategy: making decisions about what to do and what not to do for your long-range competitive advantage. Your strategic plan is the means to an end, and the end is your strategy.

Here is the thing. Many of these assessment tools can cause the consultant, CEO, or entire retreat team to focus so much on data and information that they miss an essential piece of the puzzle: insight. I have written and read hundreds of S.W.O.T. assessments and P.E.S.T. reviews that contained accurate data and information. It's good practice, and you should conduct and capture them in writing. But don't forget the additional (and incalculably valuable) step: *produce the insight.* This can be where a strategic retreat—the epic type—gets going on the right footing.

Imagine a scenario in which a comprehensive and detailed internal and external strategic situation assessment has been performed. There is plenty of supporting data and information. All of the top leaders coming to a planning retreat have had ample time to digest the reams of reports and do all of their pre-retreat reading and internal focus group work. Then, top leadership goes to that next step and coordinates a two-day offsite retreat to absorb, reflect, and develop an assessment of where the company is now, strategically. Rather than conducting a one-hour perfunctory S.W.O.T. and taking a tepid (and premature) dive into the "new" mission, they set aside a full day for a strategic situation assessment developed by and for the entire team and also a full day of establishing consensus on the insights. Then, from this sea of information, they spend the third day distilling everything down to just the handful of key actual strategic challenges. This assessment-style retreat says, as does the kiosk map at any picturesque Minnesota State Park, "You are here."

High-Performing Organizations Identify Their "We Are Here" Strategic Situations

This sort of meaningful strategic situation assessment happens routinely in high-performing organizations. They know with certainty their exact strategic situations very early in their planning process. Secure in this knowledge, they proceed with extraordinary decision-making in the retreats and next phases. Five is the highest number of actual strategic situations facing an organization that I have observed. Not 25, or even 15. If you have done an effective job of separating symptomatic and causal strategic issues and opportunities (i.e., surface from underlying), you will find there are very few strategic situations facing any organization. Usually, I observe two or three of internal nature and two or three of external nature.

So, how do you get there? How do you help a team of leaders who hold in their hands pages and pages of pre-retreat strategic data and information to narrow everything down to just the key strategic insights? This is the first phase of activities, the Research phase of the Strategic Clarity Roadmap. I have never performed the process the same exact way twice for any two of my clients. Use this Process Roadmap to help track where you are in the process. Road trip!

THE STRATEGIC CLARITY ROADMAP

JUST FOLLOW THE SIGNS

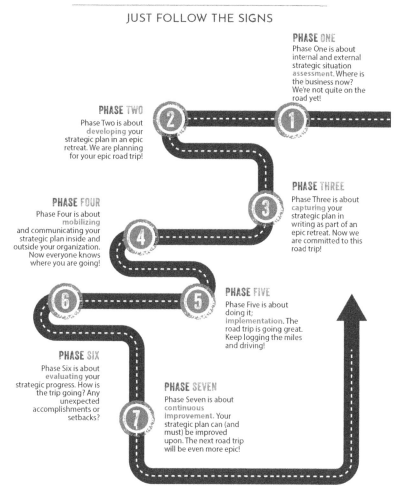

PHASE ONE
Phase One is about internal and external strategic situation assessment. Where is the business now? We're not quite on the road yet!

PHASE TWO
Phase Two is about developing your strategic plan in an epic retreat. We are planning for your epic road trip!

PHASE THREE
Phase Three is about capturing your strategic plan in writing as part of an epic retreat. Now we are committed to this road trip!

PHASE FOUR
Phase Four is about mobilizing and communicating your strategic plan inside and outside your organization. Now everyone knows where you are going!

PHASE FIVE
Phase Five is about doing it; implementation. The road trip is going great. Keep logging the miles and driving!

PHASE SIX
Phase Six is about evaluating your strategic progress. How is the trip going? Any unexpected accomplishments or setbacks?

PHASE SEVEN
Phase Seven is about continuous improvement. Your strategic plan can (and must) be improved upon. The next road trip will be even more epic!

Internal Analysis

1. Collect, analyze, and then summarize a massive amount of company information. Buckle up.

a. Audited (or reviewed or compiled) financial statements from the past three years

b. Board of director's meeting minutes

c. Current and past strategic plans and any associated action plans

d. Corporate communications plans

e. The entire suite of marketing communications materials

f. Organizational charts and associated information

g. Standard operating procedures

h. Strategic technology plans

i. Corporate culture or employee engagement surveys

j. Marketing plans

k. Primary and secondary market research they have or have commissioned

l. Sales pitch materials, including proposals they had won and lost

m. Anything else they deem important, such as confidential internal memos on direction, governance documents, etc.

2. Conduct a brand assessment of company marketing and sales support materials and website, focusing on the audience, image, and message, or A.I.M. Often, a company's current A.I.M. does not match the intended A.I.M. If nothing else comes from this entire strategic planning process, now you know where your opportunities are with your marketing communication programs.

3. Send a message from the CEO to the entire company (or a discreet subgroup) announcing the strategic retreat and intended goals.

4. Conduct leadership strategic interviews with the CEO's top team. This could be either an existing strategic leadership team (perhaps added with other leaders, some newer to the company, some gradually exiting, and so on). Generally, the interviews last an hour and feature about 8 to 10 questions designed around the topics the CEO wants to focus on. After about 10 to 20 such interviews, it is not hard to discern the patterns of their strategic business situations. The real value here is the search for meaning, truth, and patterns. My *ah-ha* moments have been based on both data I had reviewed and insightful listening sessions with leaders. Some questions you might ask include:

   a. What did (CEO's name) tell you about this planning process?

   b. Is this hour still the right time frame? Do I need to speed it along for any reason, or would you prefer even more time together?

   c. Start by telling me about your role. (People like to tell newcomers or outsiders what they do and how.)

   d. What is your goal for this planning process? Your outcome?

   e. What makes you anxious or concerned as we start this process? Why?

f. Tell me the top three strategic situations facing your organization and what makes them "strategic"?

g. In your view, is this strategic planning process about running the same race faster or a new race altogether? For your company, does strategy now need to be about competing differently, not just better?

h. What is going on externally and competitively that is either an opportunity or a threat?

i. What drives this organization? How do your top leaders make strategic decisions? Why? Has it changed in recent years?

j. How might your current culture pose a problem for lasting innovation in your company?

k. How well does the company perform financially? Can we examine the financial performance of the business in light of your strategy or lack of strategy?

l. What makes your organization unique in the marketplace? Does this unique selling proposition match up with your strategy? How?

m. If you were king or queen for a day, tell me one new direction you would take and one current initiative you would sunset.

n. Anything else you want to tell me? Anything else I should know?

5. Have a financial professional (unless, of course, you are one) conduct a financial performance ratio analysis

using the past three year's audited (or reviewed or compiled) financial statements and their current year projected budget. Look into their recent or planned capital appropriations. Finances tell their own story. So, capturing this accurately helps support other observations and conclusions.

6. Write an initial draft of your report so far for a confidential audience of one: the CEO. You will need to get to work in a marathon strategic thinking process of your own. Write your analysis. I often referred to these reports as an internal strategic situation assessment. In writing your report, your goals are, in fewer than 30 pages, to produce a clear, compelling, and accurate strategic situation assessment, to separate symptoms from causes, and to use this to scope the next step—strategic market assessment. This internal analysis needs to feature the right blend of data-driven observations as well as anecdotal observations. I have frequently organized my report this way (below), but you may have your own approach. Again, I do not like a cookie-cutter method to strategic planning. This outline below is just a sample outline from a strategic situation assessment report:

  a. Introduction and methodology: two or three pages explaining what this report is, is not, a few caveats, how it was developed, why, and how it will be used.

b. Executive summary: two or three pages of your highest-level strategic analyses written at the board level.

c. Top 10 internal strategic observations, conclusions, and recommendations. For each of 10 things you have learned, write your observations, the conclusions you are able to draw, and your recommendations not only for that company but also for the remainder of the strategic planning process. For me, this was often about 10 pages in length and sometimes up to 30.

d. Next steps in the process: a brief page or two on where you go together next in this process.

e. Appendix: include much of the data, information, and reports you used in preparing this analysis.

All of these steps illuminate the strategic situations from a purely internal view. But what about the questions of external, or marketplace, situations?

External Analysis

Strategy consulting purists will argue external market analysis should be done before the internal analysis steps described above. Empirically, yes, great strategy can be an outside-in proposition. But, in the real world, an epic retreat advisor or facilitator should invest in internal client relationships and rapport before doing the market or environmental analysis. Get acquainted before getting serious.

Just like the internal analysis, in this phase of work there are countless primary and secondary market research steps or activities to consider. I chose to focus only on the market research that was needed as part of this strategic business planning process, not *all* of the market research the client organization needed, which was always substantially more. I was getting them ready for an epic retreat, not doing all of their company market research for them. I would, for example, often find the client needed to do customer satisfaction studies more often than they had been, but I would not do the studies for them. Instead, I would recommend they do that later. You might do the same. I would tell the CEO, "You know, you really could be doing a better job of qualifying and quantifying customer satisfaction. But, for strategic planning purposes, all we need to do is a voice of the customer process for you,[10] focused more on strategic growth opportunities for your company, not customer satisfaction. You can do, and should do, more customer satisfaction measurements later. But you do not need that now, not for this phase of the planning process." This illustrated to the CEO I was focused on one role: strategic planning excellence.

Another critical body of market research is strategic trend identification. This can be a massive part of the research. You will need to oversee (and maybe perform) and package primary and/or secondary market research to help the client team understand the long-term nature of their end markets, their competitors, their supply chain, the broad societal and economic climate, etc. Your goal is to not only gather and package this data, information, and insight but also to answer, "So what?"

1. Digital transformation is redefining the supply chain and two key competitors are out ahead of your organization; so what?

2. Your four primary market sectors are not countercyclical, economically speaking; so what?

3. There is a great deal of private equity group investment happening that is driving consolidation of your competitors; why, and so what?

Your goal is not to perform and package all the strategic market research the client organization needs, just the key insights of strategic relevance the leaders need to import into their strategic decision-making process and (eventually) the retreat. A lot of organizations commission simply too much market research in this phase and the process becomes convoluted and stuck in analysis paralysis. I cannot state it strongly enough: focus on the market research needed for an epic retreat and avoid the temptation to enter into colossal amounts of market research that will confound your process.

My other favored body of research at this phase is a voice of the customer analysis, as prescribed by business strategists and planning retreat facilitators for decades. This process engaged my clients' customers directly in one-to-one settings or sometimes in focus groups. Either way, I was able to design, research, and summarize for my clients the quantitative and qualitative findings from *their* customers to help shape their business strategy and support an epic planning retreat. My stated objective was exactly that. My *un*stated objective was to bring my clients' customers into the strategic thinking room, metaphorically. In some cases, I did so literally by bringing my clients' customers into video-recorded sessions or in a few cases inside the room for the first hour of the strategic planning retreat itself. Nothing says, "we need a new strategy" like solid voice of the customer findings. Moreover, it gives a CEO confidence that their strategic business plan is built on direct customer insight in addition to the many other internal and external findings.

Then, have your entire internal and external analysis, including the many "so whats?" with your answers, peer-reviewed by a colleague before you share it with the CEO. Input from your colleagues is important. Seek edits that go beyond the cosmetic level. Ask them to be honest and blunt with you. Is your internal and external strategic situation assessment clear, concise, and compelling? What are you missing or not connecting? What comes across as too soft or too hard? Since this is not an operations review, have you kept it truly strategic? Have you avoided strategy jargon? After incorporating their input and edits, your strategic situation assessment report is more complete. For me, I called it a Phase One internal and external strategic situation assessment. It included all of the previous sections I have mentioned plus the Top 10 external strategic observations, conclusions, and recommendations. For each of 10 things I had learned, I would write my observations, the conclusions I was able to draw, and the recommendations for their company and for the remainder of the strategic planning process. This was at least 10 pages in length and sometimes up to 30.

Then, ruminate on this report for two days or more, during which time you can start to detail out the next steps in your project. This rumination process was really important for me, and it will be for you, too. Often, when re-reading a strategic situation assessment I wrote a few days earlier, I would gain a fresh and important insight and would then rewrite portions.

Then, meet with the CEO and present your Phase One internal and external strategic situation assessment. What you want (and what I have sought) is the blended effect of your Phase One internal and external strategic situation assessment, in writing, and your own added color comments, all real time. So, what I am suggesting is contrary to many consultants who may suggest forwarding the Phase One internal and external assessment report to the client days, or even weeks in advance of a meeting to talk it over. It has been my experience that CEOs are good on their feet, so they may want to think on their feet with you. They need to know that *you* know how to present complex information and insight and that you have the self-confidence to labor right alongside them. Plus, it's always fun when they add to the strategic situation assessment in the moment. Unlike some other business advisors, I often looked at my Phase One internal and external strategic situation assessment as a well-constructed strategic report, the most clear, concise, and compelling strategic analysis of their company ever. But I was open to the CEO telling me their observations and conclusions. I did this out of respect and for two additional important reasons.

1. First, engagement. You want the CEO to really engage with you and this report, to read this report, re-read it, mark it up, ask you questions, perhaps restructure portions of your analysis, ask you to fix mistakes you made, from an innocent typo to a major conclusion you have misstated. (Oh boy, I had some fantastic conversations with CEOs using this type of a report as the conversation catalyst!)

2. Second, the value of Socratic consulting. Socrates believed knowledge was something ordinary people possessed. All a good advisor or consultant has to do is ask the right questions. Then, normally, the client will arrive at the right answers. Most people already have inside them the answers to many of their questions. They just need someone to ask good questions. I did not think the report I presented to the CEO was some staggering work of genius. Most of the time, the CEO already knew much of what I shared in my Phase One internal and external strategic situation assessment. However, they had never had it well presented and thoughtfully provided with a balanced, independent voice. The CEO also needs to ask many questions, which you cannot answer if you send them the analysis up front and you are not there in person to present it.

In this same meeting with the CEO, together agree to refine your Phase One internal and external strategic situation assessment report and review your proposed agenda and recommended participants for the upcoming epic strategic planning retreat. This revised strategic situation assessment report and the proposed agenda, approved by the CEO, should go out to the participants in advance of the retreat, typically with a cover letter from the CEO. Advise them on the retreat process, flow, and each of the facilitation exercises you plan to use (I have about 25 such exercises I tinker with). Coach the CEO on their opening remarks to share in the retreat. Ask for the latitude to select the retreat location, logistics, and the participants.

This last point related to retreat participants is where the CEO and I would often have different views. The CEO's goal was frequently to include retreat participants who were current leadership team members supportive of the current strategic paradigm (i.e., the current bosses). Mine was a future-focused group supportive of the current *and* future strategic paradigm. So, I would usually recommend as many as 18 participants. Strategy sticklers will say that this is a dangerously large planning group, that the more leaders you engage, the less likely you will be to produce an extraordinary strategic business plan. They would be right, if the planning retreat was one day long or perhaps two. But mine were often two, two-day planning retreats punctuated with a month of breathing time between retreats. The result was that the strategic leadership team I facilitated was bigger, better informed, and broadly united and that the planning process was more robust. Having a larger cadre with the right sort of crazy is what gets you past compliance and commitment to a group that shares the same strategic obsession.

If your client has agreed on a strategic planning retreat team of eight, bring an illustration of a retreat table set for eight with no executive names on it yet. Then, together, start plopping names right in the table illustration.

Explore the best possible retreat *place* for their upcoming retreat experience, from your dream venue for this client, to a good venue, to one that would suffice. You will need to research alternative sites, meet with location contacts, explain to them your client situation, and uncover what they can bring to the client and to your planning process. Based on this reconnaissance, advise your client on the perfect place, if you have not already.

Then, package and distribute the entire pre-retreat reading kit with the proposed agenda, and make sure all the participants have at least two weeks to digest this information before the retreat. Most are so busy with their regular jobs that they will not read it until a few days prior to the retreat. So, consider providing a personal cover letter from you to all of them explaining this pre-reading kit and describing your excitement as you approach the offsite retreat. This is frequently when you might introduce a theme for the retreat. I am not always one for corporate retreat slogans, but often, when a CEO selects a retreat theme, it can bring important focus to the retreat conversations.

Connecting back to the importance of prescription before diagnosis, hopefully you see now the importance of conducting a thorough strategic diagnosis, both internally and externally, before diving into a retreat. Epic retreats do not just happen. I have not shared all of the methods I use in this research phase; this is just a sampling. Add mine to yours and I think you will have more than adequate information and insight.

Chapter Summary

Music therapy for heart problems? Wow, medical science is amazing. If a doctor prescribed that, and only that, before a thorough diagnosis, that would be unethical. The key is the early diagnosis of strategic situations before you start to solve them. We call this "What are we solving for?" in many businesses. The process up front involves a deep and broad internal and external situation analysis, and there are dozens of ways to accomplish this. Purists will tell you great strategy is an external-then-internal proposition, which is only partly accurate. Invest in a lot of diagnosis before planning. Sharpen the saw before attempting to cut down the tree. For an epic retreat to happen, provide ample data, information, and insight in a big pre-reading assignment for the participants. Make sure that pre-reading arrives to the right people ready for the next phases.

Chapter Challenge Questions

1. There are many tools for strategic situation assessment, making it easy to get caught up in analysis paralysis. When has this happened in your organization? Have you ever got too caught up in analysis and failed to identify the actual strategic situations? What were the consequences of that?

2. How might previewing the strategic situation analysis with the CEO in a lengthy meeting help with developing strategic clarity later? If you are the CEO preparing this report, who is one person you can share it with prior to the retreat?

3. There are many steps in this phase, which are never done exactly the same way twice. Why is it important to

follow the protocol of the Strategic Clarity Roadmap? What are the specific steps within each phase that your company needs to take? How can maintaining the core process while customizing the steps within that core process make all of your strategic planning retreats effective for years to come?

CHAPTER FOUR

Discovering Your Strategic Essence

 *"Life is a monumental phase full of opportunities to chase, but it is up to the adventurer to explore his quest with prayer."*
Excerpt from "True Essence"
by Marvin Brato, Sr.

The Language of Strategy Got Hijacked

If you spend some time in Washington, D.C., you may learn about Rare Essence, a local go-go band formed in 1976 (who can resist that handle?). Listen to their tunes, party to their music, and you will see how they have earned their name. The sound is infectious, and the huge crowds at their live performances are sick! To me, they perfectly encapsulate what essence means, that indispensable and undefinable quality of something that you can just feel. Between the hopelessly academic discussions about how to define strategy and the pile of technical jargon around analysis and frameworks, we lost touch with another important concept somewhere along the way: *strategic essence.*

Decades ago, business school MBA types hijacked the vocabulary of strategy and strategic planning. Some of them appear unaware that strategy formation is a human and, therefore a group, creative process; it's not just business. *People* develop strategy and strategic business plans for their companies. This is a key point in developing exceptional strategic planning experiences. While it may seem obvious, many strategic planning advisors overlook this. And, if they do agree with the notion that people and not companies develop strategic plans, then why do their consulting processes focus on so much of the science and so little of the art? Where is the balanced perspective? Where is the creative thinking that can disentangle a leadership team from their deteriorating corporate strategy? Where is the opportunistic dreaming that will help a company not only survive but thrive in entirely new and unexpected ways? Why do almost all lousy strategic business plans include action plans that are new work the leaders and others have to do in addition to their so-called day job instead of their newly focused job. The whole idea is to reimagine your organization and quite likely your role in it. Plans that just add more to an already overworked leader are doomed from the start.

I am reminded of the most frequently mentioned concerns I have heard from leaders when they look back years later on their company strategic plans. A client confessed to me, "Well, looking back now years later, I just kept with this notion of 'I have a day job' that has to get done. So, I figured I would get around to strategic thinking and implementing change in the organization when my day job allowed it. But it never did. I never had time. None of us did. Our 'day job' mentality hosed the strategic plan from the start. We forgot that for the plan to be wildly successful, we had to rethink our leadership roles and delegate pieces of our day jobs. Once we learned that, we created new capacity for company growth."

Look, here is the reality. On the cover of any strategic business plan, you will invariably find the name of the company. It is usually on the "Welcome to Our Strategic Plan" page of a company intranet and often their external website, too. The name of the company is presented in the first few seconds of any strategic plan video. It is often on the cover of a binder, in the first major section of an annual report, or on the first fold of a brochure about the company's strategic plan. It always reads "Strategic Business Plan for (fill in the blank) Company." But, if the plan is brilliant and truly strategic, it could just as well (probably should) have the names of the specific leaders who developed it on the cover or in the opening moments of a video. The best strategic plans, the ones most likely to be implemented and achieved, reflect more than the commitment of the company. For my best clients, the ones who consistently understand things like *process* and *place*, the strategic plan reflects a deeply personal commitment to them. They share the vision. They believe in the direction. They are mentally and emotionally aligned with the direction. If they use my Strategic Clarity Roadmap, they become more than mere participants in planning; they are ambassadors of the strategic direction. Some become evangelists. The strategic direction is in their *personal essence* because they have worked on their *strategic essence* together. These leaders have bounded way past "buy-in" to "I am going to make this happen." This is extremely important in order to drive sustained strategic success.

BUY-IN BELL-SHAPED CURVE

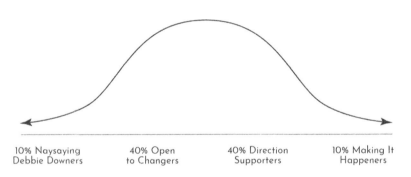

| 10% Naysaying Debbie Downers | 40% Open to Changers | 40% Direction Supporters | 10% Making It Happeners |

In every organization, there is a bell-shaped curve related to how that entire employee population will embrace the new strategic direction of that organization. I call it the *buy-in curve*. At the left end of the curve are leaders and employees who disagree with the company strategic direction. For a number of reasons, most of which boil down to ego, turf, poor internal communication, career anxiety, or stupidity, some folks will *never* support the company's new strategic direction. They will openly, but more often secretly, sabotage the strategic plan and its many associated initiatives. They may actually fight to keep it from happening. I estimate this group to be 10% of your employees right now. No matter what strategic direction you research, develop, mobilize, and implement, they may not want that. They do not all work in one department, location, or business unit, and they may not even fall into one socio-economic group. Do not, I repeat, *do not* expect your strategic business planning process to engage these folks. Do not measure your success with your strategic business plan by how well you engage *all* employees to your final chosen strategic direction, especially this whack 10%. My advice is to disregard them or eventually part ways with them. In fact, some turnover of personnel is actually a necessary outcome if your strategy is bold and your strategic plan is well articulated. Your goal is not a strategic business plan that retains 100% of your personnel. I can promise you, that strategic business plan is garbage. An outstanding strategy and strategic plan are going to produce changes, often fundamental ones, through your entire organization. Bright clients have taught me repeatedly that these strategically mandatory changes can frequently bump into these Naysaying Debbie Downers who would not agree with a new strategic direction if it doubled their salaries. These 10% will never get it.

In addition to the 10% of Naysaying Debbie Downers I just rather rudely described, another 40% will require coaxing in order to comply with your new strategic direction. I know, right?! 40%! These Open to Changers are open to suggestion, ready to learn, and perhaps curious. Most important, they can be outstanding judges of the culture shifts needed in your company so that your strategy and strategic plan are achieved. They are the skeptics. If your strategy and strategic plan falter at first, they may sarcastically point that out, usually to one another. Your strategic direction may not engage them at first. But, when they do catch the momentum, look out: they will become your most credible and effective leaders *because* they were initially skeptical. Perhaps their doubts about the direction were initially founded on past failed attempts at strategy formulation or strategic planning. You never know. Some degree of healthy skepticism is nourishing. I am attracted to the strategic direction skeptics because I learn so much from them, especially about their company culture defects and strengths.

Further to the right on this bell-shaped curve are the 40% fully in support; they buy in right away to the new strategic direction. These Direction Supporters are also valuable, like the Open to Changers, but for a different reason. Their swift support illustrates that they were able to quickly grasp the new strategic direction, internalize it, and will help implement that strategy. They often make outstanding leaders of the first-year strategic initiatives because they are already modeling the behaviors consistent with the new strategic direction. With their words and actions, they show the company the new ways to be effective and contribute. They are not skeptical, but they do think about things before just doing them. They may just be more change-oriented, or quick learners. Following visionary leaders comes naturally to them, although they are not followers. They just inherently "get it" more quickly than some.

Far to the right on this bell-shaped curve are the amazing and remaining 10%. These are the Making It Happeners who will passionately make this new strategic direction happen. They will enthusiastically, and in some cases immediately, refine their roles, responsibilities, job descriptions, and current workload to support the strategy itself and the strategic plan. They will assertively be part of the internal communication team to get the word out about the new strategic direction. Their attitude is "whatever it takes." They stand behind that commitment. Some of them were part of the development of the strategic plan itself. The ambition expressed in that plan is *in* them. Describing that as "buying in" is like calling Michael Phelps (the most decorated Olympian of all time)[11] "a bit interested in swimming."

Think "Strategic Perfume"

I offer that discussion above on the bell-shaped curve because epic strategic planning retreats are important for companies to survive, much less thrive. You need to know what you are up against internally. Finding your strategic essence is infinitely more important than documenting a mediocre strategic plan that does not ruffle feathers internally. Strategic essence is a bit like perfume. That may sound strange, but stick with me here…

Perfume is an essence. People have been making it for millennia to try to mask or enhance body odor by using fragrance to emulate some of nature's nicer smells. Did you know that, due to differences in body chemistry, temperature, and body odors, no perfume will smell exactly the same on any two people? It is a multibillion-dollar industry, and every single product that is made and sold does not smell the same on you as it does on me. I think it is fantastic that the intrinsic character of each person *changes* the fragrance. My mom loved to wear Chanel No. 5, but it produced a different scent on her than it does on my wife. The product is the same, but the *essence* is different.

Your business strategy is the same way. Like different perfumes, there are different business strategies from which to choose. It may appear I am oversimplifying, but if you do your research, you will see there are actually not that many *organizational mentality* choices, or mindsets, you can make for your organization. Not even a dozen. That's it. But, choosing wisely is of great importance. Think of your organizational mentality as the main ingredient in your rare strategic essence. When you spray this strategic perfume on your organization, it will take on a unique essence.

Years ago, I met a CEO who later became a client. He was very interested in the topic of market mentality as a central strategic idea for the future of his company. It is one of very few (fewer than a dozen) organizational mentality choices I referred to above and which I will describe later in this chapter. As CEO of this organization, he was 110% sure this was the right mentality for his leaders to take on. So, he read up on it. He studied case histories on how to become a more market-driven company. He became an expert in market-driven organizational development. He analyzed other businesses and several competitors who had deployed this strategy. He weighed the market-driven mentality against other strategic choices and became utterly convinced it was the right play for at least the next five years, maybe more. He observed that his organization should do what so-and-so (the competition) was doing with their strategic choice. In other words, he recognized he did not yet have a market mentality leadership team, but strongly believed he should have such a team in the next several years, like so-and-so. He looked forward to presiding over this transformation. So, he socialized his market mentality idea with his board and top leaders. It took a few weeks. And, to his executive joy, they agreed with the braininess of his concept. So, he held a planning meeting for a half day in a company conference room to metaphorically spray the strategic perfume of market-driven greatness on his leaders. He showered the group with insights about what it means to be market-driven, and they agreed with his insight. As a group, he wrapped up the meeting an hour early. It was all very efficient.

But nothing happened. Nothing changed. Weeks went by. It was as if nothing happened. Because he forgot important steps in this *process*; he overlooked the intrinsic nature of his organization, and he forgot *place*. He simply reduced the retreat to a half-day meeting in his conference room. Worse, he peddled the market mentality strategic perfume to the leaders in the room without engaging them intellectually and emotionally. Out of respect, executive ignorance, or some combination, they feigned agreement. They nodded their heads. When leaders smile and bob their heads effortlessly like that, one should worry. What he probably received was not agreement at all, but cheerless compliance. They were privately thinking, "*There goes the boss again.*"

He provided no critical thinking *process* through which they could deeply examine this in conversation, to explore their cultural readiness, to discover their leaders' individual preferences, to investigate how this might impact the organization, to consider the operations' impact, to contemplate the unintended consequences, and to take adequate time to do all of this and more. He did not select a facilitator to lead an independent discussion on this. So, there was no objective input from all of his leaders. He allowed no time to think about it in a great retreat *place*, to talk about it first while on a stroll through the woods, then over cold beverages, and later on the links, maybe with his spouse.

Therefore, he got nothing. He just took a good strategic choice he saw in a seminar because competitor so-and-so was implementing it. He rashly concluded his organization could utilize that formula, too. It is as if he sprayed this strategic market mentality perfume into a breeze, not on his organization. It smelled faintly sweet for a moment, and then it wafted away. There was no genuine essence. No spirit. No soul. It had no hope of sticking. No one in his leadership team was at that key moment connected to the strategy. In the end, he just gave strategic planning a bad rap.

I see this. All. The. Time. I see top CEOs—I mean, excellent leaders—read a good website, study a whitepaper, covet the way their competitor applies this in their business, learn more in some seminar, read a book (whoa now Emison!), hold a rather diminutive meeting to talk it over, and then senselessly counterfeit the strategy in their own organization. They expect transformation. But they do not get that. Even though spraying Giorgio Armani Acqua di Gio smells lovely on my neck (according to my wife), it smells harsh when it is sprayed in the air and quickly fades away.

Find Your Rare Essence

Throughout all these years facilitating dozens of strategic business planning retreats, I was in search of rare essence, not forgeries. My clients got that. We weren't going through the motions in our retreats. They understood what we were really after: the output of the retreat that would drive results, the rare essence. But a tiny handful of the CEOs I served had gone to a seminar, watched a YouTube clip, or whatever, and presumed they could install this strategic choice (like being a market mentality company) into their organization. They treated strategy like a piece of software. Wait for it. Wait for it. Wait for it…Okay! It's installed! Now, hit run and…oops. Hmmm? Nothing happens.

The best CEOs I met all those years had discernment. They would take the same steps as other CEOs in their research and selection of a business strategy. They, too, sat in the seminars. They, too, read the business strategy articles and books. They, too, socialized the idea with top leaders internally. But, when it came time to consider this strategic choice, they did not irresponsibly compress these monumental decisions to a half-day session in a conference room (i.e., recklessly oversimplify the process of considering it as a leadership team). They stopped. They reflected. They deliberated. They worked it over for days in an independently facilitated *process* with their leadership team. They invested in a serious and significant offsite retreat at an amazing *place* to really discover their strategic essence. To make it their own. To make it epic. Why? So they could achieve the promise of all great planning retreats: strategic transformation and growth. Can you think of a more important (not more urgent, more important) priority in your business right now?

Set the reimagination bar high. Put in the work. Do not take shortcuts in your process. If you want an epic strategy and a passionate leadership team that is excited with the new direction, then ask your retreat facilitator to help you hunt for strategic essence. I think Jim Collins and Jerry Porras, who brilliantly created the core ideology and envisioned future concept,[12] were in search of extraordinary conversations among intelligent leaders that *must* get drawn out. This drawing-it-out process is not unproductive time. It is the most productive a top leader can be! The same is true with the marvelous Simon Sinek and his book *Start With Why: How Great Leaders Inspire Everyone to Take Action.*[13] His insightful "why" process is a stunning manifesto for determining your strategic essence. When you know your "why," things come into focus, especially if you articulate it in plain and simple strategic language. In David Epstein's New

York Times bestseller *Range*, he encourages the reader to seek a wide variety and great depth of strategic thinking. He argues, very persuasively, that it will be this breadth and depth of input that leads to a brilliant business strategy, gifted musician, or victorious athlete. Of course, that means you have to do some strategic thinking of sufficient breadth and depth, as a team, doesn't it?

The Strategic Bundle

There is a constellation of critical decisions you and your team need to make in order to develop your company strategic essence. Put another way, when you make all of these decisions, they become your strategy. It's not just one decision. It is a bundle. En masse, those decisions *are* your strategic essence. Like the ingredients to make a particular perfume, this is your unique strategic recipe or formula. At the epicenter of these decisions is the verdict on *organizational mentality*. Add to this the essential and much-related decision about your *mission*. Like organizational mentality, mission is meant to be a statement of purpose that transcends day-to-day business and will stand the test of time, quite likely for decades. This mission decision can stem from the decision on organizational mentality or the other way around; they are *that* highly related yet slightly different. Add to this a decision about your *values and culture* that are meant to last for decades. Add to this a diagram that illustrates the *change mandate* before you, as a company. Then, add the *big picture vision* that together express your aspiration and how you will stimulate progress for the company. This conveys what you see for the company in the future, usually three to five years hence. Now add to this the decision on _growth_, how it will be measured, both financially and non-financially, the methods you will utilize, and the rate of growth you seek. The final element in your strategic essence constellation is the _unique selling proposition_ that this future-oriented company with all of these ingredients will be able to make, credibly.

The amalgam I just described is your strategic essence. Each part requires serious consideration, a great deal of research, and a number of well-facilitated and critical conversations among leaders. Each component, when finally fused together, expresses the strategic essence you will need to thrive.

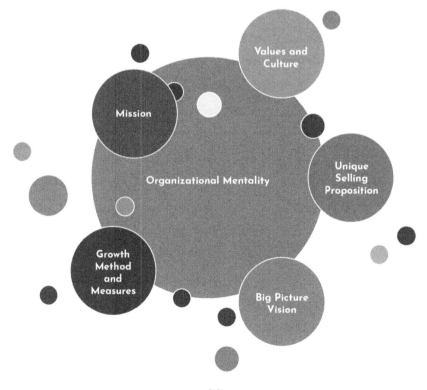

So, what is your company's strategic essence *right now*, and what does it need to be going forward? I am asking for your actual business strategy, not your strategic plan (hard to answer, huh?). Once you have an answer, and maybe have even written it here, consider whether all of your top leaders agree on the answers. This is why strategic business planning retreats are so critical. You have limited resources and you need to make strategic business choices. But you and your leaders may not all have the same mentality to start with. This is especially so in the Built Marketplace I serve, where rugged individualism, industry structures, adversarial relations, and internal corporate tribalism conspire to misalign leadership teams from the neck up. Does your industry look a bit like that, too? Are you similarly misaligned?

Strategy Is Making Choices

Earlier, I mentioned about your organizational mentality choice that there are only a few options, fewer than a dozen. Interestingly, these mentalities can be grouped by common themes. Researching your alternatives and selecting your core business strategy from these groupings is essentially like choosing your perfume or cologne. I define organizational mentality as the central decision-making outlook or temperament in your company. It is how you think. CEOs and their leadership teams often have an unspoken understanding or tacit agreement on their company mentality or character. But, more often, they do not. Most CEOs and their leadership teams have never had the talk about organizational mentality, their "why," and so on. Or, if they have, the conversation was shallow, inconclusive, and therefore swiftly lost steam. You see, leaders all think hard individually but rarely together. I found myself in countless retreats over the years helping leadership teams fully examine their mentalities. Not surprisingly, they learned in the retreat that they actually each had different organizational mentality paradigms as leaders. I discovered that this discrepancy in strategic thinking is where problems like silos, turf, tribalism, and internal competition originate. Leaders often do not know how fundamentally they disagree with their own teammates. But they know they are "not on the same page" because they will use those exact words to describe their disconnects. I can tell within an hour of meeting a leadership team if they are fragmented at the organizational mentality level. So can you, if you pause to listen.

Now for the twist: it is impossible for an organization to successfully harness more than one of these mentalities in one company at the same time. If you allow your leadership team to blend a combination of these mentalities (which is the tendency) instead of selecting the one central decision-making paradigm, you enable a weird and unproductive corporate identity dissociation to gain traction inside your company. Your business will behave a bit like that poor girl in the movie *Sybil* whose identity is fragmented into 13 different personalities or "alters." If you have a corporate culture clash going on in your company, you might have the Corporate Sybil Syndrome as a result of having multiple mentalities coexisting within your own four walls. Strategy is about choices, and your choice of one organizational mentality is where it starts. Great strategic clarity starts with discussing as leaders what your one organizational mentality will be, or should be, as an organization.

Organizational mentality plays a role in strategic decision-making in every way you can imagine and several ways you cannot. Do you invest in that new product line? Do you expand geographically? Do you hire that new executive? Do you implement that new brand strategy? Do you go fully Lean, culturally? Do you divest of that one business unit? When? Do you make that large capital appropriation? Do you acquire that supplier? Do you focus the organization on financial results more than other considerations? Is this the year to grow internationally and if so, where? These and virtually all major questions facing your organization can be answered better and more easily when you are first clear on your mentality. It is the first in a series of major decisions that make up an epic strategic plan. Please circle the one below that best describes your organization today. Place a big star next to the one that best describes your hopes for your company. They may or may not be the same.

- Ops Mentality: The strategic essence here is *operational process excellence*. This thinking is about being operationally effective, efficient, and innovative. Some will say this is not a strategy but a necessity of any business. They are wrong. I have seen this mentality wisely chosen as a core business strategy, and it has

successfully repositioned some client companies
for sustained market advantage. Any Lean business
gets this, Toyota being the most notable example
globally. Ops mentality is a strategic choice, not just a
business necessity.

- Market Mentality: The strategic essence here is *market segment devotion*. This thinking is about looking at everything your company does and every decision you make in light of what the markets want or need. Markets are clusters of your customers, mostly. Markets are not your products and services but the grouping of customers (and suppliers) who buy or influence the decision to buy your products and/or services. A great example of a market mentality business is Titleist, the golf ball company. Their market is the golf industry sector, intelligently segmented behind their strategic boardroom doors, I am sure. But they do not just manufacture golf balls. They strategically research the market and deliver an array of products and services within the golf-related markets. By the way, notice I am not describing market*ing* driven. Having a market mentality does not mean, for example, your marketing department has more influence in your company than other departments. Long live the Pro V1.

- Customer Experience Mentality: The strategic essence here is *customer fervor*. Every successful company is customer-oriented. Customer-driven companies adopt thinking that leads to putting the customer at the top of the organizational chart and running the corporate culture relentlessly toward that principle. These organizations do not just believe the customer is right; they believe the customer is their purpose. Not culture. Not profits. It can be wildly inefficient in some cases and wildly successful in others. Ask Lululemon Athletica, a Canadian company. They started out in 1998 by making (and outrageously pricing) athletic apparel for fit women. They developed a near-cult following. Look at Lululemon in 2020: $3.9 billion in revenue, 15,700 employees, and multiple product lines including some that are not even apparel, like the home exercise start up Mirror.[14] Their entire product range has expanded tremendously and now includes men (thank you). They have a customer experience mentality and their customer is athletically inspired, regardless of fitness level or physique.

- Product or Service Mentality: The strategic essence here is *product or service excellence.* A product or service mentality company is centered on its product or product line, and all decisions are made based on the product line. Let's take 3M's Abrasive Cloth. To this day, 3M is so product mentality–oriented that it is almost science- or curiosity-driven. Literally, products get developed at 3M by engineers, chemists, technicians, and the like. These products have certain performance characteristics. When the product is under development, it is brought to marketing to

essentially figure out what market or customer might
want this product. Many companies make this strategic
choice, including Drift and Trello. Some do not make a
product but offer a service instead; they, too, can often
think in this same way. Genius level achieved!

- <u>Growth/Advancement Mentality</u>: The strategic essence
here is *brisk sales*. When a leadership team thinks this
way, it is choosing to make every major decision based
on its growth potential. Many might call this revenue
driven, but I feel that is a bit judgy. Many growth/
advancement mentality companies are trying to grow
margins or customer experience, not just their top-line
revenue. They know that growth may focus on other
metrics than the top line. Being growth-oriented is not
the same as having a growth/advancement mentality.
The difference is intensity. Chik-fil-A, for example, has
a faith-based leadership team and generally believes
that assertive or aggressive growth is essential, not
just desirable.
- <u>Technology/Know-How Mentality</u>: The strategic
essence here is *technological know-how*. These are
leadership teams who think and make their decisions
entirely on technology factors and proprietary
knowledge. All companies use various forms and levels
of technology. But a technology/know-how mentality
company does it faster, better, or just for the sake of
the technology itself. It is a digital culture and a digital
mindset. This does not mean all such companies are

Silicon Valley businesses. A very good example is Starbucks. I know, I know—it is a coffee company and is very customer- and employee-oriented. But, for at least the past 10 years, their strategic investments have been made in technology. For example, in 2020 Starbucks partnered with technology entrepreneurs at Sequoia Capital China to innovate the retail experience for customers through digital transformation. They are not just technology-oriented; they have the technology gift. That happens, not by accident, but because their leaders think that way. Another amazing example is Caterpillar, the heavy equipment company that makes that incredible mining and construction equipment.

- Purpose or Philanthropy Mentality: The strategic essence here is *transcendent purpose.* As the great writer Daniel Pink aptly pointed out, there has been a rise of a new type of organization in recent decades. Purpose mentality companies have a calling in mind. It is a movement for them. Their company is so much more than a business that it transcends the notion of business itself. A very interesting example of this is the clothing company Patagonia. Dig deeply into their history and culture and you can see their goal goes far beyond selling clothes; their core purpose is to protect and preserve the environment. Recently, there has been a rise in not-just-for-profit organizations across the U.S., which aligns with a philanthropy mentality. While rare, it can become its own leadership mentality.

For example, I have served a private, Christ-centered company where the culture soars way past purpose-driven and is completely now philanthropy-driven.

- Profit Mentality: The strategic essence here is *bringing home the bacon* (the Benjamins, the biscuits). Albert "Chainsaw Al" Dunlap was an American corporate turnaround mercenary. He passed away in 2019 after a career filled with heavy criticism from business press. Some thought he was psychopathic. But profit mentality companies appealed to Al; they were not just profit*able*, but profit *driven*. In these organizations, all thinking and major decisions are made entirely on profit potential. It may sound a bit harsh, but it is a choice to put shareholder return ahead of employees or customers. Believe it or not, there can be an appropriate time for this in the life cycle of any business.

These ways of reasoning are neither right nor wrong, but they are profoundly different. It is impossible and unwise to select any more than one for your company. I am not judging one leadership team's organizational mentality choice over another; I am just distinguishing them from one another. Those mentalities described above are the most common ones I have observed in leadership teams in my strategic retreat journey spanning three decades. When a leadership team has conversations about their mentality, it drives a *clearer* strategic essence. The fog of strategic ambiguity starts to *clear*. This *clarity* is essential for your business to survive and thrive.

Almost every time I have led conversations about this topic among leaders in a retreat, someone inevitably asks, "Tom, are you asking what our mentality is now, or what we want it to be in the future?" I reply that both of those are important to talk about in a retreat. Being deliberate about that choice is a key early step in any epic strategic planning retreat. Therefore, strategy in an epic retreat can actually start with that organizational mentality conversation. There are, of course, more components to a business strategy than your choice of mentality, but it is at the center.

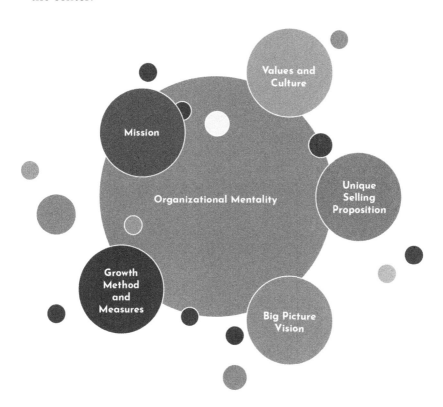

A word of caution: the leaders in the retreat room will have strong likes and dislikes about these mentalities. Persuasive opinions will be voiced on which mentality is practiced today or should be chosen going forward for the organization. Leaders may even find as a collective that they want to possess two or three simultaneously, as if organizational mentality were some strategic smorgasbord. Absolutely no. This is not the right way to approach the choice of organizational mentality. This is not some democratic discussion of these choices leading to an incongruous fusion of two or more. Nor is it selecting your mentality about the corporate silo-reinforcing notion that the marketing department is market mentality, the operations department is ops mentality, the finance department is profit mentality, the human resources department is purpose mentality, and so on. The really high-energy and transformative moment comes when the leadership team has explored all of these mentalities and boldly chooses the single and central (principle) mentality of the company, the one mindset for the entire company going forward. This later drives compelling and clear answers to your corporate "why," mission, values and culture, big picture vision, growth methods and measures, unique selling proposition, change mandate, and more. Remember, strategy is making decisions about what to do and what not to do for your long-range competitive advantage.

Model Airplanes and Business Models

When I was in seventh grade, my younger brother, Bill, took up model airplane building. He would save up his meager allowance, ride his bike down to the 7-HI Shopping Center in Minnetonka, and buy a model airplane B-52, Spitfire, or Mustang. He would carefully bring it home and then fastidiously put that model together downstairs in our recreation room while I cranked some Lou Reed vinyl on my stereo. Just as there are different models of airplanes with subtle yet important differences, I have learned that there are different models of companies in the Built Marketplace not based on what they do but how they want to be positioned. They model certain characteristics. Obviously, an architect does architecture, an engineer does engineering, a contractor does construction, a real estate developer does development, and so on. But how they want to be positioned tells us what model of firm they are trying to achieve.

Therefore, to complement the list of *Organizational Mentalities* above, here are models of companies I have observed just in the U.S. architecture, engineering, construction, and real estate sector. These are not based on what they design or build but how they want to be positioned. Maybe in your organization, assuming your organization is not in the Built Marketplace, you will find parallels to these (below). And, yes, you got it right: it is not wise to try to foster more than one of these models in any one company. Don't agree with me? Answer this: do you think a project field superintendent who works in a construction company that does all of its work with ethical negotiated contracts is different from a project field superintendent who works in a hard-nosed, low-buck construction company? Well, yes. Moreover, switching from one model (negotiated) to another (hard-nosed) is virtually impossible and will actually confuse the project field superintendent, not to mention his customers. Again, please circle the model that best describes your company today and place a star next to the one you aspire to if you are in the construction industry. If not, draw up similar business model discussions that apply in your industry.

- **The Brilliant Einstein.** These organizations are the smartest at something exceptionally complex. They might be found not just delivering architecture, engineering, construction, or real estate work, but writing about it in some journal or speaking about it from the front of a room at a major industry conference. These original thinkers can conceive of solutions to the most complex, gigantic mega-projects. They charge a small fortune, or often quite a large fortune, but their customers do not care. They are buying on proven and exceptional technical brilliance, not price.

- **The Niche Relator.** This is the focused firm that has narrowed down to just three to five sectors. They do not wish to be everything to everybody but they do wish to be everything to just a few. In their niches, they add front-end and often unexpected services, such as strategic planning offered by a niche-oriented firm. They tend to form deep relationships in their chosen niches. They have learned a powerful word: no. If opportunities come to them outside their niches, they just say no.

- **The Community Leader**. These companies lead at the local level and tend to offer a very wide array of architecture, engineering, construction, or real estate services and deliver a wide array of projects compared to their peers. They are deeply ensconced in their community (whether that is one community or many communities), serving on every important board, political, or community organization. They expect their employees to do the same. If a project or initiative of interest is gaining confidential traction in some corner of the community, you can be sure they are already there guiding the discussion. They do not want to chase work elsewhere. For general building contractors who think this way, they tend to offer a great deal of self-performed work. Self-performance does not travel well.

- **The Business Orchestrator**. These organizations know how to put together complex real estate and facilities work. They look at public-private partnerships and integrated project delivery with glee. In fact, they were at the forefront of these innovations. They know how to put together teams of organizations with potentially conflicting motives and help them form a shared motive. They tend to have more lawyers, business consultants, and finance specialists. They do not have to do all the work themselves, and in fact they often do not want to. An example might be a design-build developer who opts to go construction management

as an agent on a pursuit and have other general
contractors do the work. These firms are a lot like
consulting firms.

- **The Bare-Knuckle Antagonist**. These are the low-cost,
low-buck alternatives. They seek the low-frill work
and offer low-frill services. When I hear a mechanical
contractor CEO say to me, "I don't know how Fred
at ACME Mechanical can bid it for so cheap, he must
be losing money on every job," I tell him, "He isn't; he
just has a different profit model than you do." Often
these companies drive cost from the process by being
especially lean. But, more often, they price low and
then change-order their way to profits. Lawyer up.

- **The Green Company**. These are organizations who
long ago discovered the idea of natural capitalism.
To them, LEED AP personnel (Leadership in Energy
and Environmental Design) are not just nice to have
on staff. Green is the purpose here, and they can
prove routinely that green development, design, and
construction is less costly in the long run and better
for our environment. And, in case you think that may
be the full extent of their uniqueness, remember that a
green company is very attractive to Generation Y and
Generation Z employees. They sense the transcendent
purpose, and they dig it.

In over 30 years of facilitating conversations behind closed
doors with executive teams, I have made a discovery: your

strategic essence is what results when you start with the question of how your leadership team wants to have the company positioned. I have often used analogical thinking to help leaders explore these options. For instance, and independent of the conversation above, compare your company to those from entirely different industries. In working with Julie, the leader of a manufacturing company, I might ask, "Julie, do you want your company to be the pharmacist style company in your area, or more like a nurse, or perhaps more like a psychotherapist, or maybe the brain surgeon?" This simple healthcare analogy can help Julie and her leadership team talk for two hours in a way they never have. They soon realize that what I am really asking is what level of hand-holding does Julie want to offer in her business model and how much customization is she willing to tolerate in her business model. I am asking her to pick a strategy and pick a market position. These discussions will extract the essence, especially if you provide a strong enough *process* for doing this and if you make the *place* for these many conversations a priority. Later, you can seriously consider and then add in the other key ingredients to your strategic essence, including mission, values and culture, and big picture vision. Do all of this in the right *place* with the right *process*, and you are doing epic strategy.

Chapter Summary

Not only is the D.C. band Rare Essence amazing musically, but their name also captures what you are really after in your leadership team and with an epic retreat. Set the bar high and go for it. I have never, not once, had a client tell me that their leadership team gets together too often to think strategically. It has always been "we need more time like this together" or "this retreat was far too long in coming." A lot has been written on strategic this and strategic that. Entire business school programs are devoted to strategy. There are overly simplistic templates you can fill out if you want lame strategy from a box. But think of your strategic essence as a perfume, a strategic scent you are trying on organizationally. A business strategy in Organization A will not take on the same character as it does in Organization B because they differ culturally. Culture does not eat strategy for breakfast;[15] it enhances it. Accept the fact that a transformational retreat process cannot be reductive in nature. Draw it out. Make it big. Discover your organizational mentality and your "why?"

Chapter Challenge Questions

1. What is your company organizational mentality now? What should it be in order to thrive in current conditions? Why?

2. I have suggested that your mentality and mission are very related but are not the same. What is the mentality of your leadership team, and what is the mission of your organization? Are they related? What do you think of the constellation of decisions (the components) that I

think are a powerful and comprehensive way to express your strategic essence?

3. What are the Corporate Sybil Syndrome problems in your organization? Name each of the cultures in your organization that might be creating an us/them problem. How might it be handicapping your organization from emerging stronger?

CHAPTER FIVE

DEVELOPING AND CAPTURING A GREAT PLAN AT A GREAT LOCATION

 "Knowledge speaks. But wisdom listens."
JIMI HENDRIX

Psychedelic Strategy

In 1966 in Westminster, England, Jimi Hendrix, Mitch Mitchell, and Noel Redding formed a band that produced three studio albums and became one of the most iconic bands in rock history. The manager, Michael Jeffrey, coined the name The Jimi Hendrix Experience. I was a lad of eight and didn't know anything about them at the time. But six years later, while helping my neighbor Dave Hamilton with his basement radio station (no kidding, he ran his own radio station with a whopping transmission range of a quarter of a mile and later in life became a famously successful radio general manager), I stumbled across the album *Are You Experienced?* I still remember listening to Hendrix psychedelic rock for the first time. Many music aficionados still say it was the most successful debut rock album of all time. Since what we are after in this book is epic planning retreat experiences, let's set the bar there: create and deliver an *experience* that will be forever unmatched. It will be an experience during which you will both develop and capture their strategic direction together in two, two-day retreats with about one month between them.

Stretch Your Legs

Let's walk around this room a bit, the space where this epic strategic planning retreat is about to happen. You want to dig in and deliver an epic retreat soon. Cool!

It is one in the afternoon, and your two-and-a-half-day retreat has its toes on the starting line. Think back to any great retreat setting you have been to or imagined. It could be in an executive wellness and conference center, your own boardroom, a stellar hotel conference room, a resort with an exquisite view, a cruise ship at sea, or an upscale log cabin on a pristine lake. In that setting, there is a room where your team will do most of their work:

- Your best collaborative strategic problem-solving
- The creative moment of new strategic positioning
- That hard conversation about workforce shortages
- The new paradigm shift about what business you are *really* in now

- The mentor who gives that revealing talk on the need for executive team transformation
- The CFO's powerful retirement message in his final year with the organization
- The senior VP of marketing who persuades the rest of management to get on board with a revolutionary new brand platform
- That major investment related to complex innovations like volumetric modular construction (remember, my main niche over the years has been the Built Marketplace)

That and a great deal more is all going to happen here. The room matters far more than you think. Remarkably, and a little disturbingly, it matters more than most professional strategic retreat facilitators think. The entire setting is so much more critical than they realize. Let's keep strolling around.

Here you are, standing in the front of the room. You see an open, U-shaped table arrangement for your leaders, and those tables are not garden-variety hotel plastic folding stock. The chairs look nice but not too cozy and are spaced apart. The air smells fresh, and the temperature is on the cool side but still comfortable. Natural light is streaming in through the windows. The carpet looks new. It is quiet in here.

Hey, is that a reproduction of an Alexander Calder over there?[16] It is beautiful. Those three flat screens built flush into the front look perfect, just the right size. Based on the speaker system in the ceiling, any audio will sound perfect. It looks like everything is wireless, so there are no hideous cables running all over the floor and no trip hazards. The spot where the CEO is going to sit at the open end of the U-shaped table setup is a nice touch. It means they are in the front of the room at all times, even when seated; engaged but not dominating. Smart. That spot on the other end of the U-shaped arrangement looks like it is the facilitator's spot. In each of the nine other place settings around the table, you see a nice leather portfolio and a coffee mug branded with your company logo. Disinfecting wipes are at each seating location. Everything looks awesome.

Gazing now to the back of the room, you see a wall of whiteboards, each with important messages and information about strategic thinking and the retreat. There is a cozy seating area back there, like a living room. So, you have both the "all business" setup with the tables and tablets and the "let's chill" setup in the back of the room to kick off your shoes. Nice. You hear nothing outside those doors, even though you sense there might be a busy hallway outside. What is that you hear softly over the sound system? Is that Los Lonely Boys? La música es increíble! When you walk out that door, you see three other nearby smaller conference rooms reserved in your organization's name. You suppose those are for breakout work, small team stuff. What is the yummy aroma wafting down the hall? Are those... *fresh* chocolate chip cookies on that catering table?! And coffee and tea are there, too. Wait. Walking down the hall towards a door leading outside...are we in a resort? Walking swiftly, you step outside and take in the gorgeous view. A glance around the property further reveals a lake in the distance, walking trails, a gazebo, and a tai chi class underway on the lawn. The CEO had the executive sense to plan for, budget, and deliver an extraordinary strategic thinking experience for the leadership team at a great *place*. Despite a few tiresome guffaws from penny-pinching internal critics, this retreat setting is designed to drive corporate reinvention. While the room is killer and the resort is beautiful, what matters most is what brings people here.

You can hear the team walking up now and can tell they have some energy. Shelly, the senior vice president of marketing and business development, arrives with her husband, who is wearing sandals, Bermuda shorts, and a tee. After a brief smooch on her cheek, he is off to the boat launch with the other spouses. She sort of checks him out as he hustles away twirling his Ray-Bans. Shelly makes her spot at the table. *Anywhere is okay, as long as the sunlight warms my back,* she thinks to herself. She smiles at the leather portfolio and coffee mug. *Perfect,* she reflects; it reminds her of the retreat setting two years ago. She notices the leather portfolio has a new Apple iPad inside and is embossed outside with the message "My Executive Retreat Guide." *Polished,* she thinks. Later, she learns this small device is not just the latest company device upgrade but is loaded with all of the reports, information, reading, and more insights related to strategic business planning. She notices the retreat agenda beside her leather portfolio. She scans the topics, "Welcome, Guest Speaker, Defining Strategy, The Strategic Plan We Are

Building, Strategic Situation Today, Organizational Mentality, Mission, Change Mandate, Core Values, Big Picture Vision, Growth Strategy, Unique Selling Proposition, Markets for Focus" and more. This is real strategic stuff. Chunky, but simple. She realizes she needs tea. Like. Right. Now. As she stirs her infusion, three other top executives and the new guy, Phil, walk in. They are laughing hard at something and seem reluctant to share. It may be politically inappropriate, but you don't care. They have brought energy into the room. *Hmmm,* you think positively, *any one of them could do the CEO's job without a lot of training, really. They are all that good.* They ask where to sit. Shelly indicates wherever, except those two spots on the open ends of the table. Some big decisions are going to be made the next two-plus days. This is good, because so much has shifted externally and internally over the past several years.

Meanwhile, the new arrivals' spouses can be heard walking down the hall with Shelly's husband. Evidently, there is a spouse and significant other boat trip this afternoon. Sodas get cracked open. More leaders arrive in the retreat room and get seated. Phil looks a bit nervous, but he's new. He'll be fine. The Wi-Fi login and password are on the whiteboard, so folks are logging in to check their e-mails one last time before they are forced to go dark. A message on the whiteboard reads, "At 1:15, promptly, disconnect to connect. No mobile devices" and is signed "Your Conscience."

It is almost 1:15. Everyone is here and focused. The facilitator has an espresso with him and looks ready to deliver.

He says the fitness center here is state of the art. There is a spinning class at 5 am tomorrow and yoga on the lawn an hour later. There will be a cooking class and cocktails tonight at 5 pm. It's not just his facilitation skills; it's his servant leadership that supports your success. All of the pre-work he did to prepare for these two-plus days is on those iPads. The flat screens are scrolling inspired photographs and infographics of your corporate accomplishments the past year. No one can take their eyes off those scrolling successes. Someone had the sense to toss in a few unrelated and hilarious images. Crazy laughter erupts in the room every now and then. The staff person from the resort peeks in the room right on time and makes eye contact with you and the facilitator. "Good to go?" her eyes ask. "10 to 4," you nod back.

No indeed, culture does *not* eat strategy for breakfast, you know. That's yet another corporate cliché that has been widely misinterpreted. In reality, culture contributes to strategy and can only eat strategy for breakfast when leaders let it. You are glad you and your team devote time to really think instead of misinterpreting quotes from iconic business strategy thought leaders.

Who are you in this room? You are the CEO. You are the courageous leader who made this strategic planning retreat possible. You are the one who for the last eight years has planned for, delivered, and led four epic strategic planning experiences at exceptional locations that have helped you keep all of your top executives profoundly engaged to the strategy and to one another. You recruited the astonishing new Phil. You helped grow sales 55% in three years and doubled your gross project margins. You helped improve the customer experience. You advised investing in two acquisitions. One of those was the purchase of a profitable technology disruptor that is making it hard for your competitors to succeed. You were the one who insisted on keeping the strategy simple. Most important, you turned around employee morale with your smart corporate reorganization the past two years. And you did it all without yielding your company core values.

In 30 seconds, you will walk to the middle of the room with your opening thoughts. Deep breath now. Nervous? Yes, a bit. No. Excited. You look down at your blue jeans and those shoes your husband makes fun of. "Who wears penny loafers anymore?" he asked when you were at home packing for this retreat. You remember fondly where you were when you bought those loafers on that trip to San Jose, CA. It dawns on you that it was six years ago at a previous strategic planning retreat. By complete accident, you have just discovered a personal story to share in your opening message. It'll be about your shoes. What they've seen the past six years. How the organization has evolved. How the industry sector you are in is transforming. How the organization has matured; no, weathered…soul of the company…sole of these shoes…how you are more culturally aligned across your U.S. operations now…ready to run now, not walk…It will be about trust, vision, and real strategy, not a counterfeit of some other company's strategy.

Lucky you looked down, huh?

Over the next two-and-a-half days, you and your leadership team will again develop a new and comprehensive three-year strategic business plan. You will help these devoted leaders reestablish their personal energy and their shared executive team synergy. They will not only focus on the company but also on their own executive wellness. Absolutely everything is right, all the way down to your shoes. The culinary dinner event and the team building you are doing with the team members and spouses tonight are all set. You look forward to that because you still use a yummy wrapped-asparagus recipe you picked up from a retreat two years ago. The agenda includes a new time slot on well-being, which is important to you, the team, and all of your employees. You marvel at just how you got here in your leadership role. Gratitude washes over you along with a deep urgency to help each team leader, your "A-Team." Would you rather be out on the boat with the spouses, you briefly wonder?

Actually, no.

You have *never* felt more right about this retreat. You know that hundreds of employees and their families are counting on your leadership team to have a sound strategic vision for long-term competitive success. It all comes down to this room. Right now. You stand up and pace to the front of the room, smiling. You tuck your hair behind your ear, take off your reading glasses, look up, and smile. Go with your gut. No written notes, no overly rehearsed message. The team is excited and looking at you. *To* you.

117

Pause There

How does it feel? It probably feels epic to know:

- You have a great leadership team.
- Previous strategic planning retreats have delivered epic results.
- The walk around this retreat room was amazing; the entire resort is inspired.
- You are totally prepared.
- *They* are totally prepared.
- You would fall on a sword for anyone in this room.
- No day-to-day business is going to interfere in this revered planning retreat.
- Employees, family members, business suppliers, and thousands of customers are counting on you and your team to get it right and have a great plan for the future.
- You are, as a group, going to work *on* the business, not *in* the business.
- You have achieved record new levels of diversity and inclusion in your company.
- A new business model is about to emerge for your business in order to become more relevant in your primary target markets.
- Even new guy Phil is going to find traction.
- Your strategic advisor and retreat facilitator is known and trusted by everyone in the room.
- Those shoes still fit.

Yeah, it feels pretty good, I imagine. And it should. Because another epic strategic planning retreat is underway.

The picture I have painted during our short walk together is not fiction for many top leadership teams. There is nothing imaginary about this exceptional retreat place, the detailed process that led to it, or the transformative results that will stem from it.

A Hundred Little Things and One Big Thing

The key to these two phases of the Strategic Clarity Roadmap is a hundred little things (process) and one big thing (place). Think of place as hospitality. It's being an excellent host and listening really well to your guests, just as you would if they were visiting your home for the weekend. A great facilitator is a listener. In the retreat, you will have this special experience together, one that brings clarity to their strategic situation, galvanizes leaders together as never before, and sets the corporate roadmap for the next several years. You will want to listen unusually well and welcome them to this special place.

So, how do you select the right location? Here is how I approach it. First, the retreat location, besides being professional, needs to fit with their strategic situation developed in the first phase. For example, if the company is performing poorly, you might want to think about a low-frills retreat setting like a local school or (yes, I have seen this) in the mezzanine café above a local grocery store. That may seem counter to much of what

I advise in *Chunk*. I know that going low frills almost always backfires. But, there are times when an organization can engage leaders in strategic planning even when the pocketbook is empty. Or, if the company is located in a crowded metro area and the leadership team needs some time to rejuvenate personally and as an organization, you might want to get them out to the country, or out *of* the country. If the company is based in a rural location, perhaps it's time to bring them to a big metropolitan area for their retreat. The place needs to align with the client company culture and brand. It needs to feel right for the tone of the entire planning enterprise. It goes without saying that the setting must have the right equipment and tools. It needs to be attractive. Has the facility been renovated recently, or is it undergoing a (noisy and dusty) renovation now? You might also consider the amenities and how they align with your team. For example, if you know your retreat team includes five leaders who hike in their spare time, find a location with ample hiking. If your leadership team has a leader with a physical disability, you will want to make certain the retreat place is ADA compliant (Americans with Disabilities Act of 1990). You want to think of everything right down to wheelchair accessibility. Ideally, it offers far more than lodging and planning retreat rooms. Maybe several examples will help you to find the right place for your next retreat. Here are some examples of the right places that have inspired exceptional work in client strategic leadership teams:

- A log cabin deep in the Minnesota woods because the client company was about to pioneer a new growth strategy

- A conference room in a cruise ship in the Caribbean because the CEO and his team wanted a retreat that mixed business with pleasure—and they still managed to do three days of solid planning on board
- An arboretum with both indoor meeting space and outdoor because the client wanted to focus on growth and their markets, including agribusiness
- A spectacular country barn designed by none other than talented architect Edwin Lundie[17] because the family business owners there wanted a retreat site with farm panache
- A retreat executive learning center with an outdoor ropes course, mountain biking trails, and a kayak park, for obvious reasons!
- A hospital conference room because the client focused on hospital design-build healthcare construction
- A school because the client focused on products and services for K-12 schoolchildren
- A major university conference center because that university was my client's customer
- A newly remodeled and historic theatre because the client wanted to role-play their strategic direction in the retreat
- The jaw-dropping Harley-Davidson Museum and conference center in Milwaukee, WI because that was where this client planned to expand next

- An elegant four-star resort on a prairie with long walking trails perfectly suited for evening group strolls to talk about the company and its future, because this helps to make a retreat more restorative
- A chic hotel in Manhattan with $900/night rooms because the client knew this was by far the most convenient location for his team to gather, despite the nutty cost
- The client headquarters operations floor right in the middle of their busiest time of year because transparency to employees was key
- A community recreation center in Vail, CO because my client built it
- Several world-class destination golf resorts not because all clients are golfers, but because the venue provides an opportunity for unique team building out on the links with actual, real team-building activities
- Caesars Palace in Las Vegas because the client had a major industry exposition that same week on The Strip, and top leaders in his firm were all going to be in the area anyway. Plus, they could then easily invite a key supplier CEO in for an hour-long speech on the first morning of their planning retreat.

No Frills Can Work, and So Can Over the Top

On occasion, I found the client had a tiny budget to work with. My family is Scots-Irish, so I get frugality. I once did strategic planning consulting work for a prominent business in Cedar

Rapids, IA. The client had no budget for an elegant retreat location. Resort? Dream on. So, I did some research. Weeks before the client retreat, I discovered Cedar Rapids had one of the most robust and progressive written economic development strategic plans I had ever seen. I read that Cedar Rapids Economic Development Strategic Plan cover to cover. I learned it was also the geographic location of my client's new archrival. It turned out that it did not matter where we held their retreat, so long as it was somewhere in Cedar Rapids. This was the community where my client and his leadership team wanted to grow. We held that session in a modest hotel conference room and ordered sandwiches for delivery. The most important part was simply being in Cedar Rapids. In that epic retreat, the client really came to understand their own local community business development plan, not just their own strategic direction.

After toiling over *place*, I partnered with the right hotel, resort, conference center, or whatever to secure the best setting, right amenities, appropriate logistics, etc. In this sense, the on-site staff became members of this epic retreat experience. I did not let on-site staff stop thinking about that. I cannot tell you how many Marriott Hotels, Best Westerns, Hyatts, Radissons, LaQuintas, Ritz-Carltons, Hiltons, and InterContinentals I've worked in that were fantastic because they had the precise place and right personnel.

I've also led retreats at some singularly exclusive and over-the-top executive retreat locations, including The Thayer Hotel near West Point, The Broadmoor in Colorado Springs, the spectacular Garden of the Gods Resort and Club also in Colorado Springs, the amazing Q Center in Chicago, and The Greenbrier in West Virginia. In working with the general managers, the catering staff, the A/V staff (usually outsourced), even the bellhop, I would let them know who we were, what we were doing in their location, why we were there (if the client approved of this), and what I needed from them. I wanted them to feel connected to this process for my client. This was one of the hundred small ways I made my clients feel special. They knew that even the staff were engaged to help. For example, if I wanted to coach the hotel catering crew, I would say, "I think we need lunch served in the room at 11:45, not noon, thanks. Also, I want the break at 3 pm to feature popcorn, not cookies. The beer on our final day at 5 pm *has* to be a local brew. The planning retreat room main door needs a label that reads: 'Strategic Leaders at Work.' Thank you!"

A Professional Facilitator Cares About These Details

You may think these hundred little details are excessive, inconsequential, or an administrative assistant's job. I call them fitting, important, and very much my job. I once asked the dean of a small private college to talk to a client CEO and his leadership team because we were holding the strategic planning sessions on that college campus. The dean was not only very thankful to the client but also shared his strategic plan for the college and how it had transformed that institution the past five years. This simple retreat add-on cost my client $0, but the client team still remembers his leadership wisdom years later.

Since the 1970s, executive retreat centers have popped up all over the U.S.: in urban centers and out in the country; in association with Fortune 500 corporations, academia, and independently; some hi-tech or hi-touch; some with military-inspired ropes courses or exceptional cuisine and culinary team-building events. Moreover, hotels and resorts have sought alternative revenue by revamping their business model and facilities to gear up for executive strategic planning and corporate wellness retreats. These locations can be stellar for epic planning retreats. It is not an exaggeration to say there is a great location for an epic strategic planning retreat not far from where you are sitting right now.

Chapter Summary

Jimi Hendrix delivered an experience, God rest his soul. This is what a great leadership team can do—must do—in an epic strategic business planning retreat, too. They must have and co-create a memorable experience. The process used to create this experience, and place, are critical. Developing and capturing this plan for the leadership team real time in the retreat, well, that is part science and part art. Chunking it out is the best approach. The retreat location is a critical part of strategic thinking. Not all great strategic business plans are forged at five-star resorts, but the odds improve when the environs are killer. I have delivered epic strategic planning retreats in about every conceivable location. I took great pains to make certain the location aligned with the client situation, and you can, too. Partnering with the onsite team at a retreat site is important. They are pros at hosting such gatherings. It is a huge load off the minds of the participants if everything is just right for their very best strategic innovation.

Chapter Challenge Questions

1. Think back to a long-range planning meeting of any type in your background or experiences. If the meeting was held in an ordinary location with ordinary methods, how did that ordinariness affect the outcome? Conversely, have you been in a strategic planning retreat or executive retreat in which the location was inspired, and if so, how did that affect the outcome?

2. Not every organization can afford to take top management away to a spectacular retreat location. Or can they? How is this decision (i.e., the investment in the right location) an indicator of what will come from the process itself?

3. Why might it be very important for top leaders (after a planning retreat) to not boast to others inside or outside of their organization about the elegant retreat location and stunning amenities? In other words, if a leader has participated in an epic strategic planning retreat, why should they not crow about it with others inside their company?

CHAPTER SIX

LET'S GET CHUNKY!

 "Diamonds are nothing more than chunks of coal that stuck to their jobs."
MALCOLM FORBES

Chunking Out Your Retreat Process: The Meeting Agenda

Now that we have thoroughly explored place for our two, two-day offsite retreats, the second consideration is ginormous: the agenda and flow. The stream of information sharing, decision-making, and additional sidebar conversations needs consideration in advance. The different learning styles and preferences of the group need to be accounted for. In doing this over many years, I have learned how to organize the major pieces of a strategic planning retreat agenda into chunks. Some decisions need to be made before others, and some need to be revisited after making seemingly unrelated but smart decisions in another area of the business. For example, the decisions on the topic of corporate mission need to be made fairly early in any retreat process. Decisions made by the team later in the same retreat (e.g., the next day) may create the need to go back to the in-process mission and slightly revise it in real time at the retreat.

When I chunk this all out in advance and appropriate one hour for this—three hours for that, two hours for this, and 45 minutes for that—the chunks flow together into a retreat cadence.

This process of connecting the retreat and its chunks into one contiguous process reminds me a bit of Queen's "Bohemian Rhapsody." Freddie Mercury crushed it with this renaissance rock classic with bits of guitar licks mixed in with references to Galileo and Figaro, a little bit of straight-up opera, and, well, "...very, very, frightening!" It was one of the few rock songs to emerge from the 1970s progressive rock movement that had wide appeal. It rode atop the U.K. singles charts for nine consecutive weeks. In the U.S., it only reached #9 on the Billboard Hot 100 until it appeared in the film *Wayne's World*. Then, it popped up to #2! The song was groundbreaking in how the artists (and producer, Roy Thomas Baker) placed seemingly disparate pieces of music into the same overall melody. It's one song in perfectly orchestrated chunks.

So, I want you to see these two phases (Develop and Capture) as contiguous. Like "Bohemian Rhapsody," the retreat is one song organized into chunks. To help you keep track of where you are in the Develop and Capture process, I am once again providing the Strategic Clarity Roadmap. There are two distinct but interconnected phases. At first, the retreat process begins with very divergent conversations and thinking with many points of view and perspectives. At this early stage, there is no sense of urgency for the retreat participants to decide anything. Gradually, the retreat becomes convergent and decisive. That is when I get a little pushy and move the team members toward decisions. So, I organize an epic strategic business planning retreat meeting agenda into broad sections of decisions (1) to build and then (2) to make. Each chunk can be thought of as an ingredient in a delicious gumbo; if you miss an ingredient or two, it will not taste epic. The facilitator is the roux, the base of the gumbo made up of butter and flour, holding an epic strategic planning retreat together with connection and flow.

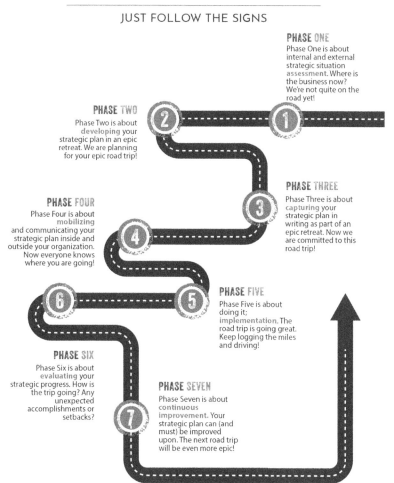

THE STRATEGIC CLARITY ROADMAP
JUST FOLLOW THE SIGNS

PHASE ONE
Phase One is about internal and external strategic situation assessment. Where is the business now? We're not quite on the road yet!

PHASE TWO
Phase Two is about developing your strategic plan in an epic retreat. We are planning for your epic road trip!

PHASE THREE
Phase Three is about capturing your strategic plan in writing as part of an epic retreat. Now we are committed to this road trip!

PHASE FOUR
Phase Four is about mobilizing and communicating your strategic plan inside and outside your organization. Now everyone knows where you are going!

PHASE FIVE
Phase Five is about doing it; implementation. The road trip is going great. Keep logging the miles and driving!

PHASE SIX
Phase Six is about evaluating your strategic progress. How is the trip going? Any unexpected accomplishments or setbacks?

PHASE SEVEN
Phase Seven is about continuous improvement. Your strategic plan can (and must) be improved upon. The next road trip will be even more epic!

129

Before I begin each retreat, I walk the room. I am typically in the retreat room a solid hour before the first arrival. During that hour, I go over the agenda in my mind one last time, make sure the room A/V is working right, coordinate with the onsite staff, make sure the handouts are in the right order, and so on. But mostly, I think about their unfolding strategic direction. In my world, this is like standing on the starting block for the 1,500 meter freestyle swim race, amped but relaxed. Focused. Hungry. It's gonna be a long and exciting couple of days. This is a bit personal, but I also pray. I pray for wisdom and insight. I pray for each of the participants. I pray for the client's customers and suppliers. I even pray for the retreat site staff. This moment of reflection then enables me to sort of "let go and let God," as they say. To each his own.

I am always completely ready, as is the room, at least 30 minutes before the retreat day begins. There are two reasons for this. First, there are always early birds, a retreat participant or two who like to come in early. Maybe she is as enthused as I am or, more likely, is just a morning person. Either way, I do not want to be too busy working on my A/V or the handouts when she saunters in. I want to greet her, welcome her, and encourage her. It's basic respect and preparedness. The second reason is she may want to talk to me about a specific idea, strategy, or concern. She may arrive early specifically to talk to the facilitator on a matter of some importance. More often than not, the matter she mentions is very helpful for me to understand. But, if I am too busy getting the room arranged, I just pilfered that opportunity from her. Not cool.

Then, I sit down before the official retreat start time (e.g., sitting down at 6:55 am if the retreat starts at 7:00 am) and let the CEO stand up and really get things going for as long as he or she may like. For some CEOs, I coach them on what to say. Others need no help at all. Some need serious coaching, but never seek it! Either way, as the CEO talks, I take notes. When the CEO wraps up, my approach is to draw from my notes, stand up, walk around, and reinforce key thoughts from her. Then, I reinforce the retreat objective as part of their larger objective of strategic clarity. We may do some form of introductions, if needed. Usually, they know each other very well and know me, too. Then, I give us all a quick tour of the whole agenda and how important it is that we follow the process and trust the agenda (one of the retreat guidelines). Often, I organize them into groups of two people to come together and tell the large group their main objective for the retreat in the form of one word, which we then discuss openly as a group.

Then, I *ask* if I have permission from the leadership group to proceed, unless, that is, anyone has a final question about the ground rules, objectives, or agenda. I keep asking for such permission at each step of the agenda. As each chunk of the agenda ends, I document what we have decided and ask if we can move on.

Chunk One: Welcome, and Why Are We All Here, Exactly?

This is usually just as the actual retreat is getting going. It is about getting acclimated to the retreat goals and process. This is the obvious time for the CEO to ask everyone to be seated (or stand up!) before really getting going. Assuming the retreat room(s) is completely arranged according to your specs, this is now about assuring everyone was able to do their pre-reading, which was extensive if you planned this process well. It's about the room and facility *now*, logistics, location of restrooms, break periods, break-out room locations, special dietary needs if not already addressed, room check-in and check-out times, and so on.

It is also important to have the CEO and the facilitator, together, explain the ground rules for an epic strategy retreat. As facilitator, I ensure the gathered group does not mistake this retreat for a seminar. A strategic planning retreat is not a workshop or a seminar! The CEO often reinforces the importance of staying high level, or strategic, and not getting lost in the weeds. It can be important for the CEO to point out to the group why these particular participants are in the retreat and how they were chosen. As a facilitator, I want them feeling a sense of stewardship or servant leadership in the retreat, not like some secret clique. Some of my epic strategy retreat meeting ground rules are obvious, like:

- Start and finish on time
- Unplug
- There are no stripes in this room
- Stay at 30,000 feet to work *on* the company, not *in* the company
- Speak for yourself
- No hijacking the conversation

- This is your retreat, not mine
- Be present

You can find lists of such meeting ground rules online easily. However, other guidelines of mine are unconventional or very specific. Like:

- Seek conflicts of opinion
- Sacred cows will be eaten here
- Dream big or go home
- We did not inherit this company from previous owners; we are borrowing it from future owners
- Disregard your specific role and be as objective as you can
- It's not negative to think critically
- Your industry changed a little bit today. Did you?

In other words, I use meeting guidelines to set the tone right from the start that this is not going to be ordinary or canned. I always ask if they have some of their own leadership team meeting guidelines they like to follow. They very often do.

I do not know why, but there does seem to be a misguided myth out there suggesting that executive teams should work without heated disagreement, that argument in a planning retreat *is* dysfunction. Retreats based on that hypothesis (typically from rookie facilitators) are doomed. When strategic conflict conversations are avoided, it sets entirely the wrong retreat tone. The truth is that, with executive teams, strategic conflict is good. Friction is good. In fact, disagreement in the strategic retreat room is a necessary part of the process along with peaceably resolving disagreements. I make that one a meeting guideline, too. Avoiding conflict as a rule is how leadership teams fall into groupthink and their companies grow obsolete in their markets.

Chunk Two: What Is Strategy, and What Is a Strategic Plan?

The next chunk in the agenda helps the group recall why we are all here. When leaders arrive at a strategic business planning offsite experience, we have to recognize they have made a sizeable mental, emotional, and even physical commitment. Some facilitators might overlook this. The retreat facilitator may think the rest of the group is just as interested in strategic thinking and as knowledgeable about it as he is. This retreat for participants is likely time away from their spouse, significant other, children, hobbies, friends, and more. They actually may not know a great deal about strategic business planning, or they could be an expert. Some of them are missing their son's parent-teacher conference, their daughter's science and engineering fair, their night out with the boys, the visit by Mom, a medical diagnosis on their low back pain, or who knows what. Some have none of those life priorities and are instead eager to engage in the retreat. The participants know this is meant to be a special retreat; the facilitator has to make that feeling possible by reminding the group what is at stake.

I do this by pointing out that strategy is the most important contribution they can make to their organization. It may never be the most urgent, but it is frequently the most important. I never apologize for the retreat and how the retreat is taking them away from their day-to-day responsibilities. I do always thank them on behalf of their hundreds of stakeholders for investing time in strategic decision-making together. I ask, "If you had a clear and compelling strategy, supported by a comprehensive and detailed three-to-five-year strategic plan, how would you use that plan as a management tool?" Interestingly, leaders will quizzically look at one another when posed with this question. They then go on, sometimes elegantly but usually clunkily, to say they will use it to drive smart decisions that will position their company for sustained competitive success out there with limited resources. Perfect.

Then, I define what strategy is, what it is not, the role of a strategic business plan, the Strategic Clarity Roadmap and its seven phases, my role as their facilitator, their role, and, finally, the informal charter we have as a group. I invite the participants to tell me stories about their strategic planning triumphs and flops. Sometimes I rely on *TED Talks* and other tools to set the stage correctly for an epic retreat. My main goal now is to make sure participants do not equate a strategic plan with strategy. I do not want them to think we're just going to fill out some generic strategy form (i.e., go through the motions). And it needs to be clear that this retreat is not a seminar or workshop. Strategy is the end, and the strategic plan is the means. It is usually at this moment that the gathered group is crystal clear why we are all here *and* they can see how the agenda is going to work well.

I usually find myself asking them very early in a retreat if they feel their company is at an inflection point and is about to change substantially. Like many successful businesses, most of my clients are victims of their own success. Let's get that right straight away. When a company grows, diversifies, improves, acquires related companies, expands, innovates, accelerates, and endures, it is a great story of perseverance and ingenuity. But it also creates a new set of challenges. Companies, like people, experience life cycles. These human life cycles are like stages in the life of a private enterprise. The topic of corporate life cycles has been written about and studied for many years. The most effective way I can communicate this topic of inflection points in a retreat is with this diagram, attributed to George Land,[18] who wrote *Grow or Die*. Below the diagram are notes I often ask my client team to talk over.

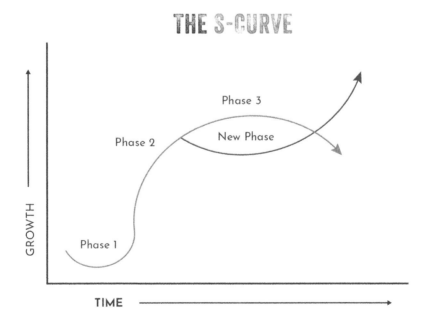

1. Phase One: The Formative Stage

    a. In this early stage of a company, there is not a lot of talk about culture, processes, structure, governance, and so on. Strategic planning? Well, not so much. This stage is about putting food on the table. Informality reigns. The company has entrepreneurial spirit and usually a breathtaking work ethic. Corporate traits include:

        i. Trial and error
        ii. Creative
        iii. Informal
        iv. Customer focused
        v. External
        vi. Hope, excitement, and fear
        vii. Leader dominated
        viii. High risk of failure
        ix. Hard to attract leaders; usually attract loyal followers

2. Phase Two: The Normative Stage

    a. In this midlife stage, the business begins to professionalize. Processes, roles, responsibilities, protocol, hierarchy, data, information, and more get established. The business now has legs, and perhaps the founding entrepreneur moves on. Operational performance reigns. Corporate traits include:

        i. Repeat, refine, and extend the patterns
        ii. Systems and policies

iii. Formal

iv. Process or operations focused

v. Internal

vi. Security and predictability matter

vii. Manager dominated

viii.Lower risk of failure

ix. Easier to attract talent

3. Phase Three: The Integrative Stage

a. This is the stage with the greatest change management peril. The company is becoming something new yet holding to its core purpose and core values. It creates a dynamic internal tension. The company *is* one thing, but leaders wish it to become *another* thing. The previous two phases have produced success, and this then produces new challenges leaders must address with solutions they integrate into the company. Traits include:

i. Change, reinvent patterns, sort new challenges

ii. Cross-functional innovation

iii. Competition and customer focus

iv. Chaos, confusion, and fear

v. Leader and manager role overlaps

vi. Higher risk of failure

vii. May lose talent

viii.Service-oriented

The George Land "S-curve" unfolds at different speeds for every company. Once the cycle is complete and the organization has moved through all three phases, the process begins again. The successful life cycle of your company is likely a series of repeating S-curves. Why does this matter? Because a well-led, determined culture shift at each stage—in support of the strategic direction—is a critical success factor for the retreat team to talk over. This is the sort of topic I get them talking about very early in a retreat.

Chunk Three: Guest Speaker or an Exercise

As a facilitator, one of the great favors you can do for the client is to arrange for (and pay, if necessary) a speaker who may have the right message for the epic retreat you hope to host and facilitate. I learned this on my silent men's retreats at the Demontreville Jesuit Retreat House in Lake Elmo, MN. They always brought in one or two such outside speakers to complement the talks we heard from the Jesuit priests. A guest speaker can be an industry expert, a former client-company executive, a key supplier to your client, a key customer to your client, a local business luminary, you name it. You would be surprised at how interested some such leaders are in supporting your company's success with strategic planning. I once had the privilege of sitting right next to the retired mayor of San Francisco, the very dapper Willie Brown, because someone had this kind of foresight. He made excellent points to my client group that day. He said that group visioning is hard work and requires compromise as well as leadership and that it is the *only* way and has *always* been the only way to move forward as a society. He did some of my work for me that morning! So, such guest speakers are motivation, not retreat fluff.

However, the goal of an outside resource is not just to add credibility to the proceedings. Rather, it is to reinforce the importance of what they are doing in this retreat and to reach for the epic. If that method is not a good fit, I use my icebreaker options. I avoid the canned familiar ones and seek exercises that fit my client. For example, many retreats I lead focus on strategic connections between rival inter-company business units. So, I tailor the well-known yarn exercise. It is a team-building exercise using a ball of yarn to connect everyone to everyone in the retreat room while sharing stories about strategic successes in the company history. When complete, after 30 minutes of such storytelling, the web of yarn connecting everyone is visually arresting. Plus, it gets them up and out of their seats for a few minutes, learning and laughing. It reinforces that a little inter-company rivalry may be cool but flat-out competition is not. I then invite them to lay the room-sized web of yarn on the ground, to cut out a three-to-four-foot section, and, what the heck, wind it gently onto their wrist as a strategic connection bracelet of sorts. Corny? Maybe. Effective? Yes.

My preferred icebreaker exercise for a strategic planning retreat is a storytelling kit called "Zoom" (and its later version, "Re-Zoom"). The kit is made up of large, colorful, laminated sequential story cards from a book written by Istvan Banyai. In

the one-hour exercise, teammates quickly learn that they must make certain in this epic planning retreat to develop and capture a strategic plan that is easily communicated to their many stakeholders. If they cannot connect the 30 individual cards in the right sequential order to tell the story, how are they ever going to be able to tell their interconnected strategic direction story? There is just one trick: they are not allowed to show their cards to one another. They must place the cards into the one and only correct sequence to tell the story. The only way they can make sense of this dynamic puzzle is to talk to one another. In order to solve the problem together, they have to really listen to each other. Every single time I use this, it beautifully reinforces that their company needs one core strategic direction that is easily communicated; they don't need fragmented strategies, plans no one can comprehend, or silly worksheets with obscure strategy references on them. To move into the guts of the retreat, I might say something like this:

"During this retreat, amazing accomplishments will happen. I do not know exactly what they will be or when they will happen or even who will drive them. However, I do know that, if your company is like others, an exceptional decision is going to be made, probably more than just one, then supported by additional decisions that will redirect your entire company onto a new three-to-five-year trajectory. It is almost inconceivable that in only two days now, and another two days a month from now, that a small team of leaders will establish a comprehensive and detailed strategic business plan for the next three to five years for your entire company.

"There is a lot to consider in this process. There are different learning styles present in this room today. There are several exercises I have custom designed for you and your team. These exercises have been proven effective, if you just trust the process. The strategic plan you seek? It will not be like a light bulb going on over your head, nor an epiphany really. I do not think anyone is going to howl, 'Eureka!' No, if you are like most leadership teams, the strategic plan will emerge out of the retreat process gradually.

"As we complete one decision-making exercise after another, let's please remove politics and other factors from the planning process. The decisions build upon one another until your sense is that the strategy is clear and smart and the plan to support it is feasible.

"A month from now, your strategy will be crystal clear and your strategic plan to support it will be brilliant, too. But, you have to trust the process today and tomorrow. Friends, you have made a personal and professional commitment not just to be here but to be co-architects in that strategy development process. It will probably be the most exciting leadership work you do this year, maybe for several years. So, I am grateful as a facilitator you have made this personal and professional commitment to be here, engaged and primed. Thank you. I know it is hard to be away from family and the rest of life, as you know it. But great strategy and great strategic plans simply are not produced in ordinary processes at ordinary locations. The retreat, this retreat, now represents Day One of where this entire organization is about to go."

Chunk Four: Reducing to Situations in Need of Attention and Your Change Mandate

Those first three chunks of the agenda may have taken an hour. The next chunk in the agenda will be a big one: the current strategic situations facing the company. To do that, the retreat team is going to have to reduce down the massive amount of data and information so far from this strategic business planning process. They will need to get down to the shortest, most concise description of the strategic situation(s) facing the organization.

Reducing complexity is the key very early in an epic strategic planning retreat after the first three chunks. We need to reduce down to a short, accurate, and condensed sense of where the business is today. To do this well, the facilitator needs to be able to make certain every participant feels that Phase One (Research) before the retreat was well conceived, well performed, and the resulting Phase One internal and external strategic situation assessment report is accurate. Usually, the retreat itself is not the right place to walk through the entire report in granular detail. The facilitator needs to let the group talk about that report and any other pre-retreat reading. Then they need to reduce it all down to the "here is the strategic situation facing XYZ Company" in about 200 words or less. Think that is plenty of words? This paragraph has 147 words.

I have discovered a powerful and simple way to do this strategic reducing. This method enables the retreat facilitator to lead a group down to what really matters, to take literally hundreds of pages and hours of research from Phase One and boil it way down to a small yet accurate set of strategic situations that need to be addressed. Again, if Phase One was done fully, all one needs to do is break the retreat group into teams of three people (a 15-person retreat group would therefore have five, three-person groups). Ask each small group to break away for an hour and agree on at least two but not more than four strategic "situations that need attention," or "SiTNAs" (a term coined by John Jones, PhD).[19] Typically, a SiTNA is an especially large, complex opportunity or problem that is facing the leadership team. Think gnarly and hard. Even very large corporations may only have three or four SiTNAs. It's a tool for high-performance problem-solving and goes deeper than your typical S.W.O.T., S.P.O.T., or P.E.S.T. Invite everyone to speak up in their small breakout groups. Ask one of them in advance to serve as a scribe for their small breakout group. Remind them this is not an operational review but a high-level strategic review.

A SiTNA could be a key corporate strength identified in Phase One. It could be a weakness identified in the voice of the customer research. It could be an opportunity the company has always wanted to tap but never quite tackled. It could be a fatal strategic weakness no one likes to talk about much. Perhaps it is a great corporate financial strength. But a SiTNA is not a solution. It is simply, and only, a statement of a strategic situation in need of attention. It does not prescribe who needs to give the situation attention, how to do it, or even why it needs to be done. Here are examples I have seen over the past 30 years. Notice none of them prescribe a solution. They just state a strategic situation in need of attention:

- Merger and acquisition activity; consolidation of competitors; it is eroding our supply chain, which has always been our strength.
- Industry-wide margin squeeze.
- We have outgrown our current top executive leaders. Success has brought us new challenges we do not know how to address.
- We are too dependent on three market sectors, none of which is countercyclical, exposing us to undue corporate risk during slow economies.
- Our brand is unidentifiable.
- Our organizational structure does not mirror our strategy; we just seem to keep dead wood around here too long.
- We cannot win on price, but that is how our salespeople are working.
- We have a great opportunity for a vertical market acquisition this year or next.

- Our technology leadership far exceeds that of our competitors.
- Nontraditional competitors from other industry sectors are entering our arena.
- Our market research functions internally and consistently place us in a position to win, which is driving our best ever win-rate now three years in a row.
- Ownership is unclear on what they expect in terms of return on investment or return on equity.
- We are not on the same page as top leaders on important strategic components like mission, values, and vision. We are just each doing our own thing. Nobody really knows our actual mission.
- Lack of diversity and inclusion is making us noncompetitive. We are losing the war for talent because of our own lack of diversity; a group of well-intentioned white men; still, we lack diversity.
- We avoid conflicts and our culture does not hold mid-managers accountable to lead or drive growth. We are frozen and have not grown substantially in five years.
- We solve problems by putting out fires; we are inherently reactive, not proactive, on all big decisions. It is good to be so responsive, but it prevents us from ever dealing with the company systemically.
- Ownership and leadership transition has always been a strength here. We are primed for our next wave of growth with a large cadre of 30-somethings and 40-somethings ready for more leadership.

- We can double revenue and profits in less than three years, but not with our current mix of products.

Again, notice they are not all positive nor all negative. They are strategic whoppers, though, right? Each SiTNA could launch a number of initiatives later in the planning process, but we're not quite there yet. Each is a strategic situation told to me by real people about real companies in real client strategic planning retreats. Their hope in identifying these SiTNAs was to say to one another, in a retreat atmosphere, that if the company addresses their SiTNA, their strategic position as a company will improve considerably and sustainably.

When the small groups come back to rejoin as a full group is when it gets powerful. Now I encourage each team of three people to stand and come to the front of the retreat room to share their SiTNAs, uninterrupted. The role of the epic retreat facilitator is to let each group share their SiTNAs, not a lot else, and ask them to avoid solutions. Thank each group. As you do this, you will experience an *ah-ha* retreat moment. All five of the groups will have very similar, or at least overlapping, SiTNAs. If you lead the process as I have described and facilitate as I have recommended, this will happen *every* time. With five groups asked to identify up to four SiTNAs each, you could potentially end up with 20 SiTNAs. But you won't. You won't even end up with 10. You will arrive at three to five. This *ah-ha* moment feels exhilarating to the participants because it means they are really actually close to consensus on the most important first step in a retreat: accord on where the business is today. As a group, that feels effective. The epic retreat is working. "These are the right strategic situations in need of attention," someone will say.

Often, the process through this chunk will fill an entire day, sometimes less. This chunk requires that you have an appreciation for solving the right strategic problems. Every day across the U.S., employees and leaders in hundreds if not thousands of businesses are working hard to achieve sustained strategic differentiation. That sounds admirable, but, in my experience, these well-intentioned people are busily working on the wrong problems from the start. The entire SiTNA process I have described is designed to prevent the wrong strategies from gaining early traction. I cannot tell you how many misguided efforts are underway, perhaps in your company right now, under the heading of "Strategic Initiative X" that are not even the right initiatives. Carpenters wisely tell us to measure twice and cut once. It is the same with the SiTNA process. Resist the temptation to race to the SiTNA because the retreat agenda says so. If you are going to go overtime on the retreat agenda in any one portion of an epic retreat, the strategic situation assessment is the portion to do it in. Here are actual examples of four well-intentioned SiTNAs that appeared obvious but upon further dialogue in the retreat were not. These important conversations were made possible because we were not rushed in the retreat. These healthy banters took an extra hour or two out of our day but prevented the companies from working for *years* on misguided strategic initiatives:

- Employee attrition is making it hard for us to compete.

  » No, it was not. Upon deeper examination, employee attrition was not the SiTNA at all; it was the result of the SiTNA, which was actually poor hiring practices and mediocre internal career mentoring because of archaic internal beliefs about the value of employees.

- Our gross margins are thinning due to industry commoditization of our services.

  » No, they were not. Gross margins were not thinning for all of the competitors out there. On further examination, margins were thinning only in my client company and it was due to poor sales training and lack of operational excellence, leading to high operating expenses and high cost of sales. It was not only commoditization, but sloppiness.

- Lagging technology adoption by employees is handicapping our utilization of tools to streamline our work.

  » No, it was not the SiTNA, it was the result of the SiTNA, which is that no one in upper management or on the board had a technology background. Therefore, CapEx investments in technology were for many years never even on their radar. Employee technology adoption was not the issue. An outdated technology mentality among top leadership was the issue. The "handicapping" was the result, not the cause.

- Customers are turning over due to poor service, and we are getting less and less repeat business from our tried-and-true customers.

  » This one was pretty close to the actual SiTNA. But, on further examination, the SiTNA was leadership succession and transitions within multiple client organizations. The reason customers were turning over was that the customers were not being managed as accounts. Service delivery was actually okay in this client company. Customer personnel, and personnel in this client company, were all getting long in the tooth. Many of them were retiring. The SiTNA was succession, not service.

I believe it was Samuel Clemens (Mark Twain) who said, "I didn't have time to write a short letter, so I wrote a long one instead." That sums up just about perfectly the importance of a strategic situation assessment that is clear and concise. Long strategic diatribes or novellas do not work. Short and to the point works, and getting it short, clear, and concise takes time.

Our change mandate is the last portion of this chunk of the agenda, and things are about to get real black-and-white. This is about the facilitator asking the group to recap in writing the 8 to 10 ways in which the business needs to change in order to establish a sustained competitive advantage. It is sort of a bundling of the SiTNAs, all on one page. But, importantly, it makes extremely clean distinctions by literally separating the state of an organization today from its state tomorrow. This mandate can be written by the facilitator in a tried-and-true simple T chart. On the left are aspects or characteristics of the company today (i.e., current reality). On the right are necessary aspects or characteristics of the company in the future (i.e., future by comparison). Let the strategic retreat group tell you these. Here is an example:

Today	Tomorrow
Marketing and sales pursuits are reactive; we chase leads	Marketing and sales are proactive; building relationships; we get paid during our sales efforts
Leaders are too busy to develop talent and just ask HR to do it all	Leaders only become leaders when they develop talent in partnership with HR
Customers are frustrated and frustrating	Customers are better as a direct outcome of their relationship with us
Gross project margins are better than last year	Gross margins are better than our competitors
Organizational structure is unclear	New organizational structure erases role ambiguity

Departments do not match up to our processes; lots of misalignments and redundant processes internally	We are strategically aligned, our processes are proven effective and efficient, and we are newly reorganized around those processes
Outside disruptors are entering our industry and dumbing down the markets	We have acquired three disruptive market entrants and have become the preferred choice among customers

What About Just Chillin'?

So far, we are at least one day into a solid retreat and are through the first four chunks. We have not done any detailed future-oriented visioning yet and at least one day has already been invested. This is what I mean when I say an epic retreat takes time and it is the best quality time you can spend together as an executive team. However, there is more to do in subsequent days. It may be the very next day or perhaps two weeks later. If it is the very next day (for my clients, it typically is), I try to plan for an event together in the evening. I often coordinate in advance an offsite dinner excursion to a local haunt, a top-rated restaurant, a private club, a boat cruise, a museum tour, or something. Here, we cut loose and discard the brainy burdens of strategic planning. We celebrate a hard day's work, break bread together, get more strategically intimate as leaders, and in some cases just chill in front of ESPN.

Is this strategy? Well, no. Does it fit into some pathetic online strategy template? No. Does it emotionally move the retreat participants? Yes. Does it grease the relationships between them and with me, which in turn increases our shared strategic capacity for innovation? Ummm, yeah! And that is how they show up the next day lighter, amped, and relaxed, even if they are a bit tired. Before I leave this section on merriment, let me say I typically do NOT hand out a work assignment for the strategic planning retreat participants to work on overnight (i.e., between retreat days). I have done that before and it can be effective and a real agenda time-saver. But, more often than not, the leaders dislike the extra ask and just want to drink, eat, chill, or work out. Me, too! I recognize there are times when the client has had enough of me for one day. Maybe we just need the night off from one another. Perhaps they need to go out and enjoy their evening together as a team. I get that, totally, and I am happy for them; plus, that means more time for me in the fitness center or with a U.S. Masters local swim club.

Chapter Summary

The epic planning retreat is off to a great start. Not only is the retreat team totally prepared for the retreat because of their excellent pre-reading, but the first day of the retreat has been informative and insightful. The team has successfully reduced the massive amount of strategic situation pre-reading all the way down to a small group of actual strategic situations that need attention, or SiTNAs. They've been channeling their inner Mark

Twain. There are no solutions yet, just a new and very clear appreciation within the retreat room of the current situations facing the organization. The team has realized the importance of this reduction. The SiTNAs have great credibility because, when the small groups broke out, they independently arrived at very nearly the same SiTNAs. They are already starting to get on the same page. For the folks who respond well to black-and-white thinking in the retreat, we created a change mandate that lays out where the company is today and specifically what needs to change (not how or why it needs to change). The retreat team is going to want to work next on the strategic business plan that will resolve these SiTNAs. With any luck, we have prevented the organization from spending the next several years resolving the wrong challenges and opportunities.

Chapter Challenge Questions

1. I advocate for an abundance of time in a planning retreat, if needed, to determine the correct strategic situations in need of attention facing any company. What future strategic problems might be avoided in your organization if the retreat team takes plenty of time to think through the current situations facing the company? How might taking so much time to talk over current situations cause some of your leaders to grow impatient with the planning process?

2. Sometimes a clear business opportunity or challenge appears clear until the retreat group talks it over. Think of strategic situations in your organization that seem obvious but, upon deeper reflection by an informed retreat team, are not the right situations at all. Why is it essential to narrow it down to the right and small group of SiTNAs?

3. If you took a sheet of paper right now and converted it into a simple T chart, what descriptions of your organization would you place in the "Today" column and what descriptions would you place in the "Tomorrow" column? If 10 of your top leaders did this independently, would each list be identical? (hint: the answer is probably not; why not?)

CHAPTER SEVEN

BUILDING YOUR STRATEGIC BLUEPRINT

 "You don't have to be a genius or visionary or even a college graduate to be successful. You just need a framework and a dream."
MICHAEL DELL

What Are We Building When We Build a Strategic Plan?

Building a strategic business plan is made much easier when you know in advance the basic structure of that plan. It's the same with a good book, for example. When an author has the framework in mind before writing in earnest—even a raw initial table of contents—it helps the entire process. What gets built needs to be structured first. Perhaps that is what Starship should have done before releasing "We Built This City" in 1985. Starship was preceded by Jefferson Airplane and Jefferson Starship, two grand contributors to rock and roll history. I have no argument with those mavericks! What Starship was thinking when it wrote, produced, and played "We Built This City" is beyond me. *Rolling Stone* listed it as one of the worst songs of all time. *Blender* magazine rated it one of the 50 most awesomely bad rock and roll songs ever. The song purported to be about anti-commercialism in the music industry but reeked of '80s music commercialism. Ironically, *Blender* magazine folded, and Starship was left still standing after that harsh criticism. So, there is that. For my tastes, it still persists as one of the worst '80s MTV videos I have watched. The word "mamba" or "mambo" is used in the lyrics, although there seems to be debate about that and neither word makes any sense with the rest of the lyrics anyway. Maybe they should have built a better song to communicate their disgust with rock commercialism.

Chunk Five: The Strategic Framework We Will Build Together

This portion of the agenda is about function following form. In other words, it is helpful to tell the participants how a solid strategic plan is built or organized (now that "strategy" has been earlier defined). It's like being a strategic plan architect (hey, that's a good job title!) of sorts. If you have been painstaking in the entire process so far, you have a clear and compelling strategic situation assessment and a well-oriented strategic thinking team at an inspired place all following a proven process. Now, let them decide what they are going to build together in terms of the scaffolding of the strategic plan (not the actual decisions yet). Most executive leaders really like this approach of designing the plan framework before making the decisions about that plan. It will be a comprehensive and detailed three-to-five-year strategic business plan that, when implemented, will deliver sustained competitive advantage and will transform the company and its leaders. This plan will include:

1. Our *strategic situation assessment*, including the SiTNAs described by them earlier and their *change mandate*
2. Our bedrock, permanent decisions on who we are and why we exist:

   a. A decision on our *organizational mentality* going forward
   b. Our *mission*, our *raison d'etre* as a company or, as author and leader Simon Sinek says, our "why?"
   c. Our *values and culture* as a team that will preserve the company for the long term, typically not more than four core, genuine, nonnegotiable values

3. Our *big picture vision*, including both a broad *"stretch for"* statement and an often paragraphs-long *detailed vision*. In addition, it includes the barriers to each detailed vision and the strengths needed to achieve each detailed vision.
4. Our *growth method and measures*, including a detailed examination of the many growth methods the team considered, the pros and cons of each, and a quantitative ranking of the preferred growth option. This is then complemented with choices on how to measure growth (both financially and non-financially) and the rate of growth desired.

5. Our *unique selling proposition*, including the brand character, brand promise, and unique features and benefits of the company to its different audiences, mostly external.

6. Our *primary markets for focus*, including a clear delineation of the market segmentation method used (there are many) and the resulting primary markets for focus.

7. *Broad financial plan and assumptions*, including a three-year look back at the income statement and at least a three-year look forward, plus the current year (total of seven years), and the assumptions that went into this model. This is frequently work I do with the client between retreat sessions, with a month or so between them.

8. *Action plans* for Year One, including at least three but not more than five strategic action plans. These are often linked to the SiTNAs uncovered earlier, but not always.

   a. I prefer to follow a manage-by-objective method of action planning that allows the team to lay out the Year One roadmap in sequence. Manage by objective is a method for goal setting made popular way back in 1954 by Peter Drucker in his book *The Practice of Management*.

   b. For every action plan, there should be a goal, a measure, and two or three strategies and/or tactics to help accomplish real progress. Most companies want to align an organizational objective to the strategies and tactics that will make it a reality. Frequently, I have then used the R.A.C.I. (responsible, accountable, consulted, and informed) method for aligning leaders' workloads with those strategies and tactics. R.A.C.I. goes back to the 1970s. It can be an effective and simple way to redirect a leader's new role in light of the emerging strategic plan. Leaders who enter a planning retreat who think their role may not change much as a result of the retreat are not used to being in effective retreats. If every action item outlines who is responsible, accountable, etc., then there will be very little mystery as to who is leading an initiative and the other roles people play in that initiative.

i. For example, let's imagine a company has a marketing objective to grow market share of one of its product lines. This is a fine objective but needs to be broken down into smaller, action-oriented strategies, or tactics, to accomplish that market share growth. Breaking it down this way, the leader and his or her teammates can more easily sequence the right steps in the right order to drive that market share growth. Each of those strategies or tactics should be assigned to a leader who can help make the objective a reality. To do that, he or she is going to need to have a team of others supporting his or her success. Those others? He or she needs to know who is responsible, accountable, consulted, and informed in those strategies or tactics. Interestingly, R.A.C.I. comes from three Norwegians, Kristoffer v. Grude, Tor Haug, and Erling S. Andersen. Reads like the names you find on groups of mailboxes at northern Minnesota lake country cabins.

9. *Communication plan* for the strategic plan, including internal and external messaging about the planning process and the resulting direction. I have discovered something exceptional about this part: nearly every organization overlooks this phase of the process.

10. The *system* we will use for implementation, measurement, and evaluation. A strategic business plan exists for one reason: to be achieved. The focus at some point has to be on execution, doing it, implementation. So, this section of your strategic plan spells out the progress review meeting cadence, sample meeting agendas, and more. It illustrates how the overall direction provides input to annual budgeting, capital appropriation planning, location planning, department planning, and so on. This section is about how the strategic plan will "live" in the company.

At that point of the agenda, it becomes clear to the retreat team that their work is going to consist of making decisions that result in this framework being built. This may be at the end of the first two-day retreat or toward the end of the first day of a two-day retreat. This provides a nudge to the retreat team to get to work on the decisions that will produce that plan. Once they know how their completed strategic plan will be organized, it is as if they are free to get to work on it. Function can follow form.

Chunk Six: Organizational Mentality

In this exercise, I explain what organizational mentality is (the decision-making mentality this leadership team will use going forward on especially big decisions that I described in Chapter Four of *Chunk*). We discuss the pros and cons of each of them along with real-life examples of companies they think marry-up well to these Organizational Mentalities. I find it helpful to ask a three-part question and then just listen: Which organizational mentality best describes your past, which best describes your future, and why?

Then, I capture in real time and in writing their choice and a swift synthesis of their many thoughts into a cogent *group* thought (that is very important). I write a customized description of what this organizational mentality choice means for the company. This could be on a large whiteboard, on a flip chart sheet of paper, or on a large PowerPoint displayed in front of the group. I literally write it on the spot in front of them. As I do so, I make sure to mention they are doing the heavy thinking and I am just pulling together their excellent thoughts. I ask if what I have crafted captures their decision. It usually does. This is typically at least a two-hour exercise. Then, I set that aside, literally and figuratively, and we move on.

Chunk Seven: Mission

I do not approach this conversation on mission the way many strategic planning facilitators might. Maybe I am jaded, maybe I notice body language in the room, or maybe I am a discerning judge of effective vs. ineffective missions. A lot of lip service is paid to corporate mission statements. But most companies' mission statements are not missions at all, are too long, are thinly veneered marketing, or do not even make sense. So, I tell the group this. First, I let them know we will be crafting their mission in the retreat and it is going to fundamentally change the organization. It is not going to get wordsmithed by HR a month later. Nope. We are actually in the room to develop this sense of mission, their reason for being. Second, I let them know good standards for excellence with company mission statements:

- Genuine. Not a tagline. Real, not magical, thinking.
- Short. Less than 25 words. One sentence if possible. But not too short.
- Answers "Why do we exist?"
- Instantly obvious to any reader what business you are in.

- Going to last a long time; many business cycles.
- Receives top leaderships' total commitment, not just buy-in.
- Gets the group in the epic retreat excited.
- Does not validate the past decisions as much as it supports future ones.

I explain the importance of diagramming the mission sentence. This diagramming is not intuitive to a lot of people, but it is to rhetoricians, linguists, and the like. They know that, by breaking the mission statement down into the smallest pieces, you develop sort of a mission schema. If you do this well, your team will not only know its new mission but will also understand the nuanced "why" behind each and every word or phrase, which then makes it far more meaningful for years to come to employees and other stakeholders. I often advise on matters like:

- Why the mission should usually start with the word "To…"
- Why the next part of the sentence should usually explain the organizational mentality of the entire entity (e.g., To emerge as the foremost thought leader in the way the market buys screen print supplies.)
- Why the next part of the sentence can often be "…so that…"
- Why the mission should answer the "why?"

In this example above, the resulting mission may be "To emerge as the foremost thought leader in the way the market buys screen print supplies so that customers can focus on their businesses and dreams." In retreats, I share examples of clear, compelling, and concise mission statements that have transformed other businesses. I do not have a canned grouping of those mission statements. I custom tailor the list for each client. I then ask the retreat group to simply start talking with those points I have already made as the context. As they talk, theme after theme makes its way into their conversation. I catch these and put them on a whiteboard, flip chart, or PowerPoint display. Some of these conversations last 30 minutes and others last over two hours. However, keep in mind that this entire process reflected in the Strategic Clarity Roadmap has now taken this client several weeks of time. To the impatient folks who think we are at that moment wasting valuable leadership time on wordsmithing, I ask them to kindly suspend their judgment momentarily. I make 100% certain I hear from everyone in the retreat group as equally as possible. I draw also from the SiTNA and organizational mentality discussions earlier.

Then, it happens.

The strategic mission coalesces in their minds, into mine, and out onto the display where everyone can see it. It is never perfect at first. But, it gets reactions, typically, "That is amazing. I feel great about that, but there is one word I want to change" or "No, I don't like that. Here is what I feel our mission is." Then, they start editing and thinking together. Examples:

1. <u>To</u> set a new standard for tenant-improvement construction services in our region <u>so that</u> small business owners and operators can focus on their dreams.

2. <u>To</u> connect architecture and engineering firms to their general contracting partners with a project-based SaaS <u>so that</u> they can all minimize corporate risk.

3. <u>To</u> build the Midwest's first totally integrated on-line sign and screen print supply distribution channel <u>so that</u> our clients can compete with the big boys and we achieve balanced, profitable growth.

4. <u>To</u> relentlessly pursue safety and employee well-being in U.S. construction <u>so that</u> we reverse negative industry stereotypes and dramatically cut addiction and suicide rates.

5. <u>To</u> bring positive inspiration and insight to every stakeholder (customer, suppliers, and even one another) <u>so that</u> we build a fitness app brand that commands premium margins.

6. <u>To</u> inspire strategic clarity by giving clients a compelling strategic planning process and retreat experience <u>so that</u> they exceed their company transformation expectations.

   a. That last one is my mission statement.

When the first cut at this emerging mission is complete, I tell them we are just going to set it aside for a day. I write it in bold, clear, legible handwriting and place it in the front of the retreat room for all to see. I ask permission for us to proceed, knowing we will be coming back to this mission from time to time as the retreat continues.

Chunk Eight: Values and Culture

When a leader works offsite on his strategic plan, one of the topics on his mind is change. Fundamental change. Industry change. Paradigm changes. In fact, more often than not, the entire purpose for a strategic planning retreat is to develop an approach to managing fundamental change. So, in this decision-making chunk, let's eliminate those aspects of the organization that the retreat team feels should *not* change. Economies soar up and sink down, competitors come and go, industry trends accelerate and others vaporize, technologies gain acceptance and change again, top leaders come and some retire. But what is the solid, unchanging, enduring character of the company no matter what strategic plan we develop? In the swirling seas of industry transformation, what aspects of the company are like granite and must be UNchanged? That is how I get to the values and culture part of a retreat, by laying down those questions and the expectations associated with values and culture.

I define values and culture as nearly synonymous: *beliefs and attitudes we hold to be essential, not up for negotiation, and with observable behaviors anyone can clearly see or feel.* When a team meets to talk these over, the tendency is to drop to the most common expressions of values and culture we see in corporate America: honesty, integrity, commitment, innovation, and so on. Well, I actually have a list of over 300 values and culture statements I have used in planning retreats. Remember, the goal is not only determining a very small set of values and culture statements but the right ones, the real ones. Not the ones we think will sound good to the board, look right on the website, or appear cool to the CEO's friends at the local country club. We are after the ones that we as a leadership team think are beliefs and attitudes we hold to be forever unchanging. Once again, as with mission, I let them know my standards for excellence with company values and culture.

- Genuine. Not a tagline. Real, not magical thinking.
- Short. Not more than five statements. One sentence each.
- Answers "What do we believe in?"
- Instantly obvious to any reader what you value most in life and business.
- Going to last decades, many business cycles.
- Receives top leaderships' total commitment, not just buy-in.
- Gets the group in the epic retreat excited.
- Does not validate the past values of long-dead founders as much as it communicates core values now and into the future.

The process and the sentence diagramming then begins in a similar way as the mission exercise, so I will not repeat that here. The difference is it usually does not take as long. While a rich mission discussion could last over two hours, the values and culture statements can unfold in a slightly faster time frame. This is likely because it immediately follows the mission chunk. Again, as these are written, I place them up on the wall. They are tentative, not final. Then, we move on secure in the knowledge we will come back to them as the retreat unfolds.

Chunk Nine: Our Big Picture Vision (Where We Are Going Together)

This is similar to, but not the same as the big, hairy, and audacious goal and envisioned future concepts prescribed by the brilliant Jim Collins and Jerry Porras. There are two parts. All told, it is a one-day exercise, if you are efficient.

The first is a short statement of what we are trying to "stretch for" as a company. These are best expressed 5, 10, or even 15 years into the future and starts with the words "We will…" It is meant to be a real reach, friends. In a retreat, I recommend a challenge or dare mentality, with this prompt: What would you dare to do, if you could? Steve Jobs had the most spectacular "stretch for" I ever read: "To put a ding in the universe."

So, I ask the retreat group questions like the bold ones below, and I take a lot of notes on the conversation, again doing so from the front of the room and on display for all to see as I write them. Sometimes I will combine individuals into two-person teams for this exercise, sometimes not.

1. If you were going to triple market share, what would you dare to do?

2. If you wanted to win 100% of the projects you pursue, what would you do fundamentally differently?

3. What goal would you have for this company if you were a kid again?

4. When you are long gone from here, what do you hope the company accomplishes that would be breathtaking?

5. What would be the "stretch for" that would cause serious heartburn for all of your competitors?

6. What would you do culturally as a company so that your team members are not just superior to the competition, but are transformed as the direct result of working at your company?

7. Pretend your company is boldly on the cover of a major industry publication 15 years from now because of this exceptional (some said crazy) thing you did as a company. What is that exceptional thing your company did (i.e., is about to do)?

8. You are headed home to your loved ones after this planning retreat. You want immediately to tell them you committed to a spectacular goal for the company the next 10 to 20 years. It is a transcendent goal. It has lit a fire inside you like never before. You have never loved this company more. What is that "stretch for" goal?

I ask them to each individually write that down in less than 15 words. Then, one by one, without stopping, we listen to each and every one. As we listen, an amazing thing happens: many of their "stretch for" statements are along a certain vein. There is a theme. So, I real-time synthesize and capture that "stretch for" theme in writing. I place it, too, at the front of the room for all to see. I describe it as emerging or tentative. I set it aside and ask if we can move on and come back to revisit this "stretch for" vision periodically.

The second part of this big picture vision is a written and detailed vision, often paragraphs long, three to five years into the future. The more detailed these are written, the more likely they are to be achieved. It also starts with the words "We will…" I am not a fan of a carbon copy of another company's vision. I am especially not impressed with slogans that sound good but are just not honest. What you are really after here is a shared, genuine dream expressed in detail. The "stretch for" statement is short and aspirational. But, the detailed vision is richly itemized and only three to five years out there. It reads, feels, and functions like an intermediate vision. What it lacks in brevity it compensates for with depth.

People from all walks of life have their own personal visions: you may wish to run a sub-3:30 marathon, stay married for 50 years or more, open your own store, put your kids through college, produce a play, climb peaks on all continents, raise a million dollars for cancer research. However, developing a shared detailed vision for a company is exponentially harder than developing a personal one. These shared visions take time and co-dreaming. Inspired? You bet. Relevant to the strategic situation assessment (the SiTNAs)? Yes. The vision of only the CEO? Nope, usually not. Authentic, genuine, and truly yours as an organization? Ab-so-lute-ly! It turns out the best detailed visions are developed by the group, for the group, to transform the company.

Remember, unlike a mission statement that is about your *raison d'etre* and is designed for permanence, the entire big picture vision is only about what you want your company to become. We use this term "vision" quite a lot in the business world overlooking its obvious purpose: to give everyone in the company, and many outside the company, the same picture or image of the future state of the company. I use a method for developing a detailed vision that works exceptionally well, but it is work. It is viewed by leaders who may be in a hurry as "taking too long." Well, just keep in mind that the tortoise won that race against the hare.

First, we need to make a very important assumption that everyone on this planning team in the retreat has vision. If not, they can develop vision. The capacity is there. They just need a way, a tool, to express their vision of the future. They may feel non-visionary, but that is probably just because they have not had the opportunity. They have never been asked, "Sally, what is your vision for operational performance of XYZ Company?" Some of the most inspiring corporate vision statements I have ever read came from foremen, office staff, young engineers, field surveyors, heavy equipment operators, floor equipment operators, regional salespeople, accounting personnel, and good people who humbly told me they were not visionary.

Second, another assumption is that vision statements should be actionable, aspirational, and written in a three-to-five-year time horizon. I have had some disagreement with colleagues over the years about this particular point. Some of them feel a vision statement should be bold, brief, and set far into the future. I argue that this is what a "stretch for" statement is for and that the detailed vision should be in the three-to-five-year time horizon.

The third assumption is that a detailed vision statement needs to be balanced in several dimensions of the company. It expresses the detailed vision for the entire company, all departments, functions, locations, product lines, personnel, aspects, traits, results, and more. It does not say how it gets to any of these visions. It is literally and exclusively the detailed vision. It is 0% how, 0% why, and 100% what, describing the destination in vivid detail. This is why the most effective detailed vision statements are actually management tools: they are specific.

I get to this level of specificity by using a unique method of visioning. Before the retreat, I create and distribute a vision assignment for each retreat participant to complete. Let's get them thinking weeks before the retreat. The assignment includes instructions and coaching. I ask them to write several pages in advance about their vision. My typical pre-retreat vision assignment asks the retreat participant to spell out their vision for several aspects or dimensions of the company that need to be achieved or in place by either three or five years from the end of their current fiscal year. Usually, I ask them to do this in isolation. I ask that their visions address at least six such aspects or dimensions, such as market position, brand character, growth, culture, bottom line, technology utilization, industry innovation, operational excellence, leadership, safety, industry partnerships, internal conflict resolution, and so on. So, let's do some more math. If we have 15 participants who, in advance of the retreat, spell out their detailed visions in six dimensions, I will receive 90 specific detailed vision statements to review before the retreat. As I read them, I invariably notice four extraordinary things:

1. These people are amazing leaders. Their love of their company is inspiring to me as a facilitator. People are friggin' great!

2. These leaders, given an opportunity and a clear writing assignment to complete in isolation, have *synergistic* visions of the future for their company. Another set of patterns!

3. There are a few truly spectacular thinkers and writers in their midst.

4. We have a few contrarians, too. We have outliers. We have unspoken conflict about the vision for the

company. Good thing we will be behind closed doors in an epic retreat to debate the different visions.

From these 90 detailed visions in at least six dimensions, what I often find is that there is a theme to each of the dimensions. A pattern, again. Frequently, I am the first to learn of this pattern because they send me their completed pre-retreat vision summary and because they do not talk a lot about their shared visions in day-to-day business. They do not even know how close together on strategy they actually are. Some are not as aligned and actually have diametrically opposing visions for the company. Those are the outliers I mentioned above. Let me ask you, do you think those opposing visions should be swept under the rug, never surfaced in the first place, or perhaps, just maybe, intelligently talked about as a group in an epic offsite retreat?

I also ask them in that same pre-retreat assignment to list the top three strengths needed to achieve their detailed vision (whether or not the company possesses these strengths now) and the top three barriers that could derail their detailed vision. I ask them to send the entire completed pre-retreat vision assignment to me several days before the epic retreat. I always tell them to bring copies of their work for discussion in the retreat. Then, in the retreat, it becomes a matter of selecting the first topic area or dimension of the company for a detailed vision conversation (e.g., operational performance and accountability) and asking every person in the room to tell us their vision. One. Person. At. A. Time. As we do this, a phenomenon unfolds that some clients have told me is so energizing that they cannot find words for it.

Well, I can. It is called alignment.

One topic at a time, we listen to the retreat individuals, giving each person the floor with uninterrupted time to share their vision for three or five years. Is this laborious? A bit. Is this inclusive, resulting in a truly shared vision for three or five years, consistent with the SiTNAs, change mandate, organizational mentality, mission, values and culture, and "stretch for" vision? Indeed, it is. Will it later be actionable because it is so specific? Yes. I capture in writing each of the emerging detailed visions as the hours unfold. I post them on the whiteboard, flip chart paper, or PowerPoint for the entire retreat group to see in real time. As we near the end of this detailed vision process (i.e., after we have 5 to 10 key aspects or dimensions of the company envisioned in detail), the retreat room is now pretty well redecorated with white flip chart paper and carefully, brilliantly crafted visions in neat handwriting. They have essentially written everything; all I do is synthesize and summarize. This is now when I recap, recap, and recap. I read them aloud. I show the connections and interdependencies between their detailed visions. I do not hide my excitement for them. Then, I deliver a message of sorts:

"This work you are doing is simply great. All of the pieces are detailed. They are balanced across major functions of the company you deem to be important. They fit with where your markets and general industry are headed. Everyone in this retreat has shared in shaping these detailed visions. They are built on the foundation of the SiTNAs we developed earlier, plus your change mandate. They also greatly mirror your choice of organizational mentality, mission, values and culture, and your "stretch for" vision. These detailed visions you have crafted are a roadmap of where you want the company to end up in three or five years. This is what strategic leaders do and what you are doing right now; you are spelling out for the company where you *wish* the company to be and where it *needs* to be in the same breath. We even have a list of the main strengths the company needs to possess to achieve these detailed visions and the primary barriers to your detailed visions. Kudos!

"What we will do now, if you agree with all of the work in this strategic planning process so far and in this offsite retreat, is build the remainder of your strategic plan around these detailed visions. Your Year One action plans? They will later in this process be organized into the same groups or dimensions as your detailed visions. Your broad financial plan? It will need to support the strategic plan expressed in these detailed visions. Your marketing plan will receive its cues from this strategic direction you are capturing. Each year, as you make progress on your annual action plans, you will be gradually closing in on achieving your detailed visions. You will likely meet monthly or quarterly to assess progress and drive accountability for results. My recommendation is weekly or monthly, but only if you all agree to start delegating your day job to others so you can meet your new strategic leadership role. If you do all of this, you will be in the 98th percentile of U.S. businesses because you have connected your plan and knitted it together well.

"As Year Two unfolds, you will probably work with me to recast the annual action plans, implementing and measuring just as you did in Year One. In Year Three, we will yet again recast your annual action plans. By about Year Three, having lived your corporate life according to your plan and these detailed visions, no doubt making continual and agile adjustments to the annual action plans, we will realize something: the company has fundamentally changed, the markets have changed, your competitors have changed, the economic and regulatory environment has changed, and more. It will be time for an entirely new strategic planning process.

"This is why I often say that all strategic leaders live their lives the same way, and it is the exact opposite way other leaders lead. Strategic leaders like you see the future they wish to co-create. They can practically taste it. They painstakingly lay it out together in vivid detail as you just have. They build it all on a solid foundation of smart strategic situation assessment. Their grasp of their shared vision is so strong, it is almost as if they have already experienced it. Then, from that unique perch (really seeing the "stretch for" vision and three-to-five-year detailed vision in their collective mind), they look *back* at Year One and answer this simple question: What must we accomplish in our Year One action plans so that we make immediate progress in Year One toward the detailed vision for the next three or five years? In other words, what must our trajectory be on our Year One action plans so that we make a significant move in the right direction? Then, in Year Two, having accomplished what we set out to do in Year One, what must our Year Two action plans be in order to continue or accelerate progress toward our detailed vision? This is what strategic leaders do and it is the exact opposite of how most other leaders lead: *strategic leaders live life backwards*. They mentally march out into the future, almost as if they are in a time machine, then turn and *look back* into Year One and then implement actions in Year One to make that first great year of progress. Most average leaders do the opposite; they have no vision of the future. So, they just develop their annual action plans hoping they will magically align. They do it in a vision void and react to the fire du jour. They are fundamentally reactive while strategic leaders are profoundly proactive.

"So, friends, we now know where you wish to go with the company. We have your big picture. But how do you get there? That's what comes next in this retreat."

Chunk Ten: Growth Methods and Measures

Growth is the next logical step in the epic retreat process. It is an interesting word, as is the word "growing." It is commonly used to describe healthy companies and yet it is misunderstood. So, after the SiTNAs are known, the organizational mentality has been chosen, the mission has been stated, the values and culture have been stated, and the big picture vision ("stretch for" and detailed) has been so thoughtfully stated, we have a new question to address in the epic retreat: growth. How are we going to define and measure growth? How fast do we want to grow, and how will we actually do it? What method will we choose so that we achieve the big picture vision? Remember, the big picture vision only spells out the destination, not how to get there. Now, we are getting into the "how?"

This next exercise, which lasts at least three hours, allows a team to select and define growth strategies that align with and drive toward the big picture vision. Growth is not just about top-line revenue growth, though that is the common misconception. While it is true a healthy company is always somehow growing, a growing company can be unhealthy. This is why I work in the epic retreat process to ask the gathered leaders their more fundamental thoughts on growth.

First, how are you going to define or measure it, in both financial terms and non-financial terms? I have frequently found the financial growth measures of greatest importance to my clients are the obvious ones: sales/revenues, margins, EBITDA, various performance ratios (quick ratio, return on equity, etc.), and frequently some other balance sheet measures. The more time a group spends on this growth discussion in a retreat, the more they realize the relationship between the various financial performance factors. They usually come to see that top-line growth (i.e., sales or revenue figures), while attractive, is best accomplished when it is more profitable growth, too. They will also understand that improvements in financial gross margins, for example, can be accomplished without adding to the top line, and then it all drops to their bottom line (EBITDA). During this exercise, another fact becomes evident: not everyone has the keen financial acumen of the CFO, controller, or CEO. This is why I often share or co-facilitate this exercise with the CFO, controller, or CEO. This is why growth planning, especially in terms of financial growth planning, is both goal setting and educational for the participants. I ask the CFO to raise the education level in the room about how the company operates financially. You would be amazed how much this is appreciated by everyone in the retreat room. Leaders in many companies are so professionally segmented by role that they actually do not fully understand how the company operates financially. It is critical to erase this knowledge gap in strategic planning because every strategic plan must align to a financial plan that supports it.

Another fact becomes even more evident during this exercise: there are many important growth measures that are not financial. I have seen a top leadership team choose three financial measures of growth (e.g., sales, pre-tax profit, and return on equity) and three non-financial growth measures (e.g., client satisfaction, market share, and employee learning and development) in the same strategic business plan. It turns out that growth is important to measure holistically, not just financially. For most enlightened CEOs, this has always been their view. Most high-performing CEOs are quick to tell me, "Tom, there is more to success than our bottom line." Therefore, this exercise includes first listing the many financial and non-financial ways the company *could* measure growth and then selecting only the measures they *will* use to measure growth. I often see a combined list of over 20 such measures in just one client company, which they narrow down to 4 that really matter.

The next step in this exercise is to explore the many ways in which the company could achieve growth. These are the methods, not the measures. This is where I prefer to use a quantitative tool to drive smart growth decisions. I first provide them a list of the 8 to 12 primary methods I have seen client companies use to achieve growth:

- Grow organically with current customers, products, and services
- Reach out to adjacent markets
- Boldly enter brand new markets (geographic or otherwise)
- Form supply chain alliances
- Develop and introduce new products and services
- Open new locations
- Engage in acquisition (horizontal or vertical)
- Reduce growth and focus instead on better profitability

We get all of these methods written up on the front-room display and then start drawing on the collective wisdom of the group. I ask them to tell me the pros and cons of each of these different growth methods. We take one growth method at a time and spend at least 10 minutes just talking about its generic pros and cons. Perhaps this company has experience with three or four of the methods. That is good experience for them to talk about. Again, it can be educational for all. Maybe two of the retreat participants were not even in the company six years ago when the company performed two successful acquisitions and an unsuccessful one.

Then, using a simple matrix, we rank the options. As I said, I like this to be a quantitative growth analysis, which accomplishes the twin objectives of engaging the more analytical leaders in conversation and minimizing politics in the room. We rank the options using a simple high, medium, or low designation for each growth alternative. I ask them to just give me a rank, not a discussion. It is very analytical at this moment, not conversational.

1. Total growth potential (H, M, or L?)

2. Long-term nature (not a short-term win) (H, M, or L?)

3. Ease of us managing; degree of ease (H, M, or L?)

4. Consistent with the big picture vision so far (H, M, or L?)

When we are done, we have a table with 10 to 12 growth methods on the vertical axis of the whiteboard. Across the top, we have the four measuring criteria. Within each intersection in the matrix, we now have an H, M, or L. If a growth method has HIGH total growth potential, HIGH long-term nature, HIGH ease of managing, and HIGH consistency with the big picture vision, we may have a winner. But, MEDIUM, HIGH, MEDIUM, HIGH could also be a winner. It is important for the retreat group to talk these over. Eventually, I ask, "Based on the planning process so far, on the decisions you have made already in this retreat, and on the pros and cons discussion earlier, which are the two growth methods that jump out as your best choices?" I tell them the table drawn on the whiteboard does not make the decision; they do. But I ask them to agree to only two or perhaps three growth options for the next three to five years. This often proves to be a controversial and lengthy talk. Here is why.

Most companies, perhaps yours right now, are pursuing too many growth methods simultaneously. So, actually capitalizing these many growth initiatives with financial and human resources is difficult. It's like eating too much spinach at once. Growth is unsuccessful because the company is attempting too many growth options at the same time. These numerous growth methods are diluting real growth, confusing employees, stripping major company functions of resources to do their jobs, and worse. So, I ask the group to consider that maybe, just maybe, using a focused growth strategy will get the company further ahead in the long run as opposed to trying to grow every way possible. I pose my opinion as just that: an opinion. However, I ask them to make the decisions. I will even ask them to vote on the choices, if needed. Strategy at this moment in a retreat is about focusing on the two or three growth strategies they can realistically capitalize that will move them toward their "stretch for" vision and detailed vision.

When these decisions have been made, we now know how they feel about corporate growth, the pros and cons of various ways to grow, the financial and non-financial measures they agree to use in measuring growth, and the two or three methods that will drive that growth. Now we add the key performance indicators, or metrics, to each growth option chosen. This is the process of setting a measure or an indicator so we can keep an eye on progress as the subsequent months and years come and go. Now, we are planning to grow in the right ways and measure the right stuff.

This entire exercise typically lasts three hours, or longer. It is analytically challenging but really gets everyone in the room talking, contributing, disagreeing, resolving, and more. In the end, the leaders now understand corporate growth better, have made growth decisions that align with their shared vision, and have agreed that focused growth is better than shotgun growth. Best yet, they have discovered that growth can be measured by more than dollars and cents. The next thing I do is summarize this growth program in writing at the front of the room. I tell them we are just going to set those growth program decisions aside and that we will come back to them from time to time in the rest of the retreat. Here is a sample product of this growth methods and measures exercise:

> "Consistent with our SiTNA addressing our gross margin fade and our big picture vision to reverse that fade, we are going to improve our sales win rate by 50% on our existing products and services, resulting in $65,000,000 in sales, at 16% gross margins by FYE 2009. Plus…

"We are going to eliminate the current sales incentive programs and migrate to a sales performance management system that rewards quality of client relationships, not quantity, while increasing our top sales producers' income potential to over $450,000/year. Plus…

"We are going to grow our industry recognition by winning six local and three national design awards in our primary markets, which will lead to unsolicited inquiries from not fewer than 10 high-end design professionals to join our company and a new sense of employee morale about our industry leadership."

Chunk Eleven: Unique Selling Proposition (USP)

We are now well into the second round of the two, two-day *Chunk* retreat process. Between these two-day sessions, I document a confidential progress draft of the emerging strategic direction. After one quick bounce off the CEO and some edits, I route it out to the planning team along with the agenda. It is just a progress draft. Between these retreats, the CFO or controller starts to evaluate the broad financial plan and assumptions that will be needed to support this strategic plan. This individual shares their emerging broad financial plan with the team in a subsequent retreat. Similarly, often the human resources leader will evaluate the organizational structure implications of the emerging strategic direction. He, too, comes back to the team in a subsequent retreat with insights about long-range organizational design implications of this emerging strategic plan. The general counsel and IT leader go through the same process. The plan is emerging from the retreat, and their direction is becoming clear. At this point, with much of the strategy and strategic plan more or less crafted, there is one more vital step to complete—and it is *vital!* This step is the development of a written brand platform and/or USP for this company to grow into. The company may not be ready right at that moment to adopt this new USP. In fact, that is almost certain to be the case right in the retreat room. What the retreat team needs to do is explore and then commit to the USP that this company *aspires to and can credibly make in less than two years* if the marketing department (or outside marketing agency) gets on it right away this year.

To do this, I share a great deal with the client team about what a USP is and is not. I usually co-facilitate this portion of a retreat with the client company senior marketing leader. Together, we have to remind the team that strategic planning is about competitive differentiation. We educate the retreat participants on how many options their customers probably have other than buying from my client company. In addition, 100% of the time, we have to help the top leaders in the retreat understand that the features of their company, products, or services are *not* their USP. The good news is I do not have to go back to square one and start having them dream about their strategic direction because we already know that. What they need to do is align a USP to that strategic direction.

So, what does make Brand X different from Brand Z? If they both have the same or similar features at the same or similar price point, then what is the customer to do? If so-called USP attributes like, "Our people are better here at Brand X than at Brand Z" are just not true or are irrelevant, what is the customer to do? What if the strengths of the Brand X company are the same as or similar to those of Brand Z? The answer does not lie in a slogan or a special 10% discount for repeat customers or some happy talk on your website. A USP is like a photo negative (to use a film photographer's expression) of the organizational mentality and mission the team developed earlier in the epic retreat. Remember the organizational mentality? The mission? A USP is supposed to be a statement that not only differentiates your products and services but also reflects your mission, culture, and the entire company. That way, no matter what products and services you have in your company portfolio and no matter the markets you serve, the USP is generally constant. It is strategically consistent. This is what great brands do: they are consistent. Of course, in some companies, the product *is* the company. There are one-product companies, like Crocs and Birkenstocks. But, for most, it is important to not completely reinvent new USPs repeatedly as products and services come and go.

- Tip: if your USP is constantly changing, unclear, or boring, then you are probably hung up on features (not benefits) of your products, services, or processes and not the actual company USP. You may forever have reactive marketing, or USP du jour, if that is the way you want to compete.

There are numerous methodologies you can use to develop a strong USP. At this point in an offsite strategic retreat, a solid USP is going to be at least a two-hour effort. I prefer USP methodologies similar to the Strategy Canvas tool espoused by Business Strategy Hub.[20] Later, with marketing department input or input from your outside marketing communication agency, this USP can be thoroughly evaluated. In doing that, the marketing departments usually improves upon the work from the epic retreat. They build on the USP without fundamentally changing it. Excellent.

Chunk Twelve: Wrapping Up, Summarizing, Connecting, Testing

The strategic retreat team has now accomplished the following (below) in two, two-day strategic planning retreats that have been epic and were facilitated in discreet, sequential chunks. It is time to pull it all together, to knit their strategy and their strategic plan together. It is time to let the leaders just talk about it overall. We chunked it out using something like this agenda:

1. Chunk One: Welcome, and Why Are We All Here, Exactly?

2. Chunk Two: What Is Strategy, and What Is a Strategic Plan?

3. Chunk Three: Guest Speaker or an Exercise.

4. Chunk Four: Reducing to Situations in Need of Attention ("SiTNA") and Your Change Mandate.

5. Chunk Five: The Strategic Framework We Will Build Together.

6. Chunk Six: Organizational Mentality.

7. Chunk Seven: Mission.

8. Chunk Eight: Values and Culture.

9. Chunk Nine: Our Big Picture Vision (Where We Are Going Together).

10. Chunk Ten: Growth Methods and Measures.

11. Chunk Eleven: Unique Selling Proposition ("USP").

If there is more work to do strategically, such as market segmentation (primary vs. secondary vs. tertiary), then this gets addressed now. Perhaps ownership transition planning needs to be discussed. That may also get addressed now in the retreat. Every client, and therefore every epic retreat, is slightly different. There are strategic decisions coming up in the next phases outside of the epic retreat that are not well suited for a retreat. For instance, detailed conversations about financial performance and organizational structure are not always suited for group retreats. So, with these major chunks, the retreat is coming to a close, almost. This is now a pivotal moment in a planning retreat: the facilitator helping the group recall everything they have done together and why so they see the entire strategic plan. It is a very important time to show where the client team is in the Strategic Clarity Roadmap process. Recapping is essential.

Connecting dots connects them to their shared direction and to one another. That takes time and must not be rushed. This recapping has to be done more than once, as I did just now to make my point.

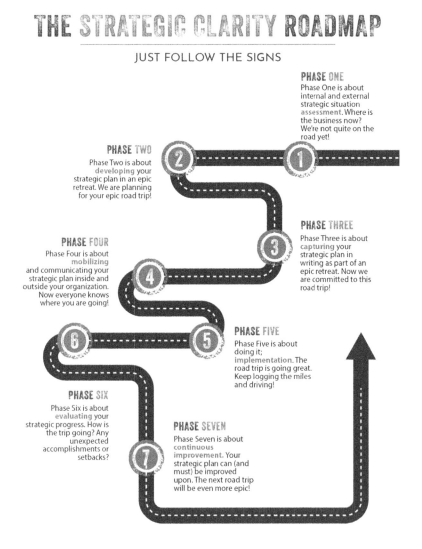

THE STRATEGIC CLARITY ROADMAP
JUST FOLLOW THE SIGNS

PHASE ONE
Phase One is about internal and external strategic situation assessment. Where is the business now? We're not quite on the road yet!

PHASE TWO
Phase Two is about developing your strategic plan in an epic retreat. We are planning for your epic road trip!

PHASE THREE
Phase Three is about capturing your strategic plan in writing as part of an epic retreat. Now we are committed to this road trip!

PHASE FOUR
Phase Four is about mobilizing and communicating your strategic plan inside and outside your organization. Now everyone knows where you are going!

PHASE FIVE
Phase Five is about doing it; implementation. The road trip is going great. Keep logging the miles and driving!

PHASE SIX
Phase Six is about evaluating your strategic progress. How is the trip going? Any unexpected accomplishments or setbacks?

PHASE SEVEN
Phase Seven is about continuous improvement. Your strategic plan can (and must) be improved upon. The next road trip will be even more epic!

I pull together a comprehensive and clear statement of the strategic essence from all of the combined decisions and outputs in this process. You remember all of those intermediate flip chart sheets, whiteboard comments, or PowerPoint summaries we set aside? Now, looking back at them all, I craft a *statement of strategic essence*. I ask the group for feedback on this. I invite them to co-author it with me. Here is a fictional example:

Strategic Essence for XYZ Company

- Based on a thorough internal and external strategic situation assessment, we have made the decision that our strategy in the sign and screen print supply business is to <u>out-relate</u> the competition.

  » We will research, win, manage, and expand on <u>relationships</u> with our customers totally opposite from our competitors. Instead of waiting to take new sales orders from customers and bidding low, we will act as an extension of their supply chain, providing <u>unmatched consulting</u> that helps our customers focus on their customers, not their supply chain headaches.

  » We decided on the customer experience mentality, not jumping from one product line (re: shiny object) to the next. Customers need us to be reliable and innovative for them and to lead them into the digital revolution. We will design our mix of products and services around what they need, not what we want to sell.

» We decided our mission is to build lasting B2B relationships in the entire sign and screen print supply chain so our customers excel, our employees have a spectacular career at XYZ, and our shareholders achieve managed and profitable growth.

» We decided our core values and culture focus on listening to understand, investing in the potential of all relationships, delivering unexpectedly positive experiences, and implementing digital technology innovations that reduce our dependence on dying distribution channels.

» We agreed to our "stretch for" vision to have an XYZ supply chain portal in every sign and screen print business in the U.S. Our detailed vision explains how we plan to make specific progress from 2021 to 2024.

» We decided to measure growth in terms of the percentage XYZ gets of the customer's total spend (we seek 50%+), growth in our leadership team effectiveness (measured by employee culture surveys), and growth in top-line revenues, exceeding 12% annually through 2024. This will be accomplished organically, without a traditional acquisition. However, we do envision by 2024 the nontraditional acquisition of a technology-consulting firm.

» We decided our unique selling proposition is to solve our clients' digital sign and screen print transformation challenges by managing their supply chain for them, all on the bedrock of mutually rewarding and transparent relationships.

• Our change mandate is clear to us. During this period of digital disruption in the sign and screen print supply industry, we have decided to lead as superior customer relationship managers and brilliant technology advisors. Everything we are about to implement, every initiative, every action plan, our broad financial plan ideally must all trace back to this statement of strategic essence.

I have crafted over 200 of these with client teams in actual retreats, wordsmithing with them real time. The fictional example above is a bit longish, but if a board member of XYZ Company asks what the strategy is for the next three to five years, that is the answer. Not a 125-page strategic plan binder. Not a financial target alone. Not an off-the-cuff quick response one week and a different rambling response the next. The essence has been developed and captured. It took several weeks of research and development and multiple days in retreat rooms. But, perhaps a bit miraculously, a comprehensive and detailed strategic business plan for the next three to five years has been thoughtfully developed by a leadership team who is now informed about and passionately committed to that direction. There is more work to be done after this epic retreat. In fact, the real work is just getting started. The Roadmap I have shared in this chapter will help you navigate the Develop and Capture phases. I encourage you to innovate within that process.

Chapter Summary

In the previous chapter, I addressed four of the major retreat chunks. In this chapter, we picked right up at Chunk Five on how your strategic plan should be built (i.e., organized), then we dove right in to the remaining chunks of the retreat. Although no two strategic planning retreats are identical, there is a pattern to the decisions that successful strategic planning retreat teams make: your mentality as a leadership team, mission, values, a big picture vision you believe in, growth methods and measures, and your new unique selling proposition. The team is not ready to implement action plans yet, but the main parts of your strategic direction are in place. Congratulations! I believe it is critical to summarize that entire emerging strategic direction back to the planning retreat team during the retreat.

Chapter Challenge Questions

1. Have you ever started a project that was not framed right from the start, say perhaps a small home repair project that quickly grew in scope? Would a blueprint have helped? How could it be helpful in your

organization to know what you are building before you start building it?

2. How would you and your leaders react to a pre-retreat assignment in which you were asked to bring your vision for the future of your company to the planning retreat? How might that sort of pre-retreat strategic thinking help a great deal with the retreat? How might it backfire?

3. Choosing your growth measures is important, at least as important as the methods for achieving that growth. What financial measures are you utilizing in your organization now? What non-financial growth measures might be important now for your organization? Why?

4. I have led executive planning retreats in many memorable locations and a few ordinary ones. Can you picture a place where you have done the same or imagine a place that would be ideal for the reimagining of your company? What did/would this place provide, and where was it or would it be? Why is it essential to get away?

CHAPTER EIGHT

Planning for Multiple Futures

"...if ever anyone discovers exactly what the Universe is for and why it is here, it will instantly disappear and be replaced by something even more bizarre and inexplicable."

The Hitchhiker's Guide to the Galaxy

Note, portions of this chapter are reprinted with permission from <u>CFMA Building Profits</u> magazine, which originally printed some of this content in their January/February, 2021 issue. That article is entitled "Uncertainty Is Not New, but Neither Is the Innovative Practice of Strategic Planning for Multiple Futures" by Tom Emison.

What in the World Is the Multiverse?

The Beatles's "Across the Universe." David Bowie's "Space Oddity." Elton John's "Rocket Man." Pink Floyd's "The Dark Side of the Moon." Frank Sinatra's "Fly Me to the Moon." Those songs taken together start to read like a playlist for traveling the universe. In fact, did you know there are *playlists* for astronauts to consider on their way into space and the great universe beyond? Or is it a multiverse? Seriously, in recent years there has been empirically supported scientific study that suggests there is not one universe, but many. Infinite. Could that mean there are multiple universes with multiple futures? This is uncannily similar to the poor justification some leaders give for not doing strategic thinking; there are just too many futures that could happen, too many aspects to consider, and no crystal ball. I agree there is no crystal ball to help any of us with business strategy. But, considering (as a group) your various futures in an epic retreat is important for that very reason: *because* there is no crystal ball. So, this chapter is written to help you plow into strategic planning even if your future looks very confusing.

I have never been in space, but I am close to a guy who has been. Rick Hieb, my wife's cousin, is a veteran of three NASA Space Shuttle missions, STS-39, STS-49, and STS-65.[21] Rick was a mission specialist and a payload commander. So, I asked him one day about astronaut music playlists. He is currently a faculty member at the University of Colorado Boulder Smead Aerospace Engineering Sciences Department. It is unreal having an astronaut in the family. When I asked about his favorite space music, he responded, "Tom, my favorite artist is Paul Simon, so I brought Paul Simon music on every mission. But my single favorite track for space flight, appropriate in so many ways, is Louis Armstrong's rendition of "What a Wonderful World." On those rare occasions in space flight when I had the chance to look out the window for a few minutes and just appreciate the beauty of the world slowly rolling by beneath us, that song was always my soundtrack of choice. Today, when I listen to that music, I am transported back to that experience more fully than any other way." On his three NASA missions, Rick was screaming along at 17,500 mph, at zero gravity, listening to Paul Simon. Mind blown here. The plan for each mission had to take into account literally hundreds of variables, contingencies, and outcomes; multiple futures. We are blessed that he and his crews came home safely. But there are many other examples of how organizations plan for multiple scenarios.

What Do These Three Share in Common?

- A 172-page scientific paper from the U.S. Fish and Wildlife Service.
- A 141-minute movie that stars Bill Murray and Andie MacDowell.
- A staggering work of genius developed by Professor Stephen Hawking in his final 10 days.

Answer: they each consider *multiple futures*. The U.S. Fish and Wildlife Service published "Considering Multiple Futures," a massive scientific paper on natural resource conservation.[22] *Groundhog Day* (1993) starred a wisecracking weatherman caught in a crazy time warp on the worst day of his life where poor Phil experiences many, many futures until he eventually prevails.[23] Ten days before Professor Stephen Hawking died, a study was submitted on his behalf to *The Journal of High Energy*

Physics.[24] Maybe the big bang created more than one universe but not an unlimited number. Random permutation of the infinite fractal reality?

Brain-bending stuff, to be sure. But, some leaders have been planning around multiple scenarios for a long time. In fact, the United States Army War College Strategic Studies Institute makes rather serious work of it. In 2019, they published "Strategic Insights: Challenges in Using Scenario Planning for Defense Strategy,"[25] which is one of the most interesting works on strategy I have read recently. High-performing executives have long understood that uncertainty is the basic challenge in strategic planning. Early in my consulting career, a few CEOs even told me that strategic planning was impossible. They had a different definition of business strategy than I did. While they wanted to plan for a future without much change, my definition made strategic change the goal. Strategic thinking is about change and so is strategic planning. Looking back on my 230 strategic business planning engagements, there is one common theme: to make sense of uncertainty and express this in a series of integrated decisions and actions that help a company in the Built Marketplace prosper by *fundamentally changing it.*

Strategic management fads I saw did not always work well when I tried to tap into or follow each fad. The amazing Richard Pascale once created a history of management fads, which when you think about it is simply a remarkable accomplishment (see next page). But I have never been fully convinced by business fads and claims. My work is with real CEOs in real companies addressing real strategic challenges. Back in 2005, I found myself designing and delivering strategic planning work using the best traditional methods (e.g., Jim Collins and Jerry Porras's excellent Core Ideology and Envisioned Future approach) and nontraditional planning methods (e.g., studying stratagems used by improvisational actors). For my clients, their future was starting to look dramatically less like their recent past. Strategic plans based on incremental growth or change (I call them Crawling Forward Plans) were not cutting it anymore. For me, strategic planning had become synonymous with change management. I began advising clients to develop strategic plans to compete *differently*, not just better. I suggested clients research their portfolio of possible futures. I would coach them as they struggled to look beyond their current business models, assumptions, and corporate cultures. I still do. I especially warned them about management fads du jour.

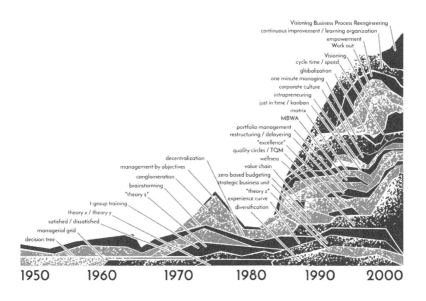

Importantly, some CEOs told me back then that their company often had several internal corporate cultures that coexisted, each different from the other. They often described these as internal silos or turf. In the same company, I would observe:

- Some smart leaders who sought and valued more structure and hierarchy in their company.
- Other smart leaders who sought and valued less structure and hierarchy.
- Some smart leaders who sought and valued more customer focus and market sensibility.
- Other smart leaders who sought and valued more employee focus and family feel.

The CEOs were permitting these silos, and, in many cases, they were creating them. In one client company, I observed six different internal corporate cultural silos: ownership silo, office personnel silo, field/union silo, office women silo, marketing and sales department silo, and technology natives silo. Six! They were busy competing against themselves internally and did not even really know it. I shared this insight with my clients to help them signal within their own company a new message, "It's time we stop competing for our limited resources internally with our silos and get back to the business of aligning around one culture focused on a shared vision. Culture only 'eats strategy for breakfast' when disconnected and uninspired silo leaders permit it."

In other words, I would try to get them to stop doing their strategic thinking at a corporate culture–inhibited 25 mph. Hey, after my advice, if they wanted a strategic plan to validate their past decisions and not build new ones and to keep their company cultures in silos, I would wish them well and move on. However, most of these CEOs wanted to grow, integrate, and grab for strategic innovation. They were ready to renew strategically at 17,500 mph, and it was exciting. They wanted to align culturally, and they felt all of their internal silos could agree on shared visions of the future. But how do you do that if there are multiple futures that might unfold?

The answer: if you want to increase your chances of surviving, you need to envision, plan for, and execute on multiple possible futures *while* the futures are unfolding in ways that are both expected and unexpected. Start thinking one or two moves ahead as you would in a game of chess. This means that strategy is an ongoing leadership discipline in your company, not a once-every-three-year event. Don't just design your strategic visions around your internal competing cultures; start developing strategic visions to align those competing cultures into one culture focused on the future. Delay your decision on your final chosen vision statements until the last possible moment. Then, go get that vision!

I mention this connection between corporate culture and planning for multiple futures for an important reason. Planning for multiple futures is complex enough, but it is impossible to plan for multiple futures with a company that is experiencing multiple personalities. Since we cannot predict with accuracy the one scenario your company should plan around, you need to plan around more than one. Read that last sentence again, please. Change is moving that quickly these days. I think Alvin Toffler got it right when he said, "Change is not merely necessary to life; it *is* life."[26]

So, let's describe another way to see the vision for the future of your company. In the previous chapter, I outlined how to develop your "stretch for" vision and your detailed vision. Here, I want you to envision multiple futures for your company. The process for multiple futures planning involves four things: *discovering* multiple futures based on intelligent market research that address a more virtually connected industry, *expressing* these multiple futures in writing, *evaluating* these multiple futures to decide what actions to take about the most likely future scenario, and *implementing* these decisions with high corporate intensity, a soldier's mentality. These four stages are based loosely on the work of creative genius Roger von Oech.[27] Let's examine each of these four stages.

Stage 1: Discovering Multiple Futures

Right now, there is a company very similar to your own that is becoming more relevant than your company in the Next Normal. They have explored through market research the many changes with their customers and their customers' customers. They have invested hours reading, prioritizing, synthesizing, brainstorming, and more or less becoming more aware of how to succeed going forward. They are exploring multiple futures. During this stage in your company, you need to make certain your top leaders are investing time researching and considering multiple futures alone *and* as a group.

- Alone: Is each top leader in your company becoming a student of market research about the future of your market sectors? Do you have an organized way to circulate among your leaders the most important articles, blogs, podcasts, links, videos, books, and other resources? Are you providing your leaders enough personal margin (i.e., time) to read such information?
- Together: Are you as a team comparing and contrasting your many observations and conclusions about possible futures? Are you having informed conversations?

In my case, this research has been within the U.S. construction and real estate industry. What is your sandbox for such research? Which of the sources for such information and insight can you rely on? What is driving these changes? How are other businesses innovating in response? Why are they not doing business as usual? Who is competing differently, not just better, and how are they doing that? If you are in a peer group, what are some of your colleagues or companies with whom you don't directly compete doing strategically? Your customers have their own customers or stakeholders; what are *their* strategic plans for reimagining their organizations? Some disruptions might happen that are game changers for your company; when might you expect those disruptions to happen?

Remember what Harvard Economist Michael Porter once famously said: "Strategy is about setting yourself apart from the competition. Strategy does not explain how you are going to get better; strategy is deliberately choosing to be different."[28] Making such choices requires excellent research. But, if you are not doing regular and high-quality research in your organization, you will never understand the multiple futures that are emerging. If you cannot or do not wish to perform this research role, then at least see if your company can provide the internal resources of money and people to perform this essential duty. That means providing financial support during lean times and allocating the appropriate research budget of both hard and soft costs. This type of research is about dropping assumptions. What unnecessary assumptions are holding your company back? Discovering is also about finding patterns (e.g., cycles, sequences, tendencies, similarities, behaviors, and probabilities). It is about looking at a problem facing your company from a different point of view. How would an architecture firm define your dental equipment supply industry problem? A construction product manufacturer? Your CPA firm? Your risk management advisors? An athlete? The U.S. Navy? As an example, many years ago, the practice of building commissioning came about in the U.S. construction industry. This is the integrated and systematic process to ensure, through documented verification, that all building systems perform interactively according to the design intent (i.e., the architect's and engineer's vision). Guess where this practice originated? It came from naval and maritime ship commissioning that is still used today to place a ship into active duty.[29]

So, a construction company can learn a lot about how to close out a retail construction project better by studying naval ship commissioning. Whoda thunk it? They are able to use this research to not just improve a process, like project closeout, but also to spell out possible emerging futures for their organization that diverge from the path they have been on. Many construction companies in the U.S. in recent years have entered the modular prefabrication fray because they have a sort of strategic sentinel in-house. Their research points to multiple futures that include offsite manufacturing or constructuring. While the long-term industry results for this delivery innovation are still unfolding, you can be sure a strategic planning retreat that does not welcome this sort of conversation is not as epic as it could be. Let's look to the next stage of planning for multiple futures.

Stage 2: Expressing Multiple Futures in Writing

There was a time, which I know will baffle most of you, when the tangible product of a strategic reinvention process was a three-ring binder! It was neatly organized into sections like a book. It included tabs labeled situation assessment, mission, vision, markets for focus, action plans, broad financial plan, and so on. The good ones told the strategic story very well and were valuable. However, some I came across were dry, uninspiring, and just mind-numbing page after page of stuff and spreadsheets. These did little to galvanize internal action toward the plan. They were virtually impossible to share with customers or other stakeholders. And worst, they did not reflect the collective imagination of top leadership and their vision. Their planning retreats must have been flops. Many such binders collected dust on the shelf.

While I worked with clients to capture their strategic direction in a binder, I also did so in creative, more communicable ways such as brochures, videos, office posters/boards, jobsite trailer posters/boards, website overhauls, new employee onboarding sessions, and all-company meetings/celebrations. One of these methods was to help the client team tell their strategic narrative as an actual story for inside their company (occasionally also for outside their company). I did this using the *storytelling* method. A great strategic plan for reimagining your company is like a narrative. You and your company leaders, if prompted, have an amazing story to tell one another internally, an account that will make sense in the market eventually, engage employees now, drive revenue growth, and more. The key in this stage is to accurately express in writing—using storytelling—the multiple futures your company is imagining. Let's explore in the next several pages of *Chunk* a fictional example of a strategic story for reimagining a general building contractor.

An Example of Pixar Animation Studio Storytelling

When you think Pixar, you think innovation. You see brilliant cartoons that are as funny as they are heartwarming. Genius level! What you may not know is that Pixar Animation Studios films follow a storytelling outline that goes back before filmmaking was an art.[30] Every film they have made is an incredible work of creativity, and each one follows a storytelling process that seems to be an innate storytelling code for humans. I have facilitated this storytelling exercise many times in epic planning retreats.

1. Once upon a time…

2. Every day…

3. But one day…

4. Because of that…

5. And because of THAT…

6. Until finally.

I used this outline above to help top leadership teams tell their story during offsite strategic planning retreats, and I still do today. It enables the leaders individually, then collectively, to step into the future and write the story they *prefer* to have written about their company's strategic success. They can write different stories for Scenario A, Scenario B, and so on. Some leaders in retreats at first exclaim, "I am not a writer!" Ironically, they are often the leaders who have compelling multiple futures in mind. With a little coaching, they really get going. Others may initially feel it is not strategic, saying, "this is not strategy." But they soon realize that is up to them. If their story is about competing differently, not just better, that is strategic. If their story is about the status quo, that is not strategic. What they dare to dream and write is up to them. Here is a sample.

- XYZ General Contracting, Inc. Scenario A

  » Once upon a time…

    ▪ XYZ GC was a strong and small community-oriented company with a great name in town, tremendous roots, community engagement, and a .45 experience modification rate (an insurance term). This is the story of how XYZ GC transformed from a local small GC to a remote work forerunner that changed for the better how architects, engineers, and construction companies interact.

  » Every day…

    ▪ Marketing and business development personnel went to market trying to distinguish XYZ GC in a community with many other excellent GCs. It was hard, and financial margins were skinny. Their brand was about strength and tradition. They were as good as their people, relying on their individual talents and heroics. Many were getting a bit long in the tooth, but wow, what great experience and knowledge they had. Customers appeared satisfied with some XYZ GC project managers and superintendents, but not with others in XYZ GC. Each project was approached entirely differently, as if the XYZ GC project managers each had their own mini construction companies. XYZ GC CEO Bob was 71 years old and sharp as a tack. He himself owned 100% of the stock of this S corp. He had been in the corner office for 35 years and presided over a company that had now grown to $125 million in GAAP Revenue/year (generally accepted accounting principles) and pre-tax profit of 1.25%, which for a contractor is not bad. Bob was charismatic, though employees were concerned for his health, misogynistic views, and his disdain for architects and engineers whom he deemed universally incompetent. The statements he made around the office about such firms were often disparaging.

» One day...

- Bob and XYZ GC leaders met offsite to dream together about the future. Bob and his wife opened the offsite retreat with a message that Bob would retire in one year. This triggered

strong emotions and even some tears in the
retreat room that day.

- Two top leaders (Julie the controller and
  Jack the director of operations) led a crucial
  conversation that day that changed the
  trajectory of XYZ GC forever and for the
  better. They clearly explained research they had
  been reviewing for weeks about the future of
  general building contracting. They elaborated
  on the troubles that are unique to midsized
  GCs like XYZ GC. They shared insights on
  new project delivery methods. They reported
  on a GC just like them, but in the Midwest,
  that had success engaging younger generations
  by becoming a more remote work–oriented
  culture. They shared a chart that showed
  their own internal succession or leadership
  retirement situations in XYZ GC. They showed
  how three projects they delivered last year were
  finished ahead of schedule, under budget,
  with zero recordable safety incidents, with
  architects that were now referring more work
  to XYZ GC. Turns out these three projects
  were delivered using virtual remote work teams
  from the architect, engineer, the project owner,
  XYZ GC, and five other main parties to the
  projects. When asked what made these three
  projects such winners, Julie and Jack answered

simply: "Our project manager, superintendent, pre-construction and estimating team, and ABC Architecture were spread out across the region and opted to do their work and build team efficiency virtually, using SilkNew." Bob was not sure what that was, but he liked the financial results. Then he recalled that his grandkids had been "FaceTiming" Bob and his wife for a couple years, and SilkNew must be a bit like that, he thought.

- "What if all of our projects were like that? And, what if we never allowed a bad word about architects to be said in our company?" a young project manager asked in that offsite. Those two "what ifs" allowed a future vision to emerge in this retreat. In fact, it showed three possible futures. The leaders discussed all three futures and agreed that they did not need to select the exact future scenario just yet. As long as they kept talking and exploring, it was good. They did so for the next several weeks. A new direction was emerging. And this direction would be about substantial change, not the status quo.

» Because of that…

- Top leadership at XYZ GC, with Bob's support and checkbook, piloted a strategic initiative to get smart on remote work and virtual effectiveness. It was a success. One year later, 11 projects totaling over $29 million in GAAP Revenue were being delivered using the new XYZ GC Virtubuild collaboration process that linked all project parties to the same technology platform. It was supported by the new alliance they had formed with MaxTable. Even seasoned XYZ GC employee veterans were engaged, being paired with XYZ GC younger mentors on this new technology (new to XYZ GC anyway). Bob wrote three messages to all of his employees in a three-week period in which he implored employees to never again say a negative word internally or externally about any architecture firm. Coming from him, it really rang the bell.

» Because of THAT…

- Architecture and engineering firms started to view XYZ GC as not only a contractor, but also a tech-savvy business partner. They began referring more projects to XYZ GC; much of this was negotiated fee work, not low-bid. XYZ GC often returned the favor to those architects.
- Local and regional media picked up on the innovation and published two high-gain media

stories about XYZ GC, giving the company new and positive marketing exposure.

- Marketing and BD personnel started realizing it was better to go out into the market with the project manager and superintendent together. Their win rate increased every time they showed the architect or project owners their younger field engineers, assistant project managers, and younger pre-construction and estimating personnel.

- Bob learned to fly (and crash) the company drone.

- Four very experienced leaders in XYZ GC did not handle this transition to a more tech-oriented culture and left of their own accord; three went directly into retirement.

- The pipeline of potential projects grew 20% in the first year and 25% again the next.

- Six interns then later joined XYZ GC full-time. Three of those have excellent long-term leadership potential.

- XYZ GC was invited to present their story of virtual work effectiveness at a local conference of the American Institute of Architects.

- Managed volume grew 25% in two years and GAAP Revenue grew 21% in those same two years—while improving project gross margins without adding additional personnel. It was a retooling of personnel, no net additions.

» Until finally...

- Bob, with advice from his CPA firm, his risk management broker, and his other business contacts, proceeded with a company ownership succession plan. This plan enabled an ESOP to take shape for a certain % of the company as well as a direct ownership opportunity for five of Bob's top leaders for the remaining % of the company.
- The entire value proposition shifted. Instead of built on tradition, the company was now built on communication, client impact, technology integration, and community leadership.
- Cost of sales dropped. G&A improved, improving working capital. The great experience modification rate of .45 was maintained.
- And, an entire cadre of younger (and a few more mature) XYZ GC employees were able to engage in new ways with one another and their stakeholders to complement the old-school handshake for which they were known and still are today. They formed a Young Professionals' Group and blended their meetings with other young professionals' groups from several

architecture and engineering firms and subcontractors. Soon, XYZ GC was zippered to about every A/E firm and other business partners in their community. They routinely heard about project opportunities months before their competitors.

I have facilitated storytelling exercises like that one quite a lot. It is an amazing experience. Without fail, leaders have powerful stories to share. Some are gifted strategic thinkers who, for the first time, are able to put it all down on paper. The epic retreat facilitator's role? Keep a broad perspective during this exercise. Listen. You might be able to see how the multiple visions intersect or combine. For instance, you might piece together parts of Hal's vision with parts of Julie's and parts of Dania's *and* you might be able to make that a more complete story by including their customer's perspective. Great corporate visions often coalesce like that.

Stage 3: Evaluating or Judging Your Multiple Futures

"Choosy mothers choose Jif" is the tagline I believe (I am a Jif guy, but my wife, Pam, prefers Skippy, sooooo we have Skippy at home). One has to go about the first two stages in order to eventually get *choosy*. When I see three or four thoughtfully expressed future scenarios for a company, I get excited. It means the first two stages have been completed and the leaders can now get choosy. But part of making the right choice is having the right timing. A great business strategy at the wrong time dies; acting too soon invites unwarranted competition and acting too late means you missed the train. When evaluating your multiple futures, the three rules are timing, timing, and timing. Is one of your multiple futures already underway in the industry? If so, your timing is likely too late.

Here are some questions to ask and answer in choosing or judging your multiple futures and then narrowing into the most likely future. The key here is to entertain all of the multiple scenarios for a long enough period of time (usually several months) to see which ones rise to the top (most likely to happen and your preferred scenario, based on your market research and instincts). Does the future you have described so well in writing appear inevitable, and is it in fact extremely likely to happen? If so, it is a contender. If it is extremely likely to happen, is it also what you would prefer to happen? In other words, is the scenario that is emerging also the one your company has been preparing for and actually prefers? Now you really have a contender. Then, there is a subset of questions:

1. What conditions will need to exist within your four walls (each department, each location, etc.) in order to seize and profit from this future scenario? And, in order for those conditions to materialize, what will your organization need to do internally THIS year?

2. How big is the gap between your current situation and the scenario? Is it a small leap, a major leap, or a

quantum leap? A quantum leap does not mean to not take the risk of leaping, but it does help leaders understand the scope and depth of the corporate change you face.

3. How about the conditions outside your four walls? Which conditions need to exist there (i.e., industry trends, policies, technologies, advancements, regulatory conditions, competitive factors, supply chain considerations, economic factors)?

4. Following the law of unintended consequences,[31] what might happen, get better, or get worse because of this scenario choice? Why? When?

5. What specific triggers will cause your organization to hone into the one scenario that you can build a strategic plan around? Examples may help:

    a. Trigger: Acme Construction down the street wins its first multifamily housing project using volumetric modular construction.
    b. Trigger: your excellent working capital exceeds $XX million for the third consecutive year.
    c. Trigger: over 90% of office employees report a strong preference to work from home during the same year you improved pre-tax profit to over X.X%.
    d. Trigger: more than five subcontractors with whom you work sign a letter of intent to invest in a new

company (often referred to as the "Newco") with your company.

6. Is this emerging direction consistent with your change mandate, mission, values, and big picture vision? If it is, it might move from a good contender to the best contender. If not, be wary.

7. What will be the expected and unexpected financial impacts to the business? Why?

8. Did groupthink creep in and play a role? This is a common leadership team phenomenon in which the desire to avoid conflict among leaders results in artificial harmony and a vision that is not change-oriented. Status quo? Uh-oh.

9. Can you put it in writing one last time—in final form—and build leadership consensus about it?

The point is not so much the examples I share but the practice of knowing how your leadership team will choose or judge the scenarios and start moving toward the right one. Here are some fictional examples to make my point more clear.

- **Future Scenario A for 123 Construction: the U.S. experiences an L-shaped recovery from the COVID-19 pandemic ("L-shaped" infers a very steep drop in economic activity *and* a very long-term recession or worse).** After all, there has never *not* been a second pandemic wave or variant. Economic recoveries in the past, including that from the 2008–2009 Great Recession, lingered slowly for years. Based on this, 123 Construction will seize this opportunity to dramatically increase its sales of small tenant improvement or special projects. Our goal is that, by FYE 2022, we deliver over $75 million in special projects under $3 million in scope. We will use this foundation to build and bring to market a new service and maintenance group no later than FYE 2023. Big construction projects will no longer be our only calling card. Small is the new big for 123 Construction. We will build a strategic business plan to do that!

• **Future Scenario B for 123 Construction (almost the same at first); the U.S. experiences an L-shaped recovery from the COVID-19 pandemic**. After all, there has never *not* been a second pandemic wave or variant. Economic recoveries in the past, including that from the 2008–2009 Great Recession, lingered slowly for years. Based on this, 123 Construction will transition to a full design-build firm through the acquisition of 456 Architecture no later than 12/31/2021. Together, we will build a vertical market strategy in healthcare and K-12 schools. We will offer fully integrated real estate development, design, general contracting, and property management services. We will build a strategic plan to do that!

• **Future Scenario C for 123 Construction: the U.S. experiences a V-shaped recovery, and we are more**

or less back to healthy sales and backlogs end of
2021. This quick bounce back will produce internal
momentum for our new strategy to be the premier
virtual contractor in our region. We will shift to a CM
agency type of contractor, almost like a consulting
firm. No more self-performance. No more unions. No
yard of iron. We will launch a new consultative selling
method that gets us into the C-suite. We will become
the experts at telling clients what to make of trends like
volumetric modular construction and how to avoid
the pitfalls. We hire the best people regardless of their
location, since being "here" is mostly moot. We will
build a strategic plan to do that!

- **Future Scenario D for 123 Construction: the U.S.
  experiences a V-shaped recovery, and we opt to
  go bare-knuckle out there**. It is clear: low cost and
  low price wins the work. We will do everything in
  our power to drive cost and waste from the process,
  becoming a Lean icon in the region. We will go so
  far with this that we prefer to work with other Lean
  owners, A/E firms, subs, suppliers, etc. Our contracts
  will become a strategic advantage as we shift from
  a negotiated-style CM/GC to a hard-nosed and
  profitable low-bid contractor. Some subcontractors
  may no longer wish to work for us. Not our problem.
  We will build a strategic plan to do that!

Stage 4: Approaching Implementation as a Soldier

The problem with strategic planning is a failure to implement. Or at least that is the lie you have been told. I hate to burst your bubble, but failed implementation is not the problem. It is the *result* of the problem. I can tell you from actual experience that these are the underlying causes of poor plan implementation. Think of these as the enemies of clear business strategy:

- Inadequate market research
- Poor leadership of the process by the CEO
- Unclear expectations internally about the process
- Purely a financial plan or a marketing plan or an (X) plan
- Compliance (not commitment) mentality from leaders
- No brilliant crafting of the plan itself; just filled out some online strategy forms
- Less-than-candid internal situation assessment
- Too many initiatives
- Boring retreats with no zip
- One person's plan, usually the CEO
- Lack of deliberate employee engagement to the plan
- Failure to mobilize and communicate direction externally
- Fear of change; let current or the old fading corporate culture "win"
- Plan that satisfies everyone but is not strategic
- Lack of measuring short-term wins

- Treating planning as an event, not a process
- Strategy plagiarism from the company down the road
- Over/under collaboration on key topics
- Turf and tribalism
- Emotional or overly political process
- Leadership team dysfunctions
- Magical thinking
- Strategy is good but is bolder than the leadership team
- No whimsy; no serendipity; no wow; no galvanizing
- Change for change's sake
- No resulting strategic essence

The multiple futures planning process you choose to use must not allow these bugs to gain a foothold. Poor implementation is not the problem but the result of other problems. Mediocre implementation of a strategic plan makes a soldier break out in hives. He is laser focused on one thing only: results. When you have completed stages 1, 2, and 3, you have now built a strategic business plan around the future you believe in. It is not time to do more research, second-guess yourselves, or get timid. The key at this stage is to incite action in your company and direct that action toward the strategic plan without marginalizing day-to-day operations. The soldier then looks very differently at the organization. He will find a way to make certain the Year One action plan is bold, aggressive, and shakes the tree. Ironically, the seemingly safer option to go slow and easy actually assures failure. A soldier understands this: you can tell everything you need to know about the next three years of a strategic plan by what changes in the first 90 days. He will help break down the annual strategic plan objectives into smaller monthly or quarterly milestones. He will align resources to the action plans. This is an often overlooked activity and, if it is not done correctly, it can stop strategic reinvention before it gets going. What I have seen in successful companies is a willingness to allocate and even repurpose key people toward the strategic plan actions. They do not ask employees who are already busy with dozens of day-to-day realities to do strategic action work in their spare time.

Reality check: they do not *have* spare time.

The better option is to recruit team leaders from both inside and outside your company to truly lead each initiative. A soldier is seeking other soldiers with whom to go into battle: a team leader who will own the initiative in its entirety and a person who is likely to overachieve the metrics associated with the initiative. He wants to communicate, communicate, and communicate. You have to tell your stakeholders where the organization is going and *why*. We are all bombarded each day with countless marketing messages and messages from inside our organizations. It is a fact of business life. This shelling has become so intense that you are literally competing for your employees' attention. If you want employees to know where your organization is headed, why you selected your particular future, the nature of that future, the specifics of your strategic plan, their role in that plan, and how you are coming with that strategic plan, then you have to communicate 10^X more than you think. Strategic soldiers know this and create written internal and external communication tactics just for the strategic plan itself. They are evangelical about this direction. They never miss a day in which they do not act as an ambassador of that plan.

Overcoming pushback becomes a skill. When composer Stravinsky first presented his *Rite of Spring* ballet, it produced riots. When Kepler first solved the orbital problem of the planets by suggesting orbital ellipses instead of circles, he was nearly killed. You can be sure that, when it comes to change in your company using the strategic plan as a management tool, your current corporate culture will push back. A soldier expects this but heads it off. When that does not work, he makes the pushback into a public example of how the company is changing. Let's imagine you lead a largish U.S. road and bridge civil construction company. Your stages 1, 2, 3, and 4 have been impeccable. Your organization has agreed to a future scenario that requires you to focus on chasing, winning, and delivering construction work in only three segments: parking structures, county/municipal roads and bridges, and paving jobs over $500,000. This is a new laser-focused approach for your company. It's a change.

In the first 90 days of implementing the strategic plan, three of your project superintendents passively protest the decision. They feel your company is more than capable of doing all kinds of flat work. They think the new focus is not needed. They promise current clients "this too shall pass" and keep asking your estimators to win small driveway paving jobs and gigantic projects for the state Department of Transportation. The soldier sees this initial mistake by the three superintendents as an opportunity to clarify expectations, reinforce the new direction, and change their errant ways. The soldier explains that a few fumbles in the first 90 days are to be expected. But the soldier also says the following out loud at a project manager and superintendent monthly meeting (without calling out the offenders):

- "Superintendents, I want to remind you that we researched a lot of choices on our strategic direction. We carefully narrowed it down to a future scenario that is very bright for our company. We put that in writing and we agreed as a leadership team that this new direction (hyper-focused only on parking structures, county/municipal roads and bridges, and paving jobs over $500,000) is real. If you think our company is capable of doing more and a wider variety of projects, you are right. I agree with you. However, being able to do that type of work is not the same as doing it profitably for the long haul consistent with our vision. We just cannot be all things to all people and build the company. Therefore, you will *not* be getting any support from estimating, or me, if you wander out of our three focus areas. If I hear about this loss of focus again, I will figure you do not understand our direction. Strategic change and our new focus are hard to get used to, I know. It has been an adjustment for me, too. But our adjusting period has ended. I need warriors who are going to help us win and win big in our three chosen markets."

Soldiers Are Party Animals

Soldiers want the company to celebrate its accomplishments toward this bold new direction. Nothing builds internal enthusiasm to a new direction like winning. These can be small weekly or even daily moments of victory or big notable wins that only happen once or twice a year. In every case, it is critical for leadership in your company to tie the accomplishment back to the new direction before you celebrate, for instance:

> "This text message is going to every employee in our company to remind us that when we focus, we win. Last Thursday, Andy and Sarah put together the estimate for the new ramp at the hotel after working for two months on this with the hotel ownership group, their operations director, and Emison Engineering. Today, we found out we were not low—but we won! This is the strategic future we are moving toward. When you see Andy or Sarah, give 'em an attaboy/attagirl! Wins like this do not just happen without focus and sacrifice. For every project we opted not to chase this year, this one win makes up for all of them and more. Linda and I are serving an entire BBQ lunch for everyone next Friday at 12 in the main yard."

Back to *Groundhog Day*

In the movie, Phil makes hundreds of blunders before he gets life right. The lesson we are to take away is about getting out of your own personal hell so you do not wake the next morning to the same thing again, again, and again. I sure hope your company does not wake up each day just doing only the same thing over again and again. Phil has an inspired moment of strategic clarity when he sees a different future for himself in his time warp. His future is unendingly multiple! Nevertheless, he uses this to his benefit. He eventually masters the piano, motivates his camera operator, inspires his fetching co-producer, saves a boy falling from a tree, changes a flat tire for some nice old ladies, and more.

Chapter Summary

Uncertainty was already underway in your organization years ago, right? There is an art to multiple futures planning, a practice that is especially well used in the military. This sets the stage for your continued success. You now have the methods and tools for multiple futures planning, and you can see how these can be used in the present day to shape the new direction for your company.

Chapter Challenge Questions

1. Planning for multiple futures by using the scenario planning approach provides agility, not red tape. What potential scenarios can you see unfolding in your

industry or for your company the next few years? Why is it important to understand all of the high potential scenarios before committing to one?

2. How could Pixar Animation storytelling work for you in your company? Which of your leaders or employees would excel at this exercise? Why is it desirable to take the time to do this creative expression?

3. Implementation is not why strategic plans fail, it is *when* they fail. And not all strategic planning efforts fail. What strategic planning efforts in your company tanked because of the shortcomings listed earlier? When did a planning effort excel and why?

CHAPTER NINE

STRATEGIC AGILITY AND ITS NEMESIS, STRATEGIC DRIFT

 "Success today requires the agility and drive to constantly rethink, reinvigorate, react, and reinvent."
BILL GATES

The Bluebird Café

On a construction industry business trip to Nashville several years ago, I had a short window of free time before I had to be back at the airport to fly home. I had always wanted to go to The Bluebird Café, which is an intimate venue where heroes behind the hits perform their own songs.[32] These folks are prolific. Here is an astonishing fact: for every musical hit song that jumps up the charts, hundreds of songs end up on the musical cutting-room floor. The songwriters behind almost all of the music we hear (not just the country genre) produce hundreds of songs for other people. At The Bluebird Café, these unknown songwriters and musicians can perform the hit song they wrote for so-and-so, or they can pull out some new number they want to play for the gathered audience. Who knows, maybe a megastar country singer is in the audience who will love that tune and want to buy it.

As we pulled up, I was shocked to find that it was not the grand, historic brick building I had imagined. The building, which was located in a strip mall, could be described as bordering that space between unassuming to bland and ordinary. But it is what happens *in* there that matters. Musical improvisation. Melodic creation. Harmonic reverberations. Lyrical genius. Moments of imaginative inspiration, played in a mostly acoustic environment. The venue follows a "*shhhhh*" policy that enables the musicians and songwriters to concentrate on their playing. Sadly, when I got there, it was closed. As I drove away in the back seat of the cab, I thought about how remarkable it was that so many creative musical contributions originate in this blasé strip mall outside Nashville.

Strategic Improvisation

Years earlier, I listened to The Bluebird Café songwriters perform live for a leadership team at a strategic planning retreat. The setting then was a meeting of Young Presidents' Organization (YPO).[33] It seems someone at YPO had the wherewithal to invite a group from The Bluebird Café to perform over the cocktail hour and into the night for YPO members. What a stroke of genius by YPO. As they performed at this business-y gathering, the musicians took breaks to talk to the YPO members about how they create, how they improvise, and how they support each other musically, making the most of their combined strengths. To the surprise and delight of the presidents gathered, the band kept going back and forth every five minutes or so between a cool song and a lesson on leadership, teamwork, collaboration, integrity, and invention. The analogy was not lost on anyone that night: leading your business strategically is no different than jamming creatively.

Let's look at the most obvious parallels. First, as leaders, we each have our instruments. For the musician, it is himself and his instrument. For an executive leader, it is herself and her leadership effectiveness. Second, a strategic business planning retreat is both informal, inspired, and well organized behind the scenes, just like a musical jam session. Third, improvised solos are okay for musicians, unless the solo goes on too long or does not fit. It is the same way with leaders who need to make sure they solo, but never too often or for too long apart from the band. Fourth, the real fun for leaders is coming together on a big strategic growth idea, just as it is for musicians with a particular big chord progression or arrangement. Fifth, a jam session may be based loosely on an existing song or an entirely new one. It is the same way with executive leaders, building their strategic plan on the existing plan or an entirely new one. Sixth, jam sessions are mostly private affairs behind closed doors. It is the same with strategic business planning retreats, which are usually confidential. Finally, a key quality in musicians who are jamming is quick improvisation, not straying too far off the path but being just agile enough to add brilliantly to the song. It is the same with strategic business agility: the ability to shift but not drift.

Strategic Agility

Strategic business plans require a new level of agility without straying too far off the path. We need to be able to improvise, often quickly. In the previous chapter, I explained how to plan for multiple futures. In this chapter, I want to explain more about why (the agility imperative) and how to avoid death by strategic drift.

So, the imperative for more strategic agility is clear enough. If you research and develop a strategic plan that is too focused or too tight, you will put in place a whole series of tactics that box in your company. You run a huge risk. If you research and develop a strategic plan that is wide open or vague, your series of tactics will be all over the board and poorly coordinated. Again, you run a huge risk. You have to make sure your strategic plan is "loose/tight." A strong strategic plan is tight (i.e., binding, constricted, stuffed, and unyielding) in some respects and loose (i.e., relaxed, movable, lithe, and flexible) in others. This quality of "loose/tight" is what helps prosperous organizations stay on track with their vision while staying open to changes that are inevitable, unpredictable, and over which leaders have no control. In most businesses, the external threats you talk about privately, in retreat settings for example, are often out of your direct control. They are external threats such as political volatility, economic uncertainty, changing regulatory environment, competitive factors, and—oh, yeah—pandemics. Using "loose/tight" wisdom, a good strategic plan must be periodically adjusted to reality out there without completely drifting from the core strategy. That is my agility imperative for your company. So, what is core? What parts of your strategic essence are so central they should be binding, disruption be damned? Conversely, what parts of your strategic essence should be flexible so you develop agility to mitigate corporate risk and seize emerging opportunities? What parts of the strategic essence are most able to be modified periodically versus those that must be like rock? The answer is simple but hugely important.

Core, Not Subject to Change	Flexible, Stay Agile
Organizational Mentality: like a rock	*Change Mandate:* can change as often as every two years
Mission: unchanging	*Detailed Vision for 3–5 Years:* recast every three to five years
Values and Culture: enduring	*Unique Selling Proposition:* can change as often as every two years
Stretch For Vision: always the aspiration	*Growth Methods and Measures:* can change as often as every two years
	Mix of products and services: needs continual refinement

Market mix (primary vs. secondary markets): can change every year

Organizational Structure: needs to be modified all the time but only changed substantially every three to five years

Broad Financial Plan and CapEx: needs refinement, of course, annually

Annual Strategic Action Plans: recast annually, measured and acted on quarterly, monthly, and in some companies weekly

The components of your strategic essence in the left-hand column must be well researched, well considered, and well crafted. They must be well communicated and well reinforced continually. These are the parts of your strategic plan and overall direction that will only change "over your dead body." In the right-hand column are components of your strategic essence that also need to be well crafted but need regular review. Notice I said *review*, not change. I am not suggesting they must be changed. I am suggesting that reviewing them as a top leadership team is important. This can keep a company tight on the unchanging staples and open to adaptation as internal conditions and market environs change. The annual strategic essence review can be as simple as a one-day offsite to reinforce and review your strategic essence. If you add to this a second day of recasting the strategic action plans for your next year of implementation—perfecto! That is a small ingredient in the recipe for remaining agile.

The Agile Company Is Like an Athlete

For the moment, think of your company as an athlete. Consider your readiness to shift to changing conditions. For an athlete, it is being ready to shift their weight to their right foot before that powerful swing of the tennis racket. For a company, it is the readiness to add a primary market sector quickly to swing into an unexpected growth opportunity. For the athlete, it is the readiness to carve the turn above the gate on a snowy slalom course, not waiting until it is too late. For a company, it is speeding a product to market 10^x faster than normal, before the window of opportunity slams shut. For the athlete, it is always being prepared to call an audible at the line of scrimmage. For a company, it is reorganizing your reporting structure to align with the strategy; after all, strategy is what drives structure (or at least it should). Great organizations seem to inherently know what components of their business are suitable for change periodically within the framework of the overall strategic essence. But there can still be anxiety, a silent concern.

The Unstated Fear

When a top leadership team wishes to develop a sound strategic plan in an epic planning retreat, there can be an unstated concern floating invisibly in the air. This unease resides in the back of the participants' minds but will not be expressed unless you probe for it. If I had to paraphrase that worry, it would say, "We do not want to research and develop a strategic plan that is too constrictive or built on fallible market research. There is just so much uncertainty. Somehow and some way, we have to be both strategic for the long term (following a roadmap) and agile in the short term." This private concern must be aired out in every epic strategic business planning retreat. To do this, I use two tools.

1. The first is the *planning for multiple futures* process I described earlier. This enables leaders to envision multiple possible futures and gradually move toward the scenario for success.

2. The second is the *cone of relative certainty* tool. I often deploy this in an epic strategic business planning retreat during the visioning process but sometimes "the cone" actually finds its way into my opening message in a retreat.

How do we as leaders think long term with so much immediate uncertainty right in our faces? The answer lies in the cone. This allows you to think and plan within a field of vision about which you *can* be relatively certain, because you can actually be relatively certain about many internal and external factors in any company. Here are some examples that may apply to your company. We can be relatively certain that:

• Customer expectations for quality will increase.

- Market competition is on the rise.
- Blurring of traditional lines that distinguish between companies in supply chains will continue.
- Marketplace consolidation of competitors is on the rise.
- Supply chain innovations will disrupt.
- Technology adoption by customers and competitors will continue.
- Corporate culture shifts to work from home will increase.
- Financial strength will continue to be critical to demonstrate to customers.
- Innovation will not just be incremental but more fundamental.
- Brand clarity will be more important going forward.
- Salespeople will need more technical training than before.
- Lean operations must gain energy internally to create new capacity for growth without adding more people.
- Employees want more mastery, autonomy, and purpose in their jobs.
- Commoditization of services will force companies to either cut costs and price to profitably be the low-cost provider, or cut financial margins, or enable some companies to migrate higher in the customer value chain to command greater fees and relevance.
- New products will come to market more rapidly than before.

- Some competitors will go out of business.
- Opportunities for vertical market integration are on the rise.

You may take issue with a few of those, and I could go on with more. In a changing world, there are many aspects about which we can be relatively certain. So, I challenge you to embrace the fact that, despite all of the rhetoric about change (some of which I myself reinforce), you can still be relatively certain about some things, at least certain enough to plan around them. You really can and must establish a big picture vision about which your company can be relatively certain. It is what leaders do in high-performing companies. They establish a detailed vision they are sure about. That vision can be either five years out into the future, four years, or perhaps only three. The closer that time horizon is to today (close being three years out), the more certain you can be. The reason so many organizations prefer three-year strategic planning retreats over five-year is precisely because they feel a bit more certain about the three-year window than the five-year window.

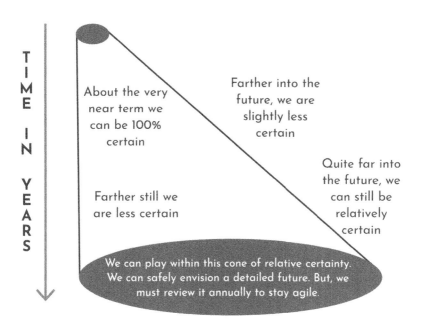

Your detailed vision needs to be researched and crafted within this cone. Or, put differently, do not craft a detailed vision that expresses statements about which you are very uncertain. Doing so would be folly. Your detailed vision needs to exist within this cone. This is not constraining. It's liberating. If you do your big picture visioning right and apply this cone in your group discussion, you will find that your vision for your company is aspirational, detailed, and realistic all at once. I am relatively certain of that…

Drift: The Unseen Enemy

Agility is one thing. Drift is another altogether. I define strategic drift as a collection of small acts (e.g., internal conversations and decisions) that, in combination, move your organization subtly off plan. When an epic strategic planning retreat has concluded, the leaders are crystal clear on the new direction. But nobody else is. That lack of clarity, left unaddressed, will increase your corporate propensity for drift. Such meandering can be insidious, really. Examples include slightly misstating your mission. Just one wrong word at an all-office meeting can start the drift process, as everyone in the meeting is now just slightly less clear on the mission. Or maybe a particular growth strategy that was chosen in a retreat is later miscommunicated to a key supplier. Now, that key supplier, and probably others, are slightly less clear on what you mean in your strategic direction. Or a branch manager in your organization may start pursuing a customer that is not aligned with the detailed vision. Left uncoached, this branch manager engages another customer also on the wrong strategic pretense. Word gets out in your corporate grapevine, and soon, many branch managers are winning new customers totally out of alignment with the chosen strategic direction. You are strategically adrift. Friends, verbal imprecision is one of the causes of strategic drift. Agility is great. Drift, not so much.

Chapter Summary

Corporate agility is one thing, but drifting away is another. Improvisational musicians jam to produce works of genius.

You can take the same logic and apply it to your business. Your leaders can "jam" on their strategic direction. Of course, things happen, conditions change, and you have to, with great agility, move in a new direction. So, what parts of your strategic essence are not up for grabs and are not changing? What parts must remain somewhat flexible? How do you achieve "loose/tight"? You do it by encouraging agility within the cone of relative certainty and greatly discouraging drift. Drift is an often unseen enemy, especially for top leaders. Verbal precision is essential on all communications related to your strategic essence. Stay on message and on your corporate toes, like a tennis pro.

Chapter Challenge Questions

1. The Bluebird Café is a center for musical songwriting and improvisation. It sits quietly in a blasé strip mall outside Nashville, TN. The way musicians jam is a good parallel for how leaders can think together, collaborate, and add to one another's genius. When have you jammed in this way on any initiative in your life? How did it make you feel? What was the unexpected and improvised outcome and how did it benefit your organization?

2. How does planning strategically within the cone of relative certainty feel? Does it feel a bit constrained or does it feel reasonable? Why?

3. What are you relatively certain about in your organization right now? List five things internal to your organization you can be relatively certain about. List five things about your industry, your markets, and your competitors you can be relatively certain about. How can you plan around these relative certainties?

CHAPTER TEN

COMMUNICATION, COMMUNICATION, COMMUNICATION

"...And O, my darling, O, my pet,
*Whatever else you may **forget***
[emphasis added],
In yonder isle beyond the sea,
O, don't forget you've married me!"
FROM A POEM BY WILLIAM
SCHWENCK GILBERT

Lost to Obscurity

It was 1974 when Grand Funk Railroad recorded *Shinin' On*, which was, amazingly, their eighth studio album. Nearly everyone my age remembers their 1973 hit "We're an American Band." It peaked at #5 in the U.S. Even though "Shinin' On" was an awesome banger, it was lost to obscurity. Some music just never flies in the charts and quickly becomes forgotten. A lot of good ideas get lost to obscurity, actually, including a business's strategic priority, usually due to inattentive leaders.

How would it make you feel if your organization invested in strategic business planning, developed a really transformational strategy, and then forgot about it? What would you do if it seemed to you that your top leaders had more or less forgotten about the strategic direction just a few short months after committing to it? I assure you, it happens more often than we all want to think. The main culprit of strategic plans never getting implemented is failure to communicate the new direction first internally and then externally. This then leads to a loss of institutional memory within the organization. Why do some organizations jump from the development of their strategic plan to implementation and fail to communicate the direction internally? To answer these and other questions, I want to recreate this conversation I had with a leadership team in a planning retreat around 2010. It was one of many similar conversations I have had with strategic retreat teams on the topic of communicating and mobilizing the strategic plan before implementing it.

"Wow," I started. "This has just been an exceptional process and retreat with all of you. Look back on all you have accomplished in this strategic planning process. I mean, you did an exhaustive strategic situation assessment before even doing any long-term planning. You did your research, listened to your customer, and participated in an epic strategic planning retreat. In that retreat, you did the hard work most strategic leadership teams shy away from. You did the deep thinking. You did the collaborative listening. You then broke your strategic initiatives down into smaller action plans. You even now have it all in front of you for final approval. Awesome. You are crushing it. You ready to implement?!"

"Yeah!" they shouted with enthusiasm.

"No, you're not," I said bluntly.

"Huh?"

"Well, I sort of tricked you into that by being so curt. Sorry! What I mean is no one is ready to implement anything—in any company, not just yours—without a rollout plan. You need to provide this plan to your organization, almost like a gift of sorts. 'Here is the strategic direction we've all been craving to keep growing our company.' So, what we need to do is start talking about communication in your company. How do you want the strategic plan to live in your company? We need a communication plan that takes into account the different audiences you have internally. For instance, top leadership is an audience. The level of confidential detail in their version of the strategic plan is probably quite high. Another audience may be your new employees who get recruited and onboarded—what is the version (level of detail) in the strategic plan you give them? For middle managers and leaders who are not in top leadership, the version might fall somewhere between those previous two examples. And, more creatively, what is the level of detail in the strategic plan you share with customers, business partners, and vendors? Some may say, 'What?! Never—we do not want our strategic plan leaking out!' I say phooey, there is without question a version of your strategic plan that is essential for them to know—so they can help you get there! So, what we are ready to do now is communication planning. Then, you can start implementing with a full force of your stakeholders' group (e.g., other leaders, employees, and eventually customers) so we achieve your goals."

"He's right," one of the team members replied. "This happened in another company I was in before, where they did a lot of planning but never told any of us about it. It was all hush-hush and weird. I knew that if our key suppliers knew some of our strategic plan, we could enlist them for their help and speed up how well we achieve our new direction. So, we had to switch from treating our strategic plan as a confidential thing to a more comprehensive and transparent way to really connect with our markets and clients." Genius level, super turbo.

I have heard this story before. We all have, haven't we? The bold new corporate direction that is never well communicated, nor understood, and then briefly lives outside the very culture it is designed to shift. It just never gets a chance to be wedged into the organization so that it must be implemented. Doomed. Then, it fades into something that was done in the distant past. Then, it is just forgotten. Two years later, someone in the company says, "Hey, we need to do some strategic planning!" They do all the strategic planning and unwittingly recreate almost the exact same strategic plan as the one forgotten from the past. I called this phenomenon "corporate amnesia" for many years before I learned that it is actually very much a studied matter. I still see it in businesses. It is more prevalent than you might think to forget something like a strategic plan, not in a deliberate act but through inaction. The words, the ideas, the strategies, and even the "why" behind it all can then slowly vaporize. It is tragic and expensive.

In my Strategic Clarity Roadmap, I call Phase Four "The Forgotten Phase." I say that because mobilizing the direction and communicating the strategic direction is often overlooked. Early in my consulting career, I helped lead strategic planning processes that were essentially sound strategic planning efforts but lacked one important step: mobilizing and communicating the direction. I would work my way through the phases of strategic planning and was conscientious and very deliberate in that work. After Phase Three in The Strategic Clarity Roadmap, my clients often wanted to go straight into action planning and implementation. They were ready to achieve results. So, I excitedly helped them get going fast on their shiny new strategic plan. I recall that, in one of my first strategic planning projects I facilitated, I lined up the client for a progress review one month after the ink dried on their plan. One month?! What was I thinking? It takes longer than that just to roll out a plan and engage employees with it. So, I learned almost immediately that their excitement to execute was premature.

The essential and often missing step is to mobilize the direction in an organized campaign to build awareness, build support, and eventually build a positive internal anxiety to implement the plan and its many initiatives. The flaw in many strategic planning efforts can simply be that: a failure to tell anyone about the new chosen direction. As a result, there is a ton of unconstructive guessing going on within many businesses about (1) who we are, (2) where we are going, (3) how we are going to get there, (4) what I can do to help, and (5) what's in it for me? When employees in any business cannot answer those five questions, implementation will be spotty. Or the sequencing of the annual action plans can be misunderstood. Or monumental mix-ups can gain traction, like the pursuit of a targeted acquisition of a competing business that is then awkwardly called off because leaders forgot to tell managers months earlier that a competitive acquisition is off the table for the next two or three years. Unclear expectations flourish when you forget Phase Four.

So, in this chapter devoted to Phase Four, let's start out on the right foot. Let's understand the importance of mobilizing the strategic direction that has been so thoughtfully researched, developed, and captured in writing in the previous phases.

10^x

The three rules of real estate are location, location, and location. If your home or business is in the right location, that proximity alone can compensate for many other deficiencies. Old HVAC system? Yeah. Cracked driveway? Yeah. Windows need replacing? Yeah. But the location is perfect. Buy it! With business strategy at this point in the process, the three rules are communication, communication, and communication.

Leaders, even top-performing executives, underestimate by a factor of 10 the amount, variety, and duration of mobilizing and communicating needed to implement their plan. Therefore, when Phase Three concludes, the strategic plan needs to be put in writing and communicated in several channels, both internally and externally. There are several versions of the plan needed at this time.

Different Versions of the Same Strategic Plan Suitable for Each Audience

Here are various versions of the same strategic plan edited to serve a particular audience:

- **Board Version:** I call this the "Joe Friday version," a nod to the old TV series *Dragnet*. This is a bare-bones strategic plan with just the facts. It is skinnied down with a heavy emphasis on the capital expenditure impacts and the process that was followed to produce this particular strategic plan. As a matter of sound corporate governance, the board absolutely has a right to review and ratify such strategic plans as soon as reasonable after a retreat process. In some cases, these board members are the same leaders who researched, developed, and captured the strategic plan in writing. But, if a board also has outside directors or an advisory board, this is an important version of the plan for them.

- **Leadership Team Version:** This is the entire strategic plan. It describes not only the decisions that have been made but also how they were made. Though there is more work to do, it is appropriate to get it all in writing at this point in the Strategic Clarity Roadmap. This version is big and significant, often including sections on:

  » Our *strategic situation assessment*, including the SiTNAs described by them earlier and their *change mandate*.

  » A decision on our *organizational mentality* going forward (our strategic decision-making mentality).

  » Our *mission*, our *raison d'etre* as a company, or as Simon Sinek says, "our why?" Always begins with the word "To…"

  » Our *values and culture* as a team that will preserve the company for the very, *very* long term. Typically, not more than four core, genuine, and nonnegotiable values.

  » Our *big picture vision*, including both a broad *"stretch for"* statement and a detailed, often paragraphs-long *detailed vision*. In addition, it includes the barriers to the vision and the strengths needed to achieve the vision.

  » Our *growth method and measures*, including a detailed examination of the many growth methods the team considered, the pros and cons of each, and a quantitative ranking of the preferred growth option. This is then complemented with choices on how to measure growth, both financially and non-financially, and the rate of growth they desire.

» Our *unique selling proposition*, including the brand character, brand promise, and unique features and benefits of the company to its different audiences, mostly external.

» Our *primary markets for focus*, including a clear delineation of the market segmentation method used (there are many) and the resulting primary markets for focus.

However, by Phase Four, some components of a solid strategic plan have not been addressed yet. Even though you have made enormous progress in your planning process so far, there are decisions that need to be made *outside* of the retreat room in order for the entire plan to be complete. There are two decisions in particular that are best discussed in a very small group before having a facilitated discussion at a retreat:

First, there is the broad financial plan and assumptions, including a three-year look back view of the income statement and at least a three-year look forward, the current year (total of seven years), and the financial and operational assumptions that went into this financial model. This is frequently work I do with the client between retreat sessions or after the retreats. But I cannot state enough the importance of connecting the three-year financial plan to the strategic plan. If you want your capital expenditure decisions to align with your strategic plan (and who doesn't?), this is the section of the plan that spells it out.

Second, there is the organizational design to drive success, including the current organization of the company(ies) and the future-oriented organizational design that is consistent with the strategic business plan. Organizational design work should *never* be performed as a group during a planning retreat. It is best performed by just one or two people in the client company, someone like myself, a very well-trained organizational design expert, or possibly human resources and legal experts *after* the epic strategic planning retreat has happened. However, it is essential to do this. A powerful strategy and strategic plan will cause leaders to consider minor tinkering with the organizational structure or in some cases wholesale structural reengineering. The organizational design reengineering needs to be at two levels: the legal entity level (hence the need for legal experts) *and* the organizational chart level (for reporting relationships, hence the need for human resources experts). Effective strategy should drive smart changes at these two levels of organizational design (entity and organizational chart). If your plan is missing the migration plan to the new organizational designs that align with the strategy, then the current organizational structure will soften, or erase, the impact of your new direction. Effective strategy can also force you to reengineer your core business processes, which means that the process architecture in your company may need to shift to support the strategic plan. This is why so many epic strategic business planning retreats can lead later to process remapping efforts on processes like marketing, sales, operations, project management, field delivery, safety, research and development, human resources, facilities management, and at least a dozen other core business processes.

The output of this is a proposed new (three-year) organizational structure that will be in the form of charts, tables, and roles or job descriptions. This, too, should be aligned with the three-year broad financial plan mentioned above. Often, I have seen successful clients develop a migration plan that shows which organizational chart changes will be made and in what sequence for Year One, Year Two, etc. The reason this is so important is that a strategic plan, no matter how well articulated, will struggle for relevance if you do not staff the initiatives adequately. Fact: some of your leaders and others are going to have to stop doing some duties in order to fuel this strategic plan with its brilliant strategic essence. In fact, some will have to switch jobs entirely. Bigger fact: none of your leaders has spare time to work on this strategic plan no matter how epic. No one in your company is sitting around with spare time. Leaders are going to have to be reallocated to the strategic initiatives, or new leaders will need to be brought in. Do not overlook this nuance. Your outside stakeholders may be willing to step up and modify their scope of engagement with your company in order to support your strategic plan. This can be almost like an additional bench of personnel to draw upon, if needed. Of course, you will have to tell them about the plan first, right? Communicate it? Yes.

In your action plans for Year One, include at least three but not more than five strategic action plans. These are often linked to the SiTNAs uncovered earlier but not always. Why at least three but not more than five? Well, if you have fewer than three strategic objectives for the first year, it reflects a modest start, a quiet start to the new direction. If you have more than five, it is likely too much to ask of the current leaders. I have found that three to five is about the right number to provide a balanced scope of actual strategic objectives for the first year.

I prefer to follow a manage-by-objective method of annual action planning that allows the team to lay out the Year One roadmap. For every action plan, there are a few components. The vision alignment statement (10–15 words) explains what part of the detailed vision this action plan is connected. The goal and measure (1 or 2) explain the year-end objective we are shooting for. This may be a key performance indicator. There are two (but not more than three) tactics using the well-known R.A.C.I. matrix, which I explained earlier in *Chunk*. For each tactic, write the now very granular activities (and who will perform them) to be accomplished in sequence to support that action plan, which ties back to the detailed vision, which ties back to the SiTNAs established in Phase One. These tie backs are the indicator that the strategic action plans your company is working on are the right plans and not just strategic busy work. The monthly or quarterly system you will use for implementation, measurement, and evaluation should also be included. A strategic business plan exists for one reason: to be implemented! The focus at some point has to be on execution. Therefore, this section of the plan spells out the progress review meeting cadence, sample meeting agendas, and more. It illustrates how the overall direction provides input to annual budgeting, department planning, capital appropriation planning, location planning, department planning, and so on. This section is about how the epic strategic plan will live in the company.

Finally, there are two versions of the strategic plan that you will want to create. A customer or market-facing version is purely for marketing and business development purposes. It's on your website, in your marketing materials, and referenced in your sales calls. Well, it should be. Do not underestimate the importance of talking to customers and suppliers about your strategic plan. What am I suggesting? I am suggesting that, as your strategic essence has become clearer and before you start implementing anything, get your strategic plan in front of your marketing and sales leaders. Ask them to research and develop a specific marketing communication plan just for your epic strategic plan.

Employee versions of the plan are perhaps the most important. This must include the strategy and strategic plan, without confidential financial information or dicey strategic situation assessment SiTNAs not ready for prime time internally. I think most leaders overlook the gap that exists between their understanding of the direction and employees understanding into that direction, especially just as the strategic plan is gaining steam internally. In recent years, I have helped clients create:

» Strategic plan onboarding kits to get employees acclimated to the new direction.

» New employee orientation materials featuring the strategic plan.

» Modest production videos about the client strategic plan.

» Strategic business plan update section of corporate annual reports.

» Corporate communications campaigns addressing everything from employees' screen savers related to the strategic plan all the way to overhauling the variable pay program to support the strategic plan.

» Website versions of their strategic plan.

» A version in Adobe Spark for more visual interest.

» Internal corporate intranet versions of the plan with Microsoft SharePoint utilization.

» PowerPoint versions of the strategic plan for use in department or business unit meetings.

» Webinars about their strategic plan.

» All-company meeting productions.

» A professional theatrical production of the strategic plan at an all-employee gathering.

» New marketing communication models and materials, new website, new value proposition materials, new proposals, new jobsite signage, and more.

Do You "Get" Your Own Strategy?

Even with stupefying strategic planning retreats that are works of pure genius and with the comprehensive and detailed three-to-five-year strategic plan laid out above, in the absence of a mobilization and communication plan, it will fail. It is a catastrophic oversight to forget communication. I have discovered two reasons why some leaders neglect the obvious and fail to roll out, mobilize, and communicate their new strategic direction.

First, they themselves have not quite got the strategy. Maybe they never quite wrapped their mind around that statement of strategic essence summarized neatly earlier. Or maybe they are distracted by other corporate priorities, or the change imperative ahead of them is mentally taxing. Any or all three of those reasons can result in leaders overlooking the importance of mobilizing and communicating.

The second reason is more common and a little quirkier and has to do with misunderstanding basic human communication and the dissemination of insight, especially to those who were not part of the planning process. We have to recognize that, even in a process as robust as the Strategic Clarity Roadmap, only a fraction of your employees and leaders know about your strategic plan by the time you reach Phase Four. If you have 500 FTEs and 30 were involved directly in the strategic planning so far (i.e., the Phase One interviews, the retreats, etc.) that is still only 6% of your FTEs. But all 500 employees need to engage in some way to support strategic plan success. There is a whole lot of education and inspiration to provide your employees at Phase Four. This is why I have been a part of so many strategic plan rollout meetings, all-employee meetings, all-company gatherings, and more: because we have to get to the other 94% inside the company in addition to your external stakeholders outside the company.

I suppose lack of leadership courage may be a third reason. Though I do not see this often, there are times when leaders have researched, developed, and captured their entire strategic plan in writing but are afraid to implement it. Fear of failing is never an emotion leaders wear on their sleeve. Rather, you will see that display of fear in the form of inaction or poor communication of their strategic direction.

Chapter Summary

Lost to obscurity is not where you want your strategic business plan to end up. What you want is the exact opposite: a strategic business plan that is so well communicated internally (and eventually externally) that there is zero unconstructive guessing going on within your organization about your overall direction. When corporate amnesia kicks in, the cost is high. You can avoid this by having a communication plan for the strategic plan. If you are like many leaders, you will underestimate the amount of communication that is needed by a factor of 10. Each audience has a slightly different use for a strategic plan, so the versions of the strategic plan can be tailored to each audience, with top leadership getting the most detailed and likely confidential versions of the strategic plan.

Chapter Challenge Questions

1. Why do organizations hedge on communicating their strategic plan internally? When you think back within your own organization, consider times when internal corporate communication was clear, concise, and inspiring. How did that make you feel?

2. What has your organization "forgotten" in recent years that just a few years earlier was the big priority? In other words, what is a specific example in your own experience when your organization circled back years later and collectively sighed, "Oh, yeah, this is like déjà vu. We talked about doing this a few years ago; I guess we forgot about that"?

3. If you independently audited the top leadership team in your organization, how many of your leaders "get" your strategic plan? 10%? 50%? 100%? How might a strong internal communication plan for the strategic plan secure more leaders to that plan and perhaps help retain top executives?

CHAPTER ELEVEN

DREAMING IS GREAT, IT JUST DOESN'T PAY THE BILLS

 "You are what you do. Not what you say you'll do."
CARL GUSTAV JUNG

Dream On

When Aerosmith debuted with their self-titled album that included the song "Dream On," it caught me by surprise. The first time I heard it on the radio, I thought, *this must be new from Zeppelin.* The guitar in the opening is *that* haunting. Lead singer Steven Tyler established himself among rock royalty, if you ask me, in just that one song. "Dream on, dream on, dream on, dream until your dreams come true!" I agreed with that then and still do, although now at age 63 I am starting to harbor wishes that I had dared to dream more boldly over the years.

Dreaming is a critical part of the strategic planning process. If you are this far in *Chunk*, you already know this. But, you also know intuitively that a strategic planning effort of that type, if never implemented, is a colossal waste of strategic planning dollars. With the strong exhortation to "dream on," even Steven Tyler would agree you also have to do the hard work. You have to make the changes. Implementation is what pays the bills. It is not enough to dream. You have to get there, one action at a time, with excellent leaders anxious to take the many baby steps that lead to achieving the big objectives. So, let's look at change as it happens at the very incremental, tactical levels.

A Lot Can Be Accomplished in Tiny Steps

When I trained for my three U.S. Masters Swimming National Championships, my daily and weekly work ethic was intense. Every factor for success had to be well researched and planned. I had to start my training for a targeted main competitive event *18 months* in advance (e.g., the U.S. Masters Swimming Long Course National Championship). This 18-month window would enable me to not just train but to train up and over the various plateaus (and valleys) that every athlete encounters. I trained in 11-to-12-week cycles, ending with a competitive race, such as a Minnesota Masters Swimming Championship or a web-enabled virtual event with competitors from across the world. Many coaches call these Training Mezocycles. After each cycle and a brief week of "rest" (during which I scaled back to just working out every other day), I would start another Mezocycle, frequently regressing in some cycles and progressing during others. I had to take into account hydration, diet and nutrition, weightlifting, body fat composition, mental and emotional state, range of motion, injury prevention. Then, of course, there were the dozens of swimming technical factors, like center of buoyancy, dive start, flip turn aggression, stroke technique, underwater stroke analysis and videotaping, final taper, and more. Swimming is technical but the great swimmers make it look so easy from above the waterline.

In my search for gold in the water as an older U.S. Masters Swimmer, I learned everything by implementing, experimenting, and just leaning into new ideas. This is a good metaphor for strategic plan implementation. As I trained, I kicked the bad ideas and tactics to the curb and honed in on what worked. My weekly workout program eventually got extreme. This enabled me to focus on very short sprint races some years, like the 50 meter freestyle and 50 meter butterfly. In other years, my focus was on the 100 free and 100 fly. Some years, the middle distance events 200 free and 400 free were my focus. And, some years, I would shift to long distance events like the 1,500 meter or open water races. It is nearly impossible to win at the national level a sprint event, middle-distance event, and long-distance event in the same year, unless you are Katie Ledecky. For me, I needed a laser focus on a key event for many months in order to win. I managed to win a national championship in each of those distances (sprints, middle distance, and long distance). In each case, in every year, the difference in my results was this: *daily action.*

Victory looks like it happens the day you win first place. But that is misleading. Victory actually happens in the preceding 18 months of draining, mind-numbing, confidence-building, and occasionally tear-filled workouts no one but the athlete understands. It is all about what you implement. Training hard, grinding out the interval sets when no one is watching, arriving early, staying late, hitting the weight room, going to sleep at 7 pm and up at 4 am, that is how it works. It is exactly the same way with implementing an epic strategic plan for success.

That is the image I invite you to consider as you approach implementation: a focused plan of implementing very few strategic initiatives, just the three-to-five strategic action plans that need attention across the entire organization. It is well known that companies bite off more than they can accomplish with the implementation of their first strategic business plan. Three or four transformative initiatives are far more important for your company to fully execute than 16 so-so operational action plans that are misstated as strategic. As I noted previously, the action planning and the R.A.C.I. formula work for many organizations. Using a manage-by-objective method works for many organizations. You can find tools galore for managing execution. That actually *is* a smart time to use an action planning template, preset format, or even an app. Far more important, however, is making certain that your action plan team leaders have the bandwidth personally and professionally to execute with precision. In Year One of implementing any strategic plan, it is essential to make sure your top leaders and your action plan leaders are not continuing with their day jobs as normal. If you want your strategic plan to fail, try to implement it without changing leaders' roles and responsibilities.

Action at the Tactical Level

When a strategic objective (e.g., grow new product gross margins to 17%) for an organization gives rise to two or three strategies to get there, action does not happen in the boardroom nor in the retreat room. Action happens in hallways, in virtual meetings, and over coffee. Action happens in a team meeting with a key business vendor or during the presentation to win new work for your company. Action happens in working sessions with people appropriate to the task. Action even happens inside your head while commuting home from work with an *ah-ha* moment swirling in your own gray matter. And, frequently, action happens in the wee hours of the morning, evenings, and weekends when teammates can be found collaborating. While implementing a major new strategic initiative, what you want ideally are teams of leaders and others working both independently and together to make maximum progress toward the strategic plan one week, one month, and one quarter at a time. This is, of course, made easier if the teams doing this implementation know the overall strategic direction (see previous chapter). This is what implementation really looks like in a company, in a slightly whimsical way.

My Name Is Fred and This Is My Life as an Action Plan

I cannot remember when it all started. I was so young. I was born in a strategic business planning retreat that had 11 people in the room. I remember that. So, I guess you could say I have 11 parents. All 11, and a lot more people now, support me and make me important. I am an action plan within our company strategic plan, and my name is Fred.

People said Fred was a crazy idea at first. Then, in a planning retreat, it turns out I was more than crazy; I was crazy important. An entire leadership team was committed to me. I was assigned a leader who used the R.A.C.I. formula to help me proceed. Under her leadership, a team of six people met weekly for the first four weeks, then monthly for nine months. I had never had such well-coordinated attention paid to me. So, I quickly evolved. Each quarter, a bigger team of leaders, including the higher-ups, learn about my progress and give me the thumbs-up, which means keep implementing, or thumbs-down, which means I am struggling. It's been thumbs-up for Fred this year. They measure the heck out of me every so often. I heard a rumor that, next year, I am going to be sharing a room with another action plan named Wilma. She has a leader and a team, just like me. We're going to have to figure out how to combine our efforts together for the company to make blended progress on both of our initiatives. As it turns out, Wilma's initiative is a lot like mine. They tell me we are made for each other. I may not live a long life in the company, but I got us going in the small steps that lead to the big accomplishments. I have been told I exist for one reason: to help the company drive lasting change at the very tactical level. I am not the only action plan. Besides me and Wilma, there are Barney, Betty, Bam-Bam, and little Dino. All of us together are working to make our company a more successful business. I am not a big deal like my friends mission or big picture vision. I am not especially inspiring. But, what I lack in size I make up for with real results I can demonstrate every week, month, or quarter. I'm a doer, not a dreamer. I get sh!t done.

The SiTNA-Action Plan Connection

To recap from an earlier chapter, your company has to identify its strategic situations that need attention before doing any strategic dreaming. We called these SiTNAs. In most strong companies, I have found that the leaders, when developing their detailed action plans for the first year of implementation, will target one or more of the SiTNAs. They will very thoughtfully craft an objective and action plan that resolves one or more of the SiTNAs. Such action plans get developed very late in the retreat process. If your company commits to two, two-day strategic business retreats, it will probably be in the second day of the second two-day retreat when you do your action planning. Here is an example of the connection I have seen in high-performing teams in epic strategic planning retreats:

271

SiTNA (Identified Early in the Planning Process)	Action Plan (Crafted Later in the Planning Process)
Customer experience needs improvement so we can drive more repeat customers and lower our cost of sales.	Create the XYZ Company Customer Experience, a three-stage process that makes life easier for our customers and harder for them to leave us.
Gross margins are getting thinner every year and our core services are becoming a commodity out there.	Target only the larger clients with more complex needs; offer them a new service that is valuable to them and which our competitors cannot easily copy.
Our technology is reactive, always last minute, never enough; and we never do the requisite training anyway.	Establish a strategic IT plan that ties off to our strategic plan and places more $ on technology utilization (i.e., training) than on the technology itself.
Our leaders need real data that has been proven accurate in order to drive better supply chain decisions; too much from the gut here.	Collaborate with ABC Technology to build a new performance dashboard that enables us to anticipate supply chain interruptions.

I could go on with more examples. I have seen this over and over and it is always exciting. The team that makes these connections between a SiTNA and the action plan is confidently connecting these two so that the company knows with total certainty that the action plan is a smart one. Moreover, because the action plan is tied to a bigger objective, which is tied back to the detailed vision, that small action plan (Fred) is actually of huge strategic importance. What you want is a leader who says, "You know, when we implemented our strategic plan, it was the small things that made the difference. Action happened in little steps, not whoppers. The big aspects of our strategic plan like our SiTNAs, organizational mentality, mission, culture and values, and growth methods are major league. But the progress for us did not happen at the big overall level. It happened in the relentless baby steps, by action planning teams who knew the big picture vision, sure, but they acted on it weekly. It was that consistent weekly hammering that drove the progress."

When a company has a small group of three or four such action plans that tie back to the big picture vision, the SiTNAs, and the overall direction, this connection matters. Seek leaders and others who also make that connection. What you want to avoid, of course, is the opposite. That is, an action plan that shows no obvious connection back to one or more of the SiTNAs nor any other aspect of your strategic essence. This means no oddball initiatives, pet projects, or leftovers from previous strategic planning efforts.

Working On (vs. In) Your Company

As I mentioned earlier, most strategic initiatives tend to be long term. Not all, but most. For example, hiring a firm to conduct an IT systems selection study is not a 10-day project. It is a months-long endeavor, typically. During that time, the team is really working *on* your company, not *in* it. Frequently, teams like this are solving for long-term problems and addressing systemic fixes or opportunities in your company. Most of your strategic action plans are going to be like that. The goal of most action plans is not to win that one new customer; the team is working on a system that will win many new customers. They are not working on closing the books 10 days after the end of one previous month; they are working on accounting and finance processes to speed up all month-end reporting. They are not streamlining one process so they can scoot home early Friday; they are working on all operational processes so that all employees can be more efficient and effective. These are usually initiatives that do not get enough attention during the normal course of running the business. This is because, frequently, leaders are too busy working in the business to work on the business. Leaders from hundreds, perhaps thousands, of businesses know what I am writing about here. They can tell you there are times when the best thing for the team to do is to work on the company, not in it. In other words, disregard or suspend your day-to-day job and work on something of strategic importance that leaders have all agreed is essential. Don't worry, your day job will be there waiting for your return, unless of course you are able to use the strategic plan as a lever to move your career in a new direction within the company.

In some cases, something special happens. The team working on the company (i.e., working on a long-term strategic action plan) is adding so much value in a dimension of the business that is so important they are literally morphing into new roles. I have seen over two dozen members of various strategic planning retreats fundamentally evolve their role based entirely on the direction taken during the retreat. In one example, a product manager was working on the company, not just in the company. He led a team working on the product development cycle. That cycle took too long and was costing my client a lot of money, so he was fixin' to fix that. As his work progressed, this product manager became an expert at all of the company's products and services. He shifted in a matter of 30 days from a product manager to a product portfolio analyst. Later, he became vice president of marketing. In another example, a very senior top leader, who was nearing retirement, was leading a strategic initiative focused on leadership succession and transition. After this energizing work on the company, he decided he would delay his retirement. He became chief culture officer and enjoyed—no, basked in—his new role for five more years. During the retreat and for about 60 days after, when these action plans were being developed, he transitioned from on his way out to *all* the way back in.

Chapter Summary

Action drives change, not just dreaming. When dreams are converted to action plans that are hit hard every day, week, month, or quarter, incredible and even unlikely progress can occur, as it did with me in my U.S. Masters Swimming exploits. An action plan named Fred may not be big and bold, but it is where the real progress happens. Epic retreat teams, late in their strategic planning retreat, get very precise and tactical in their action planning. You can, too, if you take your objective, break it down into a smaller set of action plans, and make progress on those small plans. If your team can make sure that your first year of plan implementation addresses the SiTNAs you identified earlier in your retreat, awesome work! This kind of work on your company is long term. It may not be your day job, but it is more strategically relevant than anything else you might work on in your company in a given year.

Chapter Challenge Questions

1. Think back to a time you were working on a truly huge company strategic initiative. Did it feel like you and the team were trying to "boil the entire ocean," as they say? How was that effort just too big, and how should it have been broken down into smaller, more manageable bites?

2. The entire strategic planning process might boil down to just three or four objectives and associated action plans. What would you say to a naysayer who says, "Well, that

was stupid. Your entire plan is now just three objectives and action plans. Seems like a waste of resources"?

3. Why is it important to connect your action plan to the original SiTNAs uncovered far earlier in the planning process?

CHAPTER TWELVE

EVALUATING AND IMPROVING YOUR EPIC STRATEGIC PLANNING RETREATS

 "Improvement is better than delayed perfection."
MARK TWAIN

Continuous Improvement

It was pure magic. As the Miami sky unloaded torrents of rain, Minnesota's own Prince was on stage on February 4, 2007 at the now legendary Super Bowl XLI halftime show. He was delivering the song "Purple Rain" in purple rain. It. Was. Special. Prince was different from any musician who preceded him and will remain distinctive forever. At a height of just five feet three, he was, at that moment, bigger than the Super Bowl. How is that even possible?

Like millions of others sitting in their homes as his 12-minute set unfolded, I lost interest in the game. In fact, ask people today and most cannot even tell you who played in that Super Bowl (the Colts beat the Bears 29-17). I was simultaneously stunned at Prince's bravado and skill and worried about the amount of lightning in the storm and all those electric instruments getting soaking wet on stage. It was riveting. Prince, the consummate musician and control freak, was worried, too. But, not for himself. He was concerned for the rest of the act. But they killed it. It was inspiring. His sexuality, unique brand of musical genius, showmanship, and work ethic all conspired under Floridian clouds to produce easily the most memorable Super Bowl halftime show I have ever seen. It was at once gutsy, beautiful, and a bit miraculous. Somehow, it came off without a hitch.

Here is the thing: Prince was a continual improvement junkie. Say what you want about the circumstances of his tragic passing. He was improvement driven and a studio perfectionist. When he performed "While My Guitar Gently Weeps" as he was inducted into the Rock & Roll Hall of Fame three years prior, he stole the entire show. He had perfected that song through hundreds of tiny improvements. Stories of his work ethic and drive for excellence are now so well documented it's the stuff of legend. Every musician and artist with whom he worked has the same report to share on his creativity, attention to detail, and demanding nature. And they were all better for it.

Another continual improvement icon, cut from the exact same cloth but during a different era, was none other than Malcolm Baldrige, Jr., the U.S. secretary of state from 1981 to 1987. He helped create the National Quality Improvement

Act of 1987. The Malcolm Baldrige National Quality Award is named in his honor. *Chunk* is now the only book, I am sure, that has placed Prince and Malcolm Baldrige, Jr., in the same context: quality freaks.

To win the Malcolm Baldrige National Quality Award, your organization must excel in seven criteria areas:

- Leadership
- Strategy
- Customers
- Measurement, analysis, and knowledge management
- Workforce
- Operations
- Results

Most of those above are areas you would naturally assume are important to quality in any business. I find it fascinating that strategy is one of these seven criteria. If I am to interpret this correctly, then continually improving your company strategic thinking is essential to running a quality organization. It is cyclical. The continual improvement of your strategic business planning is a cycle. So is my Strategic Clarity Roadmap. It is at this stage of the process that the next wave of strategic reasoning kicks in: can we improve on our planning? In many organizations, as implementation is underway, there is a separate effort to ask and answer three questions about the planning process itself:

- "How are we doing with execution and achieving results in our action plans? Are we just busy or busy on the right transformative projects?"
- "What midcourse adjustments to our action plans should we make to drive or accelerate progress?"
- "As we approach the end of Year One, what can we learn from our successes and failures with driving strategic change (i.e., implementation), and how should we scale up further in Year Two?"

I survey top leaders near the end of Year One with questions like:

- The last time I talked internally in a substantial way about our strategic business plan was:

  a. Less than eight hours ago
  b. Between 8 and 72 hours ago
  c. In the last two weeks
  d. None of the above

- For each of our four strategic action plans, which were established to drive Year One progress toward our shared direction for our company, what is our current percentage of completion for each?

  » Action Plan 1: _____% complete
  » Action Plan 2: _____% complete
  » Action Plan 3: _____% complete
  » Action Plan 4: _____% complete

- Our single biggest strategic success in Year One was:

  _____

- Our biggest priority for Year Two needs to be:

  _____

Unless you did a poor job of internal and external analysis back in Phase One (Research), there is rarely a big departure in strategic direction from Year One to Year Two. The focus for Year Two needs to be on additional implementation while scaling it up and expecting more. You want to consolidate some initiatives and build on them. Other initiatives will have a very short duration (less than one year), and your company will more or less complete them. You can check that box, so to speak. Still other initiatives will never be fully achieved but will require annual action. These are the very long-term transformative initiatives I addressed earlier. During Year Two, it becomes very important to make sure top leaders are leading at the enterprise level and not micromanaging the strategic action plans. Middle managers are accountable for the action plan results. You want virtually all employees to be able to answer those five questions I posed earlier: who are we, where are we going, how are we getting there, how can I help, and how are we coming along and making progress? Keeping the organization focused on implementing for results is key (i.e., not chasing new shiny strategies), unless they are well supported by internal and external research and align with the big picture vision.

And, by the end of Year Three? The entire cycle repeats. It's time for Phase One of the Strategic Clarity Roadmap again. Odds are that the markets, competitors, and political and regulatory environment have all changed. Most important, your company has changed. It's time for another epic strategic planning process if what you seek is epic and sustained competitive differentiation for your organization. If you work the Strategic Clarity Roadmap process fully, you will eventually find that you are not so much competing against Joe down the road today but against yourself yesterday. Your entire company will be motivated to compete and win against what it was and how it performed before. It is now your company improving upon your company, strategically.

Chapter Summary

The Strategic Clarity Roadmap is cyclical and brings a leadership team eventually to communication, mobilization, the development of action plans, evaluation, and improvement of the process itself. Prince and Malcolm Baldrige, Jr. may have looked very different, but they both had the same obsession for quality. High-performing leadership teams view every year as another year to reset the strategic plan, recast the associated action plans, and keep progressing. If you play your cards right, annual action planning broken down by quarters or months in a management-by-objective method can work well. So long as top strategic leaders do not micromanage the implementation, things go well. They go even better if you allocate some managers and leaders to the strategic plan. Things can go especially well if you and your company focus on nailing four strategic objectives really well instead of a mishmash of 16 strategic objectives that clog your transformation.

Chapter Challenge Questions

1. Do you think your organization has adequately communicated the strategic direction to employees? What about outside your organization? Do your key customers and suppliers "get" your strategic direction? Why not?

2. Implementation is about just doing it. Breaking it down into manageable action plans is the key. Can you describe right now the three or four top strategic action plans in your company? Why or why not?

3. How often should leaders reinforce the strategic plan by talking about it in their various journeys inside and outside the company? What do employees conclude if a top leader does not communicate the strategic direction and progress toward it? What makes communicating a strategic plan especially hard for your company?

CHAPTER THIRTEEN

Interview with Jim Johnson, CEO of GE Johnson Construction Company

 "The essence of strategy is choosing what not to do."
Michael Porter

Spinal Tap and One Incredible Museum

The 1984 cult classic *This Is Spinal Tap*, directed by Rob Reiner, has one of the most memorable and hilarious interview scenes in movie history. Created by American comedians and musicians, the movie follows a fictional English heavy metal band as they make hapless final efforts to reignite the group after years of crappy attendance to their shows. In one of the fan favorite scenes, Rob Reiner is conducting an interview with the lead guitarist who explains how their band's amplifiers go to "11" not just "10" like other bands' amps. When Rob asks him, "Why don't you just make 10 be the top number and make that a little louder," the guitarist gives him a bewildered look, chews his gum while he considers this thought, and finally idiotically replies, "These go to 11."[34] If you can manage to watch that mock interview without laughing so hard that a little bit of whatever you're drinking comes out your nose (yes, that happened to me), then, well, I cannot help you. Best. Interview. Ever.

A Day with GE Johnson Construction Company

This chapter is devoted to an interview, too. I want to go deep into my professional archive and allow an actual CEO who has taken part in numerous retreats with me to share his perspectives. You will meet Jim Johnson, CEO at GE Johnson Construction Company, headquartered in Colorado Springs, CO. He is a client for whom I have designed and delivered three different rounds of comprehensive and detailed strategic business planning retreats. In two of the consulting engagements, I utilized the entire Strategic Clarity Roadmap, that is, all seven phases. In the other engagement, the focus was entirely on their brand development. I am going to bring you, the reader, out with me to spend a day with Jim and his leadership team. I will ask Jim questions about strategic business planning, leadership development, and his organization, back then and now. I have chosen to interview Jim from a list of many clients. There are four reasons why:

1. First, Jim has overseen the managed and profitable growth of quite a fantastic business. His father, Gil

Johnson, founded the company in 1967. Jim has been in leadership roles with the company since the early 1990s. He has been president and CEO since 1997. So, Jim has seen the company through three major different economic cycles and has kept the strategic vision intact throughout. What enables a leader to be so consistently focused on long-term competitive market position, despite the inevitable ups and downs? Jim is not alone in this regard, but he stands out as a supremely strategic CEO.

2. Second, Jim is not into corporate bullsh!t.

3. Third, Jim has developed as a leader through the retreats we co-led. He has emerged as an enterprise leader, not CEO in title only. The strategic business planning process, including the retreats we co-led, have made him into a better executive, a better man, and even a better father and husband. He has shared with me how learning to think differently as a result of our retreats is one of the primary reasons for this.

4. Finally, Jim and I are both competitive athletes. He is an endurance runner who has completed dozens of marathons. His personal best time is 3 hours, 4 minutes (at the Phoenix, AZ Marathon a few years ago). In addition, Jim and I are both in recovery from alcoholism and drug addiction. Though we each have decades of continuous sobriety, we work on our individual

leadership edge continually. I wonder how that has helped or constrained his executive growth, as I have often wondered the same about myself. I want to learn from Jim how his personal strategic focus has created a setting for him to be a successful CEO, and how being a successful CEO has perhaps influenced life at home and on the open road in his arduous miles running.

So, I organized a visit to "The Springs" in March 2021. My itinerary looked like this:

1. First, I held a private question and answer session with Jim in his office on Cascade Avenue in downtown Colorado Springs. Jim's office up on the fourth floor of his building looks out to a clear and unobstructed view of breathtaking Pike's Peak. When Jim is interviewing potential new employees, he walks them down the hall to the Gil Johnson Conference Room with a wall of windows facing Pike's Peak. He always makes sure the candidate is facing that window and gazing out, awestruck, at that view. It is about as subtle as a velvet hammer. Employment candidates come to interview at GE Johnson Construction Company from all over the country. Some have never seen the Colorado Rocky Mountains. If they have, maybe they have never seen the 14,111-foot-tall, jaw-dropping mountain reaching for the heavens just outside those conference room windows. Very clever interview technique, Jim.

2. Next on my agenda, I met with his management team, discussing strategic leadership over the years at GE Johnson Construction Company.

3. After that, we hit the road to the astonishing U.S. Olympic and Paralympic Museum that GE Johnson Construction built. When a company has its strategic plan in clear focus, it can accomplish amazing results. For GE Johnson Construction Company, one of those outcomes was the ability to build frankly one of the most sophisticated museums in the world, right there in Colorado Springs. Jim's company would not have been able to win such a notable project and build it without a clear strategic roadmap.

Bears, Garden of the Gods, and Collaboration

Jim greeted me with a firm handshake, not the odd and temporary COVID-19 knuckle-bump. Jim is a thin and lithe marathon runner. What body fat he does possess belongs there and anything else has been burned off during Lord knows how many road miles training. His trousers hang on for dear life and the expression on his face is that of a very fit, joyful old friend. We took the elevator to the fourth floor, where Jim ushered me into his office. There was a sense of wonder in the air as we laughed at how long it has been. It was over 20 years ago I first met with Jim in his office and the last time I saw Jim had been a year prior. While the place has been updated and the company is now over twice as big in revenues and employee head count, the basics remain the same, including Jim's fondness for bears. Bear statues. Bear photographs. Bear coasters. Bear this. Bear that. He has been collecting bear artwork and knickknacks for decades. Jim and I closed the door to his office and got down to work. For the next hour, it was rapid-fire strategic wisdom from CEO to me. Here are excerpts from that interview.

Tom: Jim, to start, there was a time before we met in 1999 when GE Johnson Construction Company did strategic planning. What was the planning process like back then?

Jim: Before I took over as president, my father (Gil Johnson) had not been afraid to use consultants. But, back then, it was just a process of hiring a facilitator. We found a construction industry leader and it was okay for a while. I think in 1999 we were about $200,000,000 in GAAP Revenue. The planning sessions were sort of basic. But, it was good stuff.

Tom: While we are on size of the company, where is the company today?

Jim: About $1.6 billion in managed volume [a construction finance term to denote total amount of work under management in a given year] and $800,000,000 in GAAP Revenue.

Tom: Do you recall when we met in Chicago many years ago?

Jim: Of course! It was at a Young Presidents' Organization meeting. 1999, I think. You were speaking on strategic business planning and the importance of having a strong planning process. I think we had about 20 construction company owners in the room. I remember thinking you were approachable and helpful. Not like a typical consultant at all, actually. It was when I realized you have the collaboration knack. You just know how to engage groups.

Tom: That led to us getting together on our first strategic business planning project. It lasted about four months, then you and your team implemented that plan for three years. During that time, I met with you and your team twice per year. At the end of that third year, we did it again as a team, this time raising the bar. We went offsite for a two-day strategic planning retreat then a month later another two-day strategic planning retreat. I worked with you to roll that one out at an all-employee meeting. Later, you and I helped a large team at GEJCC to work on a brand-building process using your strategic business plan as the bedrock to build the brand on. I think we did that in Silverton, CO, and it involved over 50 people. As I recall, every single person was able to establish their own personal brand platform, which was cool. I also worked with you on your executive coaching, just between you and me. Then, five years ago, we held a brand and culture supercharging offsite retreat for your team at the remarkable Garden of the Gods Resort and Club, in the Springs. So, I have worked with you in your dusty equipment yard training room and some exquisite offsite locations. As you look back on all of this, what was the most important work I did for you? Why?

Jim: It's right here [he says, sliding a tattered binder to me across his office conference table]. It was the executive coaching. I knew that for our company to get past its growth barrier, I had to develop my own enterprise leadership skills. I was managing a good, strong midsized construction management and general contracting company. But, we were stuck at a certain size. In order for me to grow, I had to learn to lead other leaders. I already knew how to manage other managers. But, *leading* other *leaders* was a completely new thing. Your executive coaching forced me to look at my own dreams, hopes, strengths, and flaws. It caused a stirring in my leadership style. In just a few months, I evolved into a better big-picture, enterprise leader.

Tom: Who have you found to lead your strategic thinking and planning retreats?

Jim: Well, to be blunt, what you did over those many years converted about a dozen of us into strategic thinkers. So, we lead the retreats ourselves now [author's note: I frowned a bit at hearing this]. In fact, just a month ago, I took us all offsite down to Scottsdale, AZ to recraft our plan. Would have been better if you were there. But, you did teach us how to facilitate decision-making, and for that, we are a better company. We have not found your replacement.

Tom: What are your core values now as a company?

Jim: Actually, our mission and core values have not changed since we worked with you on these over 20 years ago. Our vision and growth plans continually change, but not our values.

Our core values are: "Integrity, safety, relationships, ingenuity, collaboration, balance, enjoyment, and excellence." Our mission is still "Enriching our communities by leading and building projects with the best people and ideas." We think of that mission as our reason for waking up in the morning.

Tom: Okay, for my skeptical readers, prove that is not just a bunch of words.

Jim: Well, our experience modification rate [an insurance term that indicates how safe a construction company actually is in reality] is down to a .62 EMR. For our size of general building contractor, doing the amount of work we do, in the [Rocky] Mountains, that is an exceptionally good safety indicator. We just keep trying to get better.

Tom: What about—

Jim: Sorry to interrupt, but I will actually go further. It is not just worker safety we want to achieve. It is overall wellness. Safety is cultural here now. In 2019, we were awarded (for the second year in a row) a mental health award by the state of Colorado. To us, we do not just want each worker to go home each night with all 10 fingers and all 10 toes. We also want them in the right frame of mind. It is a complex world and these are complicated times. If we are to really practice our core values, we have to go beyond the norm. This is why we are in the "Face it Together" initiative for our employees and their families to help with addiction, substance abuse, and mental illness. We do not want a crane operator swinging a load into place on a construction site worrying about his teenage son and the crowd he is hanging with. Want to know how to get your EMR down to a .62? Help employees be safe in ways that are both expected and unexpected. We even have the GE Johnson Foundation in place now to support that, too.

Tom: Okay, I can see you are passionate about safety! Tell my readers why it is important to have a well-organized planning process before, during, and after a retreat.

Jim: This is the thing, Tom, process is everything. You always had a process that was organized into phases. We always felt like you had a core process, but you adapted it to our situation. Every retreat you led was organized and fun. We focused on the task because you focused on the task. I never got the feeling you were going to try to sell me on some add-on services. And, along the way, we had hilarious good times. Like the time you brought an industrial psychologist out to meet with us. He was a brilliant guy, exceptionally good at his job and with impeccable references. But, after four hours of meeting with you and us, I think *he* needed to go see a therapist! We are serial intrapreneurs here, sort of like entrepreneurs but inside an existing company. I think we sort of blew him away with our radical disdain for therapeutic advice and our hunger for growth and a good laugh. This is something about our culture that is just part of who we are: we take our work very seriously, but not ourselves.

Tom: You once ran a 3:04 marathon, right?

Jim: Yeah, in Phoenix, I think it was in the fall. You know, you and I have always had this in common: a passion for self-improvement and competitive drive. You do it in swimming, Tom. You trained out here [Colorado Springs] at the Olympic Training Aquatic Center and Flume. I do it on the open road. I once read that leaders should hire athletes because in so doing, they are hiring people who inherently keep improving, learning, adapting, and being effective. They are the most accountable people I know. I long ago gave up trying to be the fastest or richest guy. Hey, go to an industry conference and you learn right away, you are not the wealthiest person in the room! No, personal income and my speed on a racecourse are now far less important, and it is the same with our company. Yes, we make consistent gross margins and our EBITDA is slightly better than the industry average. That is okay with us, so long as we stick to our strategic plan to minimize the many risks of running a large construction management and general contracting company. It is humbling to me, running a company my dad left me, without any sort of training manual. I had virtually zero training on top executive leadership when I took this job. It has all been applied learning, in this office and out on the road running marathons.

Tom: How has strategic thinking helped you at home, as a father, husband, and just in general?

Jim: Well, not much. [He pauses]. Okay, you could say that I am more focused at home now. Because of the strategic planning, I have been able to delegate major corporate processes to others, like operations, marketing, business development, finance, and more. So, how do I say this? It has made me more big picture, which has enabled my leadership team to step up, which has enabled me to frankly spend more time with my family and in our communities.

Using a Strategic Planning Retreat as a Growth Lever

After my one-to-one time with Jim, I was able to corral four of their top leaders, plus Jim, in a conference room for an hour. Peter Speiser is a 15-year GE Johnson Construction Company chief financial officer. Nick Siakotos has been with the company three years and is vice president of risk management. Chris Hanaway is the newbie in GE Johnson but an experienced executive and currently serves as their information technology leader. Kasia King is their accomplished executive director of human resources. Together, they reflected back on the role a strategic business plan has played in their individual success and corporate accomplishments. These were their top observations that I want to share with you.

1. First, at every juncture in our strategic planning together, GE Johnson made the decision to grow. They actually used the strategic planning as a growth lever. In the middle of the Y2K scare, they opted to grow. After 9/11, they leaned in and drove for growth. In the Great Recession of 2008–2010, they decided to grow. It would seem that, at precisely the time most companies choose to slow down, these leaders opted

to grow and they used the strategic planning retreats as the place to decide to do that. Why, I asked? Because if their strategic plan was sound, and if they had faith in one another, they knew that growth would be possible, even in sour economic circumstances. To them, clarity of strategic plan equals increased capacity for growth. "If we want to grow the company, we have to grow together as leaders, and that has to be continual. It's not a one-time thing, but ongoing," said Kasia.

2. A great strategic leadership team is not so much organized around their technical skills as their leadership mentality. "When I took over this accounting department here many years ago, I realized I had great people, but we had no vision," Peter said. "I needed to serve this group as a leader first and as a financial technician second. Now, many years later, my role is mostly that of an executive leader, a strategic leader at GE Johnson, who happens to be the CFO." "I agree," Chris jumped in. "My role as a technologist is, well, very technical. But, what I am doing is directly tied to our strategic plan, making me more of a CIO (chief information officer), really. Aligning our resources, which are limited, is part of my job, and that has to be done by using our strategic plan as a guide," he added.

3. Ingenuity, according to Kasia, is not just about construction project ingenuity. It is a mentality that "we can do this." Even the choice the company made

to pursue advanced manufacturing as a sector came from a core cultural value of ingenuity. "Look," Nick said, "there were very recently two high-rise projects awarded in downtown Colorado Springs. We won one of the projects and another construction company won the other. Only time will tell, but here is what we think is happening right now on these two projects. We think one team of construction companies is having an exceptionally good project because we are fostering collaborative relationships and demonstrating ingenuity and integrity every day. We cannot speak for that other project team, but we can for ours. There is just a lot of street-smart practical innovation going on every day on our job site."

A Visit to the Remarkable U.S. Olympic and Paralympic Museum

In 2020, GE Johnson Construction completed work on a very technologically sophisticated museum. It is beyond belief. As construction projects go, museums are especially complex and very much under public scrutiny. In fact, some general building contractors actually avoid trying to win and then build museums, claiming the work is exceptionally complicated and the extra hand-holding needed to deliver the project is just not worth it. If there is even one mistake, the entire community knows about it in an instant and never forgets it. That's museum work. The designs of these iconic facilities are notoriously intricate.

Some project managers (office types) and superintendents (jobsite trailer types) are not cut out for museums. GE Johnson Construction Company *is* so cut out and actually considers this project one of its best ever. This is what can happen to a company that has a clear strategic business plan: it gains the respect of the business community and can win (and, in this case, build) amazing things.

The museum was celebrating Women's History Month during our short visit. We arrived as a family of seven (me, Pam, her mom Carol Hieb, Pam's brother Terry Conrad and his wife Christine, and their two sons Jonathan and Brandon). It was a blustery, gray March Friday morning and a colossal storm was predicted to hit Colorado in less than 48 hours. Coming from Minnesota, I love big snowstorms. But, not when I am traveling. We received a private tour led by one of the senior staff. The architects of this awe-inspiring facility are Diller Scofidio + Renfro. Here is what they say about this cultural facility (from *The Journal of the American Institute of Architects*):

> The United States Olympic Museum, a new cultural facility recognized by the International Olympic Committee, celebrates American Olympic and Paralympic athletes. Located at the base of the Rocky Mountains in Colorado Springs, home of the United States Olympic Training Center, the 65,750 square foot museum takes its athletes as inspiration; the design idealizes athletic motion by organizing its programs—galleries, auditorium, and administrative spaces—twisting and stretching centrifugally

around an atrium space. Visitors arrive at the ground level of the atrium, and then ascend to the top of the building quickly and gradually spiral down through a sequence of loft galleries, moving back-and-forth from the introspective atrium to the building's perimeter and views to the city and the mountains. The museum and the landscape are designed to form a new public plaza, nestling a distant view of Pikes Peak and an intersecting axis bridging downtown across the train tracks to the America the Beautiful Park to the west.

If the exterior design and plaza are not grand enough to blow your mind, a walk into the lobby will make you wonder if you have been transported to the future. But here is the thing. You do not have to walk in. It is the U.S. Olympic and *Paralympic* Museum and it might be the most accessible museum on terra firma. The museum's ramps connect four exhibition wings, with each wing sitting inside these nested petals. There are seams between, producing skylights and windows back to the city. These soft overhead daylight seams connect the atrium. And, this atrium, whoa! It boasts an enormous portrait-oriented LED screen that projects a constantly changing array of LeRoy Neiman–styled artwork in brilliant, stunning color. As we all logged in to the museum visitor technology system, the tour was then customized for each of us. I entered some data and chose a tour that would highlight competitive swimming and downhill skiing. To my splendid amazement, the rest of my tour then featured historical and contemporary nature of the Olympics and the Paralympics, such as athlete training, technology in the games, and the role of the media, all based on what I wanted to learn: swimming and downhill skiing. Each of my family members was receiving their own custom version tour but we all walked the museum together. Mass customization. Tremendous. We even took part in a virtual Parade of Nations, capturing the athletes' experience of the opening ceremony, and every one of us teared up. Just…goosebumps. The Summer and Winter Games are each depicted. We learned about athlete training and the medal ceremony. There is a Hall of Fame and a fully accessible theater with the greatest Olympic and Paralympic moments. And, get this, the actual scoreboard from the U.S. vs. Soviet Union Olympic Hockey Game (Lake Placid, February 22, 1980) is in there! It is frozen in time at the score of 4-3 in favor of the U.S., with three seconds remaining on the clock. This is the moment when ABC broadcaster Al Michaels excitedly asked the world, "Do you believe in miracles?!" He then answered his own question three seconds later, "*YES!*" A lot of the young men on that team grew up in my home state of Minnesota. So, as you can imagine, we just stood as a family looking at that scoreboard. Not a lot was said. We just looked at it. I teared up. Again.

At the top of the museum, there is also a soaring boardroom with a view of the mountains. The façade of this entire facility is some sort of magical-looking satin anodized aluminum, which appears to be stretched like an elastic fabric over the building's angled frame. The facility looks like an athlete. Comprised of diamond-shaped folded panels, its surfaces seem to shimmer and move in the daylight.

I offer you this detailed glimpse of the U.S. Olympic and Paralympic Museum because it is also a retreat event center. Yes, friends, *you can hold a strategic planning retreat here.* I am having a hard time thinking of a better place to hold a strategic thinking and planning retreat for top leaders. If this book you hold in your hands prescribes anything, it is that place matters. And this place, this museum? It would (and I very much hope *will*) be a magnificent location for an epic strategic planning retreat. I cannot imagine the strategic plan that produced this cultural and community masterpiece, but I can see with my own eyes that the result is overwhelmingly beautiful.

Chapter Challenge Questions

1. I have told you that epic strategic planning retreats can lead companies to amazing accomplishments, like the accomplishment by GE Johnson in building the U.S. Olympic and Paralympic Museum. What might your organization accomplish years from now if you hold an epic strategic planning retreat now?

2. Does your management team view strategic planning as an event or an unfolding process; is it a mentality or a transaction (one and done)? Why?

3. The museum is one epic place, huh? Name a place right now where your team might consider holding a strategic planning retreat—a place so special, it would actually contribute to the strategy.

EPILOGUE

Getting Real

"Hey, hey, my, my, rock and roll can never die."
THE IMMORTAL NEIL YOUNG

Twice

Twice. That is how many times Neil Young has been inducted into the Rock & Roll Hall of Fame,[35] once in 1995 as a solo artist and once in 1997 as a member of Buffalo Springfield. Um. Sheesh! A spectacular accomplishment, twice. He keeps me guessing about what he will do next, write next, and release next. He remains more than a musician and is also an activist. Plus, he co-directs movies. Say what? Yes, many years ago he co-created the soundtracks to the 1993 movie *Philadelphia*. Just when I thought I had this iconic rock, folk, and country genius figured out, he became a dual citizen of both his native Canada and the U.S. in January of 2020. I am still guessing what he will do next. His persona reminds me of other genius-level artists whose boundless creative fuel keep people guessing (e.g., Bob Dylan, Prince). A real truth teller, if you ask me.

Well, you are not Neil Young. Neither am I. Heck, I bristle just at the thought of being called an expert. But I am going to surprise you a bit now. In this last section of this book, I want to awaken in you an insight you have long suspected but could not quite put into words. It has to do with a deeper truth. Your deeper truth.

An epic strategic planning retreat facilitator is not going through the motions, right? If he has absorbed even a little of *Chunk* and has put just some of it into practice, he is helping to transform a leadership team. He is connecting to the leadership team and connecting them to one another like never before. All of that is being connected to a strategy for sustained market differentiation. There is a sense of specialness in the retreat room. He is fostering that. But he is not involved directly in it. Yet. That is, this retreat is for the gathered team and their company. It's not for the facilitator.

But, the gathered leaders (if the facilitator is doing well) have an affinity for the facilitator. He has become an independent, outside friend of the company. If the facilitator has led several retreats for this leadership time, perhaps over many years, he is now a friend of the client company. To apply an overused expression, he is a most trusted advisor. He has learned things about the individual leaders that are not only professional but are often personal. This relationship between facilitator and leadership team has now reached its zenith. The level of honesty, transparency, and creative strategic thinking is exceptional. This permits the facilitator, if and when the timing is right and only rarely, to share deeper reflections with the group. In so doing, he demonstrates the leadership team intimacy the strategic leadership team is probably craving, if not demonstrating themselves. He models trust. He has license (to be used sparingly) to get real with the group and get personal. In my case, I can pick a moment to get honest or even raw with the group. For me, this rare moment of professional nakedness is an emotional perk of the work. More importantly for you the reader, it is the reason some retreats are more epic than others. Candor. Connection. For me, it is often about topics that are real for me and may help reinforce a key strategy for the gathered leaders in the retreat room. Those topics for me include alcoholism, drug addiction, competitive swimming, multiple sclerosis, faith, and in one case, coccidioidomycosis. Allow me to relate a brief story and how such authenticity may help make a retreat slightly more epic.

Coccidioidomycosis (*"Kock-sid-ee-oi-do-my-ko-sys"*)

The pain on my scalp was excruciating and unprecedented. I had never (still haven't) felt anything like it. It was February 2018, and I was on a short vacation in Scottsdale, Arizona. I had evidently caught the flu. Total buzzkill. Pam and I had rented a home for three months off Scottsdale Boulevard along with her mom. The plan was for me to split time between Scottsdale and the Twin Cities as work permitted, while Pam and Mom would stay for the whole three months. We could golf, swim, and bike, all in the same day. It is how we roll, swim, or whatever.

So, when I arrived and immediately had flu symptoms, I was more mad than sick. A total waste of valuable vacation time! For three days, my temperature rose and fell; I had the sweats and trouble at both ends. Then, gradually, whatever malady I had contracted evidently moved on. So did I, back to the Twin Cities. Nice vacation (not). I had lost five pounds doing nothing.

Three weeks later, I experienced some of the same symptoms at home in the Twin Cities. A peculiar headache in my scalp. A new rash on the side of my calves. A temperature. That also moved on. Twice more that spring, I experienced skin rashes, deep aches and pains, then extreme fatigue. I would become so tired in the middle of the day I would have to work out in our company gym just to stay awake. Then, a burning sensation when peeing. Uh-oh.

In March 2018, I admitted myself to the ER with pain in my groin and right leg. There was blood in my urine. Diagnosis? Kidney stone or perhaps a urinary tract infection. This did not feel like the right diagnosis to me. But I went on antibiotics for the next week and drank cranberry juice. In April, I was feeling flu-like *again*. With Pam home from Arizona, we walked one Saturday into the ER. I had not only these flu symptoms but also a new crackling sound in my chest when breathing. The nurses and the doctor followed their usual protocol, which by now I was getting accustomed to. The doctor felt perhaps that an X-ray of my lungs would be in order given my experiences the past three months. Picture time. Click.

Then, in a quiet ER room, with Pam and I Zillowing real estate properties, the doctor walked in. She held a file of X-rays. She looked at us both and smiled. She sat down on a small rolling stool. It squeaked on the tile floor as she cozied up to me in the ER bed. A little close, I thought. So I sat up.

"Tom. I am glad we did this X-ray. There is an abnormality. This is…not good. There is a large mass in your upper left lung. It is a bit puzzling, but it is fairly large," she said as she showed us the picture. "Several of your lung nodules are enlarged. Actually, in both lungs [seeming to notice that detail just then]. You also quite likely have pneumonia. When we add to this your skin rashes and possible blood in your urine…this is going to require deeper work than we do in the ER here. But we're going to put you on IV antibiotics right now."

Long pause.

"What do you mean 'mass'"? I asked, dazedly.

"Well, it's a blob, really. It appears like a tumor. But it could be something else. With your other symptoms, it points to…well. Your symptoms may be cause for concern."

Now, I see why she cozied up to me. She should have cozied up to Pam. Because Pam instantly went into a stone private disbelief, she later told me. Then, more questions for me. More answers from the great doc. Tears for Pam.

Tumor?

Pneumonia suddenly sounded like a good outcome. I guess we packed up our things and headed to Regions Hospital in downtown St. Paul. But it was just a blur to me. I was soon lying in an ICU bed waiting to see a pulmonologist at Regions. One overnight stay. Visits from my brother Bill, his wife Tina, our friends Cindy and Jerry, Scott and Mary Miles, Rob (who was then bravely battling cancer and later died from it), and Julie Foley and their daughter Lexi. They all wondered what was happening, as did we. I was Mr. Masters Swimming stud. Mr. Cycling-to-raise-money Guy. Cancer? Pam and her mom Carol stayed by my side every minute; they never left. Late that next day, I had a lot of blood drawn, and then a saliva test. Then more CT and PET scans. I'm sure there were other tests they administered but which I have since forgotten. Then, a few hours of waiting. It was a trifle agonizing, yes.

The doctor walked into the room, looking astonishingly like Pam's brother, Terry. Same hair, same facial features, even the same size. He was a pulmonologist at Regions. He zipped into the room with a frown and sat down. I was trying to keep the mood light, "Hi, Doc!" It had been a long day waiting for our results. *My* results. He drew close to me on his stool.

By the way, is that a thing? Do they teach you that in med school? "Students, if you have to give a catastrophic diagnosis, scoot on a squeaky stool very close to the unsuspecting patient and then…*spring* it on the patient!" The first time was nice, but this second time made me laugh.

"Tom, you do not have pneumonia."

Long pause.

"Fuuuuu…" I gazed upward.

"Your left lung has an infection underway, yes, but the mass in your left lung is not pneumonia. It is something else. It is not quite the size of a golf ball. It's in the upper hilar region of the lung. Behind it is a big infection. It is large. With the other symptoms you are presenting, we want to get a biopsy right away. There is no way to know if it is malignant until we do that biopsy. Tom, it is gnarly, this mass. We can do this a week from today, which is what we advise. If it is cancer and has metastasized, and if the skin rash and the spots on your liver and blood in your urine are all related, as well as your lung nodules and your lymph nodes, which are also enlarged, then this is quite serious. This is why the biopsy is important."

He said all this calmly, clearly, arms folded but making amazing eye contact with me. He was laying down my new truth. A perfect communicator, I thought. He wanted me clear on what he was saying: biopsy, soon. I deeply admired his verbal precision. I briefly thought leaders in all organizations should be so blunt.

I looked at him. Then I asked one of the most bemusing questions I have ever asked out loud. To this day, I cannot explain why I asked "Are you real? Is this…are you…*real?*" I honest-to-God did not know what was happening. I thought maybe, perhaps this was some new feature of midlife: the surreal lung doc, who looked almost exactly like my brother-in-law, telling me that I probably have cancer; me, a U.S. Master Swimming competitor with gigantic lung capacity. It was all sort of out of body.

"Yes. Yes, Tom. I am real. This is happening," said Terry's twin, a little miffed by my question. "You are free to go when you like. Just some discharge papers to sign here that the nurse will bring in shortly." Zip, out he went from my room.

At this point, Pam, sitting on the hospital bed with me, gripped my hand and her tears started flowing. I felt her stop breathing. She immediately put off body heat like a furnace. Carol stopped her knitting from the couch and looked up. It was sort of a haze for me after that. I know we packed up, again, drove home to our place on Lake Carnelian, north of Stillwater, MN, cuddled with the dogs, and ate a snack. Later, Pam was in the kitchen on and off her phone whispering a bit intensely. A long hour passed.

Pam Unloads

"Nope. Not Regions. Pack a bag, We are going to Mayo [The Mayo Clinic, Rochester, MN] tomorrow at 5 am. I am sure Regions is amazingly good [they are]. But the actual Mayo Clinic is two hours away. Mayo. We're just gonna park ourselves there and wait for an appointment. No arguing, I am not *asking* you. Pack your bag. I will make us food for the road. The tank is full. Mom is going to take care of the dogs. Call in sick for work tomorrow or whatever, I don't care. You are not going to work."

Pam was taking charge. If you ever want to know what it might be like for a military officer to boldly switch tactics and cut right to the point, leaving zero room for confusion, ask Pam. She missed her calling.

Over the next two days, we were able, amazingly, to have my labs assessed. We saw a pulmonology fellow (a term they use there) twice, met with an infectious disease specialist, a dermatologist, and other appointments. More tests. Pokes. Scans. Then back to work and home to Lake Carnelian for a few days to await the diagnosis and schedule a biopsy. I told my boss, Al, and our chairman, Bruce. They were totally supportive, in my corner fighting for me.

The Mayo Clinic diagnosed me with pulmonary coccidioidomycosis that had disseminated. This, my friends, is a fungus. *Not* cancer. The mass? Fungus. The infection? It was huge. So, they hammered me with more IV antibiotics. "Cocci" is endemic to the southwestern U.S. It's in the soil. It's everywhere. If one is immunosuppressed and if you inhale it just wrong, you, too, could be a winner! My diagnosis went from bloody awful to just unpleasant. But, and this was the twist, cocci can masquerade in some tests as cancer or other fungi, and some cancers look like cocci in some tests. There is no way to know for sure without a biopsy. Well, it took more tests. My first biopsy (down into my left lung through my throat!) was inconclusive. I would have to do it again. It was finally a week later we had a clear prognosis from a second biopsy (this one performed straight into the lung through my left side): one to three years of gradual recovery, and the first 120 days would require daily antifungal pills. There was an outside chance it may never go away. My lung capacity would be poor for a while. Maybe forever. By the way, they also found an actual cancerous nodule in my right lung, but it is so small and slow growing I call it My Li'l Fella.

Anyway, by June of 2018, we had clarity. We had a plan. A month later, there was a small new complication: pulmonary embolisms, or PE blood clots, and a lot of them. So, we added a real joy to my daily pill: a daily injection into my belly ("Git in mae belly!" name that movie: _____) of blood thinners for several weeks and more visits to Mayo for review, analysis, and constant resetting of the action plan. Mayo has a patient portal that is exceptional. On my mobile device, to this day, I can examine literally hundreds of my data points, notes, recommendations, answers to questions, lab results, and so on. It is amazing. Even with the COVID-19 scare in 2020, I did not run a higher risk of reinfection. Amen to that.

In this process, we learned to keep our sense of humor. One day when we were at Mayo, I said to Pam, "Told you I was a 'fungi'!" She groaned (as you did just now). A week later, our friends Geoff and Lucy Gray came over for dinner bearing a gift: a black tee shirt that said, "I'm a Real Fungi!" with a mushroom illustration that looks like the artist did mushrooms. At least one of the side benefits to the antifungal pills was that my old man toenails looked young again.

Today, in terms of the final effect three-plus years later, I feel like I am always at altitude. You know, that lung compression and dizziness you feel when you first arrive at a location 6,000 feet above sea level? Easily breathless? That is what cocci feels like to me, along with fatigue, but not every day. No biggie. By the way, it turns out that in the southwest U.S., this is a common fungus. Fungi like this are common across the planet, but they vary slightly from region to region. If such a fungus disseminates to the human central nervous system, well, it can be fatal. Mine disseminated, but not quite that far, thank God. I am back in the pool swimming easily. I have been back on the road bike training for charity bike rides. I am losing the weight I put on from a year of emotional eating. Yeah, about that, I just got lazy: bad food, candy, fast food, pie, ice cream, and so on. I got depressed. I started seeing a counselor. I got on an antidepressant. I started going to a men's group meeting. Just a setback is all and an important time to find my true north again.

And Platoon Leader Pam? She is strong. Pam was diagnosed 29 years ago with multiple sclerosis, relapsing and remitting. So, she has conquered health beasts. She is a strong soul. During this time of recovery, she was so supportive. I sort of fell in love all over again.

So, What Does This Have to Do With Epic Strategic Planning?

What does this story have to do with being authentic as a facilitator of epic planning retreats? Actually, a lot. You see, the role of the facilitator in a strategic retreat is to shine a mirror on the group, keep the process and strategic conversation moving. You gradually build decisions, inspire when you can, redirect as you can, and then help them make decisions. You remain independent, reinforce positive behavior, manage things so that people with different learning styles in the room can all benefit, and along the way there are about a dozen skills that come into play. Skills like speaking clearly, truth telling, exceptional listening, working in a small group, synthesizing various participants' views and comments into a coherent shared view, staying on agenda, and galvanizing decisions. One of these skills is analogical thinking, which I have shared in great detail in this book. That is what we do when we use information from one domain (the source or analogy) to help solve a problem in another domain (the target). I often use analogies during the process of problem-solving. Analogies have been involved in too many scientific discoveries to count. My fixation on music being analogous to strategic thinking is an example. Another skill is the facilitator offering reflections, which can be personal in nature. Participants in strategic planning retreats absorb, learn, and make decisions in many different ways, including from comparisons and personal reflections. Stories. There are key moments in any two- or three-day business retreat when the facilitator can share a personal reflection, albeit briefly, with the gathered group to draw a parallel. Here is how one of my brief moments went.

The client was a rural hospital system's board of trustees. We were in day three of their strategic innovation planning retreat. They had made the inventive decision to move from a sick-care-based business model to a well-care-based business model, to provide more preventative services and specialties and to make their communities well. They believe this is critical to addressing the affordability crisis in American healthcare. There was much more to it than just this. But their direction? In a word: brilliant. The strategic plan they built to get there is really well considered. Here is a one-minute snippet (out of several weeks of work serving this client).

"Welcome back from the break everyone. Grab a seat. Please refresh your coffee, or whatever, and let's get back to work. You know, as your facilitator, I really have to say your emerging direction is inspiring to me. The organizational mentality is market-oriented. It is smart. It has your 100% commitment as trustees and top leaders. I can see and feel that. Your market research supports this. Your seven strategic initiatives are a lot, but your fierce insistence on implementing all of them indicates to me you are really on the right road. Your commitment to making communities well…hmm.

"You know, last year, I was not well. Can we pause for a moment please so I can share this? What I am about to tell you I would like to keep just between us. However, almost two years ago, for the first time in my life, I was diagnosed with a very serious lung disease. Not cancer. But it hit me and my family like a velvet hammer, this diagnosis. We were crushed. I was drifting. It turned out after many tests not to be cancer, which was an incredible relief. I will not go into the gruesome details. However, I will tell you this: your new mission and vision? Your new direction for the next 10+ years? Your telemedicine strategies? As a recent patient in our nation's healthcare system, it feels to me like…like…I would want to be treated by your specialists. All I wanted, all I needed, all I prayed about for two years was to feel gratitude in spite of being unwell. Well care… you are the kind of healthcare system our country needs, speaking now personally. I just wanted to be well. I did not need to win U.S. Masters Swimming National Championships again. I just wanted to be well, and still do. This is why, very personally, I am excited for all of you and your very well-planned and inspiring strategic vision. Please promise me now, right now, you will really live out your new well-care mission and vision; that you will implement this direction, not just be initially excited about it here, but for years to come. Okay, let's get back to work."

It took one minute. Pin-drop quiet. Despite my many leadership flaws, this bit of oversharing was authentic, strategic, and supportive of their direction. A few smiles. A quiet recognition in the room of a sacred conversation that related to their strategic direction. They are really, really going to do well care—that was the vibe. That is when I noticed one of the C-suite leaders wiping a tear away. She smiled at me and wrote something to herself in her retreat binder. I will never know what.

So, this sh!t-just-got-real retreat moment had nothing to do with market share calculations, analysis of healthcare reimbursement rates, market segmentation criteria, or their balance sheet. Yet, it was wholly strategic. It contributed to them figuring out how to compete differently than their competitors out there, not just better. My message to you? This is the sort of one-minute conversation—well facilitated, at the precise moment in time, with the right group, at a great place—that can transform people and their organizations.

Months later at a management meeting for this same client, one of their leaders came to me during a break and remarked, "Our vision, our direction, everything we're doing now, you know you helped, right? You realize you helped make that happen, I hope. How are you feeling?" I answered, "Yes, I was there when your team made those decisions, and it was a blessing, truly. But your team did all the work. This is *your* plan, not mine. All I did was listen and capture your plan with you. I owe you, honestly. I feel great, thanks. Better. Well."

I have had other such rarified opportunities. Once, it was evident to me that the client team I was facilitating was waffling on their new core values. Among the key ideas, their ethos if you will, was whether the new core value was to be stated as integrity or honesty. They could not decide. This was happening at the time of the Bernie Madoff trial for his massive Ponzi scheme. One of my clients' top leaders had been a burned investor in that scheme. He had lost nearly everything. All I had to do was ask which of the two words (honesty or integrity) would best avert a Bernie Madoff–type problem in their company. I simply drew from recent media information.

The best such raw and naked moments for leaders in an epic retreat are always client related. In one especially memorable instance, a client team member spoke eloquently about her passion for Fischer Skis. We were in the middle of a discussion on their vision for the next 10 years. I was facilitating a question: Where do you see your company brand in 10 years, and why? I asked a two-part key question: are there other companies *not* in your industry that you admire, and how have they remained visionary during times of intense competitive pressure?

A mid-executive immediately spoke about her passion for Fischer Skis: their manufacturing, their branding, their support of competitive and recreational skiing worldwide. She stood up and kept talking. I just sat back quietly and listened. She was on fire for Fischer! She told a story about her dad teaching her to ski on her Fischers. Her dad had since passed away. She was passionate about Fischer Skis because she loved her father. I explained I have the same feeling for the brand TYR in competitive swimming, but for different reasons. Others chimed in with their parallels (Titleist, Hoyt Hunting Bows, Chevy). An hour later, they had settled on a vision about ingenuity. Every person in that room will remember her story about Fischer Skis and how that played a role in their strategic brand building.

In another retreat, a client used an orchestra analogy. The CEO was their fictional conductor (he actually really was/is an amateur cellist). He spoke eloquently of what it is like being in a chamber orchestra. Another retreat participant told us about his experience he had with a theatre troop and how that was akin to a great leadership team. But sports analogies? Most cliché sports references are dead, friends. You know what's real? *You* are, and your real, relevant, and brief story as a facilitator that may magnify a company's, the client's, emerging direction in an epic offsite retreat. Please give yourself the opportunity (within limits, of course) to get real with the gathered leaders. Try not to get off the rails with a 20-minute conversation about your child's recent divorce or your boss's flaws. That is just wrong. But, connecting—truly connecting—with the gathered leaders? That is the right sort of crazy.

Chapter Summary

As a facilitator of strategic business work, there are moments to be real and present with the client group. To speak from the heart, not spreadsheets. Perhaps you have a parallel to draw for the group, a genuine story from your own experience that will help the group really understand one another better or maybe their direction together. If so, share that. Pull yourself out of the facilitator role if only for a moment, keep it short, and relate to the client group. Be there. This is called being authentic, but I view it as being truthful. In every upcoming retreat, I think about when I might do that. When in the agenda might personal reflection be briefly fitting? What I never know until it happens is what I will say. It just happens.

References

1. "Pink Floyd Lyrics Pigs." Google search. *Google.* Accessed August 10, 2021. https://www.google.com/ search?client=firefox-b-1-d&q=pink%2Bfloyd%2Blyris%2 Bpigs.

2. "VUCA World - Leadership Skills & Strategies." *VUCA,* July 20, 2021. https://www.vuca-world.org/.

3. Danny Buerkli. "'What Gets Measured Gets Managed' - It's Wrong and Drucker Never Said It." *Medium,* April 8, 2019. https://medium.com/centre-for-public-impact/what-gets-measured-gets-managed-its-wrong-and-drucker-never-said-it-fe95886d3df6.

4. Demontreville Jesuit Retreat House, May 10, 2021. https:// demontrevilleretreat.com/.

5. Brave New Workshop Creative Outreach, March 16, 2021. https://bravenewworkshop.com/.

6. "Traffic." *Rock & Roll Hall of Fame.* Accessed August 10, 2021. https://www.rockhall.com/inductees/ traffic?gclid=CjwKCAiA6aSABhApEiwA6Cbm_ 6D1cvs8VK0tnfzmMCZyQXtIYokQiSmI8PNmYPCa aQNv8VGX_9LTsBoCwM0QAvD_BwE.

7. "Welcome to Build Me Up!" *Build Me Up Podcast,* December 4, 2019. Podcast, 18:52. https://www. krausanderson.com/podcast/welcome-to-build-me-up/.

8. "Creedence Clearwater Revival." *Rock & Roll Hall of Fame*. Accessed August 10, 2021. https://www.rockhall.com/ inductees/creedence-clearwater-revival?gclid=CjwKCAiAsO mABhAwEiwAEBR0ZjN_XoLLuZZMwo-iKiSIuxJkiBHjg SaN5A5M1enoZr9bXF23kBhwqxoCgyQQAvD_BwE.

9. "Music Therapy." *MacPhail Center for Music*, August 3, 2021. https://www.macphail.org/meta/music-therapy/.

10. Abbie Griffin and John R. Hauser. "The Voice of the Customer." *Marketing Science* 12, no. 1 (1993): 1-27. doi: https://doi.org/10.1287/mksc.12.1.1

11. "Michael Phelps." *Wikipedia*. Wikimedia Foundation, August 9, 2021. https://en.wikipedia.org/wiki/ Michael_Phelps.

12. Debbie Stocker. "Vision, Values, and Purpose According to Collins and Porras." *Stocker Partnership*, August 16, 2019. https://www.stockerpartnership.com/resources/articles/ vision-values-and-purpose-according-to-collins-and-porras/.

13. Simon Sinek. *Start with Why: How Great Leaders Inspire Everyone to Take Action*. London, England: Penguin Business, 2011.

14. Nikki Gilliland. "How Lululemon Became One of the Biggest Risers in the BrandZ Top 100." *Econsultancy*, November 20, 2019. https://econsultancy.com/how-lululemon-became-one-of-the-biggest-risers-in-the-brandz-top-100/.

15. "Did Peter Drucker Actually Say 'Culture Eats Strategy for Breakfast' - and If So, Where/When?" Quora. Accessed August 10, 2021. https://www.quora.com/Did-Peter-Drucker-actually-say-culture-eats-strategy-for-breakfast-and-if-so-where-when.

16. Calder Foundation. Accessed August 10, 2021. https://calder.org/.

17. "Edwin Hugh Lundie." *Wikipedia*. Wikimedia Foundation, February 22, 2020. https://en.wikipedia.org/wiki/Edwin_Hugh_Lundie.

18. Janice Hodge. "Model: Transformation Theory." *Creative Change Management*, May 11, 2019. https://www.creative-change-management-online.com/creativity-models/transformation-theory-contributions-by-janice-hodge.

19. John E. Jones and William L. Bearley. "High-Performance Problem Solving: Using the SiTNA Alternative for Generating Synergy And Commitment." *Organizational Universe Systems*, 1996. http://158.132.155.107/posh97/private/problem-solving/high-performance-Jones.pdf.

20. "Strategy Canvas: A Tool for Competitive Advantage." *Business Strategy Hub*, May 9, 2020. https://bstrategyhub.com/strategy-canvas-a-tool-for-competitive-advantage/.

21. "Richard Hieb." *Wikipedia*. Wikimedia Foundation, July 27, 2021. https://en.wikipedia.org/wiki/Richard_Hieb.

22. Erika L. Rowland, Molly S. Cross, and Holly Hartmann. "Considering Multiple Futures: Scenario Planning to Address Uncertainty in Natural Resource Conservation." U.S. Fish & Wildlife Service, June 2014. https://www. fws.gov/home/feature/2014/pdf/Final%20Scenario%20 Planning%20Document.pdf.

23. "Groundhog Day" *Wikipedia*. Wikimedia Foundation, August 10, 2021. https://en.wikipedia.org/wiki/ Groundhog_Day_(film).

24. Brian Resnick. "Stephen Hawking's Final Paper Makes a Hopeful Case for the Limits of Existence." *Vox*, May 3, 2018. https://www.vox.com/science-and-health/2018/5/3/17314878/stephen-hawking-final-paper-journal-high-energy-physics-hologram-multiverse-big-bang-thomas-hertog.

25. Michael Fitzsimmons. "Strategic Insights: Challenges in Using Scenario Planning for Defense Strategy." SSI US Army War College, April 26, 2021. https://ssi. armywarcollege.edu/strategic-insights-challenges-in-using-scenario-planning-for-defense-strategy-2/.

26. "Alvin Toffler Bio." *Toffler Associates*. Accessed August 10, 2021. https://cdn2.hubspot.net/hubfs/454613/Toffler_ Associates_September2017/Doc/AlvinTofflerBio_160701_ v2.pdf?t=1509109344072

27. "Roger Von Oech." *Wikipedia.* Wikimedia Foundation, June 6, 2021. https://en.wikipedia.org/wiki/ Roger_von_Oech.

28. Stan Silverman. "Understanding Your Competitive Position Leads to Success in Building a Business." *The Business Journals*, March 2, 2020. https://www.bizjournals. com/bizjournals/how-to/growth-strategies/2020/03/ understanding-your-competitive-position-leads-to.html.

29. "Ship Commissioning." *Wikipedia.* Wikimedia Foundation, July 30, 2021. https://en.wikipedia.org/wiki/Ship_ commissioning.

30. Joe Bunting. "Once Upon a Time: Pixar Prompt." *The Write Practice*, January 20, 2019. https://thewritepractice.com/ once-upon-a-time-pixar-prompt/.

31. "Unintended Consequences." *Wikipedia.* Wikimedia Foundation, August 6, 2021. https://en.wikipedia.org/wiki/ Unintended_consequences.

32. The Bluebird Cafe, August 13, 2021. https://www. bluebirdcafe.com/.

33. YPO, July 27, 2021. https://www.ypo.org/.

34. "This Is Spinal Tap." *Wikipedia.* Wikimedia Foundation, July 31, 2021. https://en.wikipedia.org/wiki/This_Is_ Spinal_Tap.

35. "Neil Young." *Rock & Roll Hall of Fame.* Accessed August 10, 2021. https://www.rockhall.com/inductees/neil-young?gclid=Cj0KCQiA34OBBhCcARIsAG32uvNxD2zOj1e-SwpcPzur3IsJFPz0NI5lTWp7bC2zgJTdXRF9abdYSQsaAp5LEALw_wcB.

About the Author

Tom Emison is a strategic business planning advisor, organizational change agent, and facilitator of offsite and virtual executive retreats. He is a "C-suite" mentor, three-time U.S. Masters Swimming National Champion, writer, speaker, charity volunteer, and podcast host. In a period spanning four decades, Tom researched, facilitated, documented, and helped implement over 230 strategic business plans in multiple industry sectors across the U.S. Tom learned that strategy is a creative process not well suited to superficial templates, toolkits, frameworks, apps, and other contrivances that dumb down your thinking. 2020 and 2021 brought the COVID-19 pandemic, social unrest, political volatility, and economic meltdowns across the globe. Everything was disrupted. Five years of change were compressed into an instant. Entire categories of leadership team interactions were suspended. You and your leadership team need an independently facilitated and epic retreat to reimagine your organization right now in a safe and healthy setting. Those who creatively rethink their businesses will be rewarded. The rest will suffer in a race to the bottom. It is that simple.

Chunk is a priceless resource that outlines how to reimagine your organization. Are you wondering how to perform a comprehensive strategic situation assessment of your business now? Tom shows you how. Are you excited about the possibilities that lay ahead for your organization, but your leaders are not on the same page? Tom explains how to align your individual visions into one shared vision. *Chunk* is a distinctive blend of strategic planning thought leadership, retreat facilitator's guide, and unexpected rock and roll.

Tom Emison is an independent C-suite strategic advisor. He is past chair of the National Multiple Sclerosis Society Upper Midwest Chapter and past chair of the Building Futures Council. He has ridden thousands of miles on his bicycle raising money to find a cure for MS and to support families hit with MS. Tom is a recovering alcoholic with a sober date of August 9, 1978. Tom and his wife, Pam, have three children, Emily, Mac, and Ashley. They are active in their church, the Salvation Army, and addiction recovery ministries. When Tom and Pam are not golfing, cycling, reading, or listening to music, they are quite likely swimming across the lake.

Made in the USA
Monee, IL
26 February 2023

28521873R10204